LONG ISLAND
SEAFOOD COOK BOOK

LONG ISLAND
SEAFOOD COOK BOOK

By
J. GEORGE FREDERICK

Recipes edited by
JEAN JOYCE

DOVER PUBLICATIONS, INC.
NEW YORK

This Dover edition, first published in 1971, is
an unabridged and unaltered republication of the
work originally published by The Business Bourse
in 1939.

International Standard Book Number: 0-486-22677-8
Library of Congress Catalog Card Number: 79-140230

Manufactured in the United States of America
Dover Publications, Inc.
180 Varick Street
New York, N. Y. 10014

Contents

LONG ISLAND
SEAFOOD COOK BOOK

I

An Introduction to the Appreciation of Seafood

SEAFOOD is the immemorial food of the gods. Ye gods and little fishes have always made good company, and the Greek gods—their home in the endless isles of the Aegean Sea—had a very rich variety indeed to choose from—and were quite evidently not above doing so! Dionysius warns that to cook one must depend upon genius, no less; and certainly this applies to the cooking of sea food in particular, because it is the most delicate material for cookery of all the foods of man—but at the same time the most rewarding to the appetite.

The lost Greek cookery books of Archestratus must have dealt much with fish, for fish and game authentically ranked first in the appetite of the Greeks. "Round a table delicately spread . . . in choice repast," as Archestratus said, both gods and men were served with *sole,* the noblest of all fish (Piscus nobilis) of Greek gastronomy, which to this day ranks high with epicures on two sides of the world —and which most of the time in America means Long Island flounder (and let no man cavil at that!).

The Greeks obtained most of their master cooks from Sicily, and among the most celebrated of these was Trimalchio, who had so very high an opinion of fish that when he could not for the moment obtain certain scarce and coveted fish, he expertly counterfeited their shape, texture and flavor! In the same way, King Nicomedes, King of the Babylonians, often had his cook serve him an imitation (made of anchovies) of the real fish which the King ardently desired out of season. We have of course all heard of Vatel, the famous cook of Louis XIV, who committed suicide when his royal master's favorite fish (sole) was not delivered in time for the banquet.

Gods, kings, ordinary mortals have in all ages spoken avidly of fish. As Swift put it, "they say fish should swim thrice—first it should swim in the sea, then it should swim in butter, and at last, sirrah, it should swim in good claret." The great heritage of savor and favor which seafood has always enjoyed, among all races and in all times, is unquestionably due to the marked piquancy of seafood flavor, and the wide available range of varying textures and flavors. Monotony of taste is the deadly enemy of appetite; all those peoples living far from seafood have always felt this monotony; whereas all those peoples living near the sea have always considered themselves bounteously provided by nature with epicurean variety. There are over 250 edible fish—almost one for every day in the year!

Seafood, let it be understood, is meant quite definitely for *food lovers*. One must love it in general—quite as one must love woman in general before one can truly appreciate any particular woman. One must—to carry the same simile forward—be ready to accept the special temperament, the changeability, the moods and tenses, the delicacy of approach, of sea food, to get the richest treasures from it— quite as one must with woman! There is no food which demands more special consideration in cookery than seafood. One cannot be careless or crude or neglectful with seafood and affect to love it—just as one cannot with woman. Act like a lover to seafood and it will reward you! From the moment it comes out of the sea it must be cherished, tenderly escorted, considerately treated, meticulously handled. *Fail* to do this and it will languish rapidly upon your hands like an unloved, deserted woman. *Do* this, and it will bloom and radiate its savor like a rose, and transport your appetite.

Perhaps one must also have a touch, at least, of romantic flair for waters and the sea, for the salt tang, for the ever-shifting, the captivating, the illimitable, the mysterious deeps of the ocean, in order to savor seafood most effectively. Then the oddities of seafood do not repel us; then the special care and labors of preparation do not irk us; they become labors of love. Perhaps it is because men are inherently more romantic than women, and are also more habitual lovers of the sea, that women care, on the whole, less for seafood than do men; and are so often squeamish about handling it. This difference between men and women was noted fifty years by a woman herself, writing about seafood cookery.

The crabbed, picky, fickle attitude toward seafood is however, often met with even in men. They like oysters, but not clams. They like salmon, but not eel. They like their fish fried, but never baked. They like fried oysters but not raw oysters; they like trout but not mackerel. They adore scallops but despise mussels. They adore a stew but look down upon a chowder.

But never the true seafood lover! He invariably has preferences, but rarely hates. He may put broiled fish first, but fish in any form (well cooked) is a gastronomic port in a storm. He may rank oyster stew high, but he will not pick suspiciously at a bouillabaisse or at a fish chowder. He may care more for finnan haddie than for smoked eel, but he will not have the familiar subjective distaste for the eel because it is shaped like a snake. He can look at a squid without gagging. He may even clean a fish and like it. And he can surely eat steamed soft shell clams, besprinkling the table cloth and the napkin, and revel in it!

Several years ago a hearing on fish was held in the U. S. Senate. At that hearing Senator Overton of the Senate Committee on Commerce asked, "Don't you think that the consumption of fish would be much greater if there were more information as to the proper method of cooking fish?" Gardner Poole of the Fisheries Advisory Committee agreed readily; and Senator Copeland then remarked that there has been a lamentable lack of publicity about the best methods of preparing fish foods. Said he, *"In the average house there is only one way of cooking fish, and usually they don't know another way."* (He meant, of course, frying.) Then C. B. McGovern, chairman of the Fishery Advisory Committee of the U. S. Bureau of Fisheries said that "the average housewife seems to be ignorant of the best way of preparing fish," and pleaded for appropriations to help educate more people to fish cookery. It is with such statements as this ringing in his ears that the author has felt that this book might be important.

The true situation was well disclosed by a consumer survey made among housewives (in San Francisco, a good fish town at that) by Barton De Loach for the U. S. Bureau of Fisheries. Here are the attitudes discovered among housewives:

26% of them disliked the flavor of fish or objected to fish bones
20% do not have the habit of buying fish at all
19% found it impossible to buy fish except on Friday
13% found it impossible to buy fish of good quality
11.5% disliked to prepare fish for cooking
6.5% found the price of fish too high
2.6% admitted they were incapable of preparing and cooking fish in a satisfactory manner

With a situation like this it is no wonder that America has not yet become one third as much a fish-eating nation as England. The expert icing and refrigerated transportation of fish, and particularly the quick-freezing of fish fillets are now at work to help. Women are not obliged to clean fish any more, which is an enormous aid, in view of their fish attitudes.

The reach of fish distribution is also very much greater than formerly. It was only about 10 years ago that 85% of all the salt-water fish were eaten within 200 miles of our coasts, and people not living near the coast were brought up on *no* fish, or poor quality fish. Also many acquired *fish fears* and *fish delusions,* such as that fish cause certain skin diseases, or that fish are likely to bring on ptomaine poisoning. None of these delusions have any foundation. A little time is needed to re-educate people—time and a good seafood cook book, I hold! These fish delusions remind one of the old saying by Ovid that "a fish once injured by the hook believes all food dangerous." Someone utterly lacking in sense may once have eaten obviously tainted fish and then forever after blamed fish for being dangerous or poisonous. Yet after the Spanish-American war beef poisonings no one stopped eating beef.

One good route by which fish has made friends has been via amateur fishermen. Another old Latin saying is to the effect that "fish is sweet from the fact of being hunted for." It is the same reason why the duck or quail or grouse-hunter adores to eat his game. The fisherman adores to eat, even to cook, his catch. He invites others to the feast, and transmits to others his enthusiasm for dining on seafood. He also learns the arts of seafood cookery and spreads them. One of the ways by which seafood was made very popular after the Civil War was the dinners at old Delmonico's, New York, of the Ichthyophagos Club. Chef Filippini of Delmonico's was a past master of the art of fish cookery; some of his recipes are in this book.

How did England rise so high in fish consumption? We would expect Norway, perhaps, to be great fish eaters, but how come England, with her notorious love of beef and mutton? The answer goes back to the great, wise Queen Bess of the Shakespearean era. Queen Elizabeth, believe it or not, compelled the English people *by law* to eat fish! She had a good economic head on her shoulders, and knowing that England's primary problem (then as now) was to make herself more self-sufficient in her food supply, saw the great good sense of training England to like the abundant food supply existing in the waters around her. The Gulf Stream, warm and teeming with fish, comes all the way from off the shores of Long Island to England, bringing Spring there before it arrives in New York, and likewise bringing plenty of seafood; one of nature's special boons to an island nation, located in a naturally cold spot, and short in food supply. Good Queen Bess made England know and use her blessings. Henry the Great had 24 fishmongers to supply him with his fish needs for his table. England had never since lost her special love of fish.

A paradox lies in the fact that England, not so good at cookery, should love fish better than France, which is so expert at cookery. France has been, possibly, the victim of her own high degree of artistry of cookery, because French cooks seem always to have taken very special delight in treating fish as a kind of backdrop or plastic material for special cookery skill. Fillet of sole, for example, has been used by French chefs much as clay is used by sculptors in modeling: it was not the fish (the clay) but what the cook did with it in shape, color, and sauce, that seems to have mattered. The diner has been asked to admire the cook, rather than the fish! This is all very well, up to a certain point, but as Martial once said in his famous *Epigrams,* "I prefer the feast should please the guests rather than the cooks!"

A modern French cook has only pity for the naive Vatel, the famous chef to Louis XIV, who committed suicide because the sole didn't arrive in time for the King's dinner. The great modern French chef, Escoffier, who died only a few years ago, was once asked what *he* would have done had he stood in Vatel's shoes at that critical moment.

Escoffier smiled in a very superior way, replying without any hesitation, "I would have taken the breast of a very young chicken, which is also very white and very tender, like fillet of sole, and cooked my dish, and the King would never have known the difference!" Nothing could better illustrate the difference between French and American cookery of fish—the French too far on the side of artificiality in cookery, the American too rough and ready and too limited in cookery scope. That is why New Orleans, standing midway between, has so notable a fish cookery, highly respected all over the world. But the New York and Long Island region, leader in amount of fish eaten per person, is just now, I believe, quite on the point of arriving at having the best and most varied seafood in the world. This does *not* mean that the *average person* in New York or Long Island knows and enjoys the best seafood cookery, but that large numbers of discriminating seafood diners can and do find it in New York or Long Island; also that such discriminating persons are more numerous there than elsewhere.

There must be a primordial connection between humans and seafood, to explain the special love so many have for it. Indeed there *is* such a connection. We all sprang from the sea; it was our primordial home. We carry in our bodies vestiges of the day our human progenitors swam in the sea like fish. Seawater is as near as anything to our blood, and doctors sometimes save lives by pumping it into the veins of humans. It is the fluid of life, containing all elements. Why, then, should we not feel a special affinity for the denizens of the salty deeps?

The matter goes, of course, further. Seafood contains elements very vital to our bodies—iodine, minerals, vitamins. Why do so many people of certain inland Mississippi valleys crave so strongly for seafood? Why are such regions called "goiter belts"? Because inland waters and foods are so often deficient in iodine and cause goiters. Furthermore, inlanders tire of the tastelessness of so much ordinarily available food. Lacking the ingenuity of clever cooks they do not so often obtain the infinite variety of taste, which nature herself has provided in seafood. Often they bog down into lamentable one-track food habits, rejecting all but certain foods which provide flavor (the ham-and-eggs complex, for example), and missing the great array of choice which seafood provides.

Nobody at Marseilles, France, or New Orleans ever complained of lack of variety in taste—for the very significant reason that seafood, with its abundant variety of taste, is so plentiful there—as of course it is also around the Long Island waters, the Chesapeake and Delaware Bays and Virginia Tidewater areas. But today, with rapid refrigerated transportation both by railroad, by truck and even by airplane, no inland regions need do without plenty of seafood. The quick-freezing process also has been amazingly extending the reach of distribution of fresh seafood. We are now at a point in national dining in America when all families, almost anywhere—even in the rural regions thousands of miles from the ocean—can and do dine on fresh seafood. The appreciation and cookery of seafood is thus now no longer a seaboard matter, but a national matter.

It should also be remarked that there seem to be people who have a *duty* attitude toward fish-eating. Doubtless this is bound up somewhat with the very old fish-on-Friday religious decree. It has perhaps bred that most unfortunate of attitudes—the same attitude that has spoilt the taste of spinach to many: the "this-is-good-for-me-even-if-I-don't-like-it" attitude. A story quoted by Scottson-Clark in England illustrates it. A typical "fish-dodger" developed this rather Freudian technique: he went into a restaurant dutifully every Wednesday and Friday during Lent and said to the waiter, "Have you got *shark*?" "No!" said the startled waiter. "Have you got *porpoise*?" "No!" was the answer. "Have you got *whale*?" "*No!*" was the astonished comment. The patron sighed contentedly, "Then bring me a steak, rare. God knows I *asked* for fish!" Fish will never really taste good when eaten on a duty basis; but on a taste basis it rises to top flights of gastronomic delight.

This book of seafood cookery, in effect, is no more Long Island than it is United States, except for its omission of specific mention of certain fish local to particular regions —for example the pompano and sheepshead in the Gulf regions, whitefish and muskalonge in the Great Lakes region, salmon and abalone in the Pacific regions. In its treatment of seafood, this book is broadly national, and few good methods of cooking seafood of any kind are omitted. I do not for a moment pretend that the fish recipes in this book all originated on Long Island. A dozen foreign cuisines and various American fish-eating regions have developed many of these recipes.

I shall hope that many people will make this book the means of broadening their taste horizon for seafood. Not even the most confirmed lover of seafood will fail to find here, I believe, some new ideas for cooking favorite seafoods—and certainly some new seafoods and subtle differences of treatment which can whet the appetite. The best cooks in the world for centuries back have contributed to the making of this modern book of seafood cookery.

Become a seafood lover—life will never be quite so dull again!

J. George Frederick.

New York
June 1939

II

The Long Island Art of Seafood Cookery

NEW YORK CITY and Long Island have the best of justi-
fications for leadership in matters of seafood cookery,
because, first, they eat the most seafood; and second, they
cook it in a wider variety of ways. The per capita annual
consumption for the U. S. as a whole is 13.3 lbs., but New
York City and Long Island eat 32 lbs. per capita, which is
higher than any other American city or region. Into the
New York market come *one half a billion pounds of fish*
each year, of 100 separate varieties, the large proportion of
which come from Long Island. They are cooked by the
world's largest aggregation of good chefs, and by housewives of about half a hundred different nationalities. There
isn't, I am sure, another place on the round globe of which
these things can be said.

Long Island, like the favored and storied Isles of Greece,
so rich in mythology and gracious living, has always been
a particularly bounteous seafood isle. It was recognized as
such long before the white man came, by the American
Indians. Hendrik Hudson in 1609 landed on Long Island,
where Coney Island now is, and recorded that he took "a
great haule of fish."

Long Island, like the famed Chesapeake Bay and Virginia Tidewater districts, had more Indians to the square
mile than most other American localities (a total of 13
tribes), quite probably because of the rich abundance of
seafood available and easily obtained.

It was perfectly natural that the abundant fish, clams,

oysters, crab, turtle, eel, mussels of these sheltered salt-water regions made these regions Indian paradises. The Indians appreciatively called Long Island *Sewanahaka,* "island of shells." At the same time, to add to the para-dise-like nature of a region like Long Island, the very presence of so much shellfish brought there the wild ducks, geese and other wild game. In addition, these regions are in a favored position for climate, which is milder both be-cause of the proximity of the Gulf stream, and the more southerly latitudes. (Average monthly day temperature 60.9°F; five year record of sunshine per month, 77.6%). Quite often there are 8 to 10 degrees of difference in tem-perature, even between New York City and middle South Shore Long Island.

At times Long Island has been visited by miracles of fish-plenty, as for example at Stony Brook in January 1939 when the Bay was found chock full of bass, ready to be picked up by the hundreds of pounds by anyone who cared to do so. The fish had been trapped by tidal ac-tion. At one period early settlers on Long Island wrote that sometimes they could walk across the river or bay on the backs of the bass solidly packed in the waters.

Now that the white man has made Long Island his na-tional and international playground a great deal of the wild *game* has flown—*but not the seafood.* Long Island remains, as it always was, a great fisherman's paradise, and one of the foremost, if not the foremost, of our shellfish centers. The Blue Points, the Gardner's Bay, the Robbins Island and other oysters of fame are elabor-ately cultivated here. Years ago "Rockaway" and "Saddle Rock" oysters were famous at Delmonico's, but New York City grew too close to these waters. It was, indeed, only half a dozen years ago that the approach of too much New York City civilization, forty miles away, compelled my family to cease picking oysters right off the sands of our shorefront property on Long Island, and dining freely upon them! But we can still dine on the clams (quahog hard shells, and soft shells), and the mussels, the eel and the fish. Fish charts of fishing gazettes show how adjacent Long Island waters are packed with fish of almost every kind and size, up to and including the largest tuna fish ever caught in any waters. "57 varieties" of fish, most of them fish good to eat, and some of them the most succulent seafood known to man, are to be had in these Long Island waters. Other regions may be rich in some one fish, like salmon, shad, mackerel or cod, but Long Island waters know them almost all; yes, even the whale! Long Island, incidently, was once a nest of whaling vessel ports, and whaling captains of that era still live on the Island to tell about it.

Twelve months of the year the fishermen fish in Long Island waters. The sea-Titans—the tuna and the broadbill swordfish, whose steaks are so succulent and nourishing—are there in comparative abundance: a 705 pound tuna, the largest ever caught in American waters, a 505 pound swordfish! Also marlins, bonitas, and bluefish, weakfish, flounder, cod, blackfish, sea bass, striped bass, kingfish, mackerel, snapper, porgies, and many, many others; indeed several varieties of some of these; two kinds of mackerel for example. (See last chapter in book for Long Island fishing details).

Add to all this the various types of clams (the Little Necks are named for a town on Long Island), the mussels, the oysters (the famous Gardner's Bay Blue Points and Robbins Island oysters are named for definite places in Long Island waters), as well as hard and soft shell crabs and other shellfish, and it is not hard to understand why Long Islanders are born with seafood in their mouths, plenty of iodine in their bodies—and the salt sea tang in their nostrils, blowing in from the north from Long Island Sound, blowing in from the East from the 3000 miles of Atlantic Ocean, blowing in from the South from the soft currents of the famous Gulf Stream only a few miles out.

Long Island, consequently, knows its seafood as few if any other regions in the United States know it. The Indians themselves taught the early white men how to make clam bakes, how to spear eel, how to roll fish in seaweed for cookery, how to broil seafood on green sticks. Ever since about 1632 the Long Islander has been dining on seafood and learning how to make palatable seafood dishes. Some of the best seafood restaurants in America are located on Long Island, and many delightful new seafood recipes have been concocted there. Nor can we forget that the concentration of many nationalities in and around New York City has made the entire world's seafood cookery experience available there. You can eat on Long Island seafood cooked by cooks of nearly all of New York's varied nationalities—French, Italian, Spanish, Mexican, German, Jewish, Greek, Polish, Scandinavian, Hungarian, and even Chinese. New Yorkers by the million drive out on Long Island and make patronage for the Long Island seafood restaurants, whether in a rough shack on a fish wharf or a gilded dining palace. Rich men's private chefs also apply their skill. Society makes its summer capital at Southampton, and has year-round country homes there and all over the Island; their high-priced cooks constantly experimenting with various Long Island seafood; indeed even, nowadays, the rich folk themselves dabble in "gourmet" cookery. "The millionaire's playground" they called Long Island, until Jones Beach and the other lovely state parks were opened to the public, and the World's Fair came. Now Long Island is for the general public in a very thorough-going way; the *average man's* playground.

The most important thing that has happened to Long Island seafood cookery in the last half century or more has been the influence of the foreign language groups of New York City. We must here recall the little-realized fact that actually *the greater part of New York City is now located on Long Island* (Brooklyn and Queens). New York City has the greatest assembly of groups of foreign backgrounds of any city on earth. But that is not all. It also has probably the most notable and varied assembly of foreign chefs of any city on earth. Thus two strong forces long ago went to work on Long Island seafood. First, the professional chefs, the pick of the world. Next, the home cooks, the housewives reared in the traditions of their native excellent cookery from abroad. These groups were further catered to by special national food shops in New York, of which there is one or more for each of 30 or 40 nationalities, and at which can be purchased the various spices and special accessories for cookery that is practiced in other lands. Both the professional chefs and the housewives of various nationalities could thus apply here, unhampered, the seafood cookery techniques of most of the rest of the world. Many of these national groups have their centers in Brooklyn, Queens or somewhere on Long Island.

The result has been that Long Island seafood cookery took on a most decided extension of repertoire. New Yorkers and Long Islanders had presented to them seafood cooked in every conceivable way. In recent years many of these nationalistic cookeries have set up restaurants along the main highways of Long Island, to meet the needs of automobile travelers, so a drive to the country could end in an Italian, a Swedish, a German, a Hungarian, a French or even a Chinese restaurant, where Long Island seafood, obtained fresh from the briny deep, could be eaten, prepared along the lines of some particular national cuisine. Driving out on Long Island on the Jericho Turnpike you will pass at least four first class Swedish restaurants, for example, equal to good restaurants in Stockholm. Thus, even before the World's Fair, one could eat seafood on Long Island prepared in the maner of 20 to 30 different cuisines (even more in Manhattan). The World's Fair of course brought the whole world's cuisine to Long Island as never before, accentuating its polyglot character.

I have been a resident of Long Island—the interior, the shore region of Long Island—for 30 years, and the cooking of Long Island seafoods has been all these years a gourmet delight and a fascinating hobby, not alone with myself, but with my family; at Mrs. Frederick's famous Applecroft Home Experiment Station Kitchen at Greenlawn; on the outdoor fireplaces at our home, and on the actual shores of Long Island waters (seafood has an inimitable special flavor when shore-cooked). I have traveled to many other fish and seafood regions of the world—the Mediterranean, the North Sea, the Spanish waters, and also New Orleans, the Great Lakes and Canada, and have been able to taste and compare the seafood cookeries of other places. Long Island, I find, is among the very richest in resources and skill, and yet its seafood lore has never before been assembled.

Thus, following the policy which the Gourmet Society of New York, of which I am the head, has consistently followed (that of drawing out and encouraging the regional cookery skills of America), I have addressed myself to the task of building a Long Island Seafood Cook Book. For this task I believe my 30-year special status as a Long Islander and gourmet gives me considerable fitness, in the same way that my origins as a Pennsylvania Dutchman encouraged me to work out my book, *The Pennsylvania Dutch and Their Cookery* (1936). If this book will infuse some of my own interest and zest in seafood to those who will enjoy it as much as I have, I shall consider myself amply repaid. I wish here very specially to acknowledge the great interest, care and professional competence of my daughter, Miss Jean Joyce, in her assistance in the compilation of this book.

What may be called the Long Island art of seafood cookery began of course with the Indians, whose clambakes on the many shores and coves of Long Island reach back nobody knows how far into ancient history. They developed the art of eating clams and mussels; how to accentuate rather than dissipate the sea-tang by means of steaming them in sea-weed. They used this clam-bake steaming process for fish and even for corn.

Long Island, more favored by nature than New England, never concentrated on one seafood so much. Codfish became "sacred" and overworked on the menu in New England, as it never did on more favored Long Island. The New Englander has always leaned heavily upon codfish because of its accessibility, but the Long Islander has always had a richer, wider variety of fish with which to provide himself. Not having the "cod complex" his meals were never quite so narrow in scope. Even in winter he has always been able to get plenty of flounder, from October to April; and striped bass from May to December. Shell fish are actually at their best all winter, and Long Island waters are rarely or for long badly frozen over.

The new commercial fishery techniques, of course, have shifted the fishing seasons and brought fish in plenty to all regions at nearly all times, but the traditional seafood standards, including the salting and drying of cod, were created in other days. A lesser volume of salt cod is now used all over the United States, because of more plentiful fresh fish supply. Salt cod is capable of some very savory cookery in the hands of a knowing cook, but it was necessarily rather dull fare when eaten so often, cooked by ordinary means, with limited accompaniments. Long Island never had to do it, and never did; therefore cod is only one among many fish to a Long Islander, and not too high-rating a fish at that.

At many points on Long Island there are unique and effective tie-ups between the fishing boats and the seafood catering. Restaurants stand on the very fish piers, or close by, so that almost literally the fish is yanked from the net or the fish line into the frying pan or broiler (which is of course the absolute ideal). At Sheepshead Bay, for example, down near Coney Island on lower Long Island, is a picturesque wharf where many fishing boats tie up after going out to sea for fish. Here fish is sold right off the boat, or from stands by the water-side, and several famous seafood restaurants are operated by fishing boat captains themselves. Dining on fish at restaurants extending out over the water with fishing boats almost within reach from the windows, as for example at Sheepshead Bay, has been for years a Long Island treat. Other somewhat similar facilities exist at various other docks on Long Island at which the fishermen tie up—Bayshore, Sayville, Port Jefferson,

Riverhead, and in the Montauk, Orient Point and Peconic Bay sections.

Really to understand the art of seafood cookery and seafood enjoyment one needs to know certain basic facts. Fish is not just fish—it divides itself into four very definite classes:

1. *Shellfish.*—the seafood that shuts itself in shells and presents a problem in cookery of making the most of its delicate flavor, much of which is closely associated with the *shells*. (Clams, oysters, mussels, scallops, lobster, shrimp).

2. *Fat Fish.*—fish which contain considerable fat (over 5%), a fact which cannot be overlooked in their cookery. (Eels, mackerel, salmon, turbot, fattened carp, sardines, etc.). These fish have high nutritive and heat-producing value, but they are less digestible.

3. *Medium Fat Fish.*—fish which have only a moderate amount of fat (2% to 5%)—halibut, trout, etc. More latitude is possible in their cookery, and they are rather more digestible. Incidentally some fish are more fatty at some seasons of the year than others, and at such times are best baked, while at other times are best fried.

4. *Lean Fish.*—fish which are dry and without much fat (up to 2%), and therefore need quite particular care in cookery from this point of view. (Cod, whiting, pike, flounder, etc.). These fish do not have a high nutritive value, but their delicacy of texture, flavor and digestibility make them extra good fish cookery materials, and backgrounds for rich, appetizing sauces. Thus flounder (and its brother, sole) have drawn more attention from the great chefs of the world in devising unique sauces than probably any other known fish. Many are the chefs who have based their reputations on a sauce for sole or flounder, and there are surely a hundred or two different flounder or sole dishes.

Possibly the first great law of seafood and all fish cookery is the utmost possible freshness. Seafood, even in cool weather, will not keep fresh (without ice) more than 16 hours; even when lying on ice, seafood loses its flavor. To keep fish lying in water, even cold water, is a particular menace to freshness. The less fish is touched by human hands the better, too! All gourmets know that the fish that would jump from the water into the stewpot without a moment's delay would be "tops" for flavor! That is why shore feasts are so popular on Long Island and other places where seafood is cherished, and why fishermen learn so often to be cooks; because they are thus able promptly to eat their catch and have a double pleasure. Ideally, the diner-out on seafood should be able to point to his fish swimming in a tank, and after sitting down to an appetizer and a soup, then be served the fish he selected! In a few restaurants, this is actually done!

In a practical world, we must accept seafood compromises, of course. The bringing to market of fish is now greatly improved, and even legally supervised. (New York City has exceptionally high food-handling standards). The quick-freezing process is still not everywhere recognized to the extent it deserves as insuring full freshness of fish flavor, but is surely a great advance, especially for fishless inland territory. Perhaps its most important contribution is to eliminate home fish cleaning and thus make women more willing to cook fish.

Thus the *selection* of fish from the market is a prime factor in seafood delight. Some points for this are:

(1) select medium-sized fish rather than very large or small.

(2) the fish flesh must be plump and elastic; the belly walls particularly full and firm and not flabby; the scales bright, the eyes full and sparkling, the gills red. Never take fish with pale gills, eyes sunken or dull, belly flabby, mouth dry, flesh soft. Eel, lobster, crab, oysters, clams, etc. should be *alive*.

(3) choose fish that are *in season,* for best seafood taste.

(4) Arrange to cook fish in the one or more manners that are best suited to the fish. A salmon for example is not so good broiled as boiled; a bluefish is never as good broiled as baked.

Shellfish Cookery Secrets.—Whether or not Long Island was first in appreciating the special secrets of the shell in shellfish cookery, I am not prepared to say. I have found evidence that the Italians and the Portuguese knew them a long time ago; at least as regards mussels and shrimp. New Orleans also knew them. But it is regrettable that so many people who cook shellfish—even on Long Island and in New Orleans—are not aware of these secrets.

This is the "secret" No. 1: all dishes containing shellfish— with the exception of the oyster—should not be cooked minus all the shell; some shell should be admitted to the pot, yes, even to the dish served on the table, because the shell holds a great deal of distinctive flavor which should not be lost. That is why the gumbos of New Orleans are cooked—and served—with some crab and lobster shell in them. That is why broiled lobster is especially delicious, and why other dishes baked in shells, such as deviled crabs, are delicious. This is also one reason why bouillabaisse is so famed and excellent a dish—it usually is made with some shellfish shell in it.

This principle is simplicity itself to follow, (and in fact should be more widely applied than it is, for some recipes even in this book ignore it)! A mussel or clam or lobster or crab stew or chowder should have a few shells placed in the pot; they do something to the flavor, probably because of the iodine and calciferous content of the shell. A shrimp soup is made extraordinarily good (see recipe) by grind-ing the shells of the shrimp and adding them to the soup, thus putting the truest shrimp flavor into the soup. A mussel soup featured in certain New York Italian restau-rants is always served with several mussel shells in it, and contrary to most people's ideas, this is decorative as well as tasteful. It is cheating ourselves to throw away shells which hold the concentrated, distinctive flavor each shell-fish possesses. In this book I have striven as much as possible that this special feature be added to shellfish dishes. We must widen education on this subject. No New Orleans lover of seafood, or Marseilles lover of bouillabaisse ever looks distastefully upon the lobster or mussel or crab shell in the dish set before him. On the contrary he knows it as the sign and seal of the best shellfish flavor. The rest of America is not yet fully appreciative of the point, not even in New York and Baltimore.

"Secret" No. 2—which is known of course to many cooks: the oyster liquid or clam or mussel broth, or the liquor of any shellfish, is of equally great importance in cookery. It is extraordinary how many cooks toss aside this liquor and do not ingeniously, in some way, blend it into the food, as it should be. Most recipes in this book are careful on this point, for good Long Island cooks know about it. New Orleans cooks are actually cranky on this subject—they highly prize the oyster liquor, for example, and without it their gumbos and other dishes would not be what they are. One *should* be cranky about this matter—just as nowadays we are cranky about the sin of pouring down the sink the mineral salts of vegetables. Clam and mussel liquor are equally as important as oyster liquor. One of the urgent needs today is for shellfish lovers to clamor and insist that when they buy opened shellfish they should get their full quota of the liquor.

Other *Seafood Cookery Secrets.*—Quite related to the above "secrets" are those of using whenever possible the head, tails, bones and trimmings of fish. First of all, we need to get over the absurd squeamishness of failing to serve the fish on the table with head and tail on. Not all fish are suited to this, it is true, but the larger (and the smaller) fish are suited. The head contains (like the shells of shellfish) especial fish savors.

Next, it is particularly good technique to make use of the fish broth or stock obtainable by boiling the heads, bones, tails and trimmings. In this way the maximum fish savor comes out and is made available. Many people who do not like fish have undoubtedly been turned from it solely by the stupid methods of cooking which make a mere pulp of fish flesh, and neglect the art of preserving sea-tang, or the distinctive taste of the particular fish. This neglect is the same sin which is responsible for reducing other good foods to an indistinguishable pulp.

The French have long insisted on the use of "court-bouillon" (fish stock) for boiling or poaching fish, and the use of it for other cookery. The New Orleans Creole cooks have gone further—they have given this "courtbouillon" an additional meaning and value, transforming it into an actual *sauce,* as for example with their famous Redfish, *Courtbouillon* dish. In both instances the fish head, tail and bones are the basis; and in some other dishes the fish, bones, head and all, are included as a matter of course. The whole family of fish chowders, fish stews, gumbos, and bouillabaisse, including even the Jewish *gefüllte fish,* count upon the fish head, tail, skin, bones for the real essence of fish flavor. We need to incorporate this homely principle still more widely in fish cookery to make seafood more popular; to raise the annual per capita consumption of fish in the U. S. from 13.3 pounds to the level of other real fish-loving countries (as for example England, 35 pounds).

Boiling fish.—Therefore, incomparably the best way to boil fish or to poach or parboil fillets, is in *courtbouillon,* and there are various types of courtbouillon for each type of fish:

(1) *For large fat fish, or large pieces:*—a choice of a Vinegar or a Milk or Cream Courtbouillon can be made. For the fattest types of fish the Vinegar Courtbouillon is best: $\frac{2}{3}$ cup vinegar added to 2 quarts cold water, with 2 tablespoons salt, 2 small sliced carrots, 2 small sliced onions, a few thyme leaves, small bouquet garni; then 12 pepper-corns, bruised, put in 15 minutes before dish is done. For the milk or cream courtbouillon the directions are: In a kettle pour cold water and salt, then add $\frac{2}{3}$ cup of milk or cream per quart of water, also a peeled and seeded slice of lemon, and seasonings as above.

(2) *Smaller fish, eel, trout, etc.*—make the courtbouillon precisely as for Vinegar Courtbouillon, but substitute Chablis (white wine) for the vinegar, adding a quart of

water. Or use red wine; but in this case add a little more of the carrots and onion. In these wine courtbouillons, the fish is *served* with some of the courtbouillon poured over it, plus some of the vegetables, plus a little butter added just before serving.

Some of the *don'ts* about boiling fish are not to let the water stop simmering for a moment; also never to let it boil. Never *under*-cook boiled fish; allow 6 to 8 minutes per pound of fish. Also, do not stick a fork into a fish to see if it is done; use a thin skewer to determine if the flesh is separating from the bones.

The courtbouillon, let it be remembered, is prepared in advance for boiling the fish, and allowed to simmer for an hour before the fish is put in. Bring to a boil as soon as you put the fish in, then skim thoroughly, and then simmer for the required time. If the fish is cut into pieces to boil, then the courtbouillon should be brought to a boil before the fish pieces are put in, in order to "sear" them; and then set aside to simmer.

For poaching or parboiling, the fish is put into a covered pan containing courtbouillon, and placed in a moderately hot oven or over a low flame, and basted often; cooking time according to size. Sauce is made from this poaching liquor to pour over the fish.

Boiling fish in plain salted water is of course a simple, old method, excellent for some purposes.

Frying Fish.—Probably more fish are fried than cooked in any other way, but they do not make the best eating. However, it is true that small delicate fish have a more delectable taste when the frying process is used, provided the fry pan is clean and the oil or butter good and not allowed to reach the smoking point. But why not go the *whole* way in frying and sear the juices in *deep fat frying?* That is tops. Even the tiny whitebait, dipped in deep fat for just a minute, comes out a delicious tidbit. Trout come out very nicely too. Ordinary fry-pan fish cooking is treacherous; too shallow pan; too much heat; fat allowed to reach the smoking point. Result, bad fish, bad digestion.

Deeper frying pans, careful attention, can improve fry-pan fish. The fish needs thorough drying with towel or paper before frying, and thorough draining on absorbent paper after taking out. As for the preferred frying oil, olive or peanut oil are probably tops.

Deep fat Frying.—This technique is used for the smaller fish only; large fish could not be cooked enough in their interior without scorching the exterior. The best method is to soak the fish to be deep fat fried in *salted cold milk,* and then roll in bread crumbs, corn meal or flour. The fat should be at the 375° F temperature, just this side of the 400° F smoking point, to be accurate; consequently it is wisest to use a deep fat frying thermometer. Higher temperatures form a crust on the fish, creating a burnt flavor. The usual hash-house common seafood restaurant which operates on a rule o' thumb basis, ruins its fish in just this way. French cooks like lard; in America peanut oil or olive oil, Crisco or Spry (which are also vegetable fats) are preferred.

Fry-pan Deep fat Fry.—This is a makeshift, but not a bad one, if care is used, for fish up to one pound in weight. Even butter (clarified) can be used, or the above-mentioned oils. You heat the pan, and melt the fat in it, to the depth of ½ inch or more, bringing the fat to a boil before you put the seasoned, rolled-in-cornmeal fish in it. This sears the fish, browns it, and does a competent job.

Broiling Fish.—There are many gourmets who are convinced that this is the ace-high method for cooking fish. But that is sheer enthusiasm and a one-track palate. We must use discrimination, classify and segregate. Broiling is not the best method for all fish; in fact broiling some fish, like flounder, is a waste.

But there are tricks in broiling fish, too. Here are some points to watch:

(1) be sure to dry the fish thoroly, *first.*

(2) be sure to grease the broiling grid well.

(3) be sure to turn often while broiling.

(4) if fish are small and fragile, be sure the broiling grids

are near together; if not, use a double-wire broiler, laid on the regular broiling grid.

(5) if fish is of dry, flaky-fleshed type, be quite sure to brush both sides with bacon fat, oil or butter, season and then roll in flour.

(6) for the sturdier type of fish (mackerel, shad, salmon, bluefish, etc.) no flouring is necessary; and for fatter types of fish, no oiling.

(7) certain larger fish (like shad) are best broiled split down the back, with head and tail removed.

(8) broiling a whole fish should be done first on the fleshy side, then turned on skin side long enough to brown.

Baking Fish.—This method brings out the bouquet of many fish difficult to handle. It is not the most delectable form, but it is savory. The common error is to forget the classifications of fish (fatty, medium, non-fatty) and get too much fat in the baking dish; or, vice versa, not get enough. The *combinations* of ingredients need to be well-chosen for good baked fish. The glass baking dish or casserole enables one to bring baked fish to the table in a particularly hot and tasty manner. *Braising* is merely baking with the lid on the baking dish, plus basting.

A Few Final Hints.—There are those who say that they hate to cook fish at home *because of fish odors*. Let us meet this objection by saying that any fish odor in a house can be dissipated by burning some sugar on a pan. Cooking in parchment paper is one way of preventing fish odors. Another is to pour $\frac{1}{2}$ cup of vinegar in the frying pan after frying fish, and let it burn. This frees the utensil of all grease odors. Washing hands in strong salt water removes fish odor from hands.

It is a mistake, of course, to be over-squeamish about fish and wash or scrub them too much. Some of that very "sea slime" which *seems* (to the eye) objectionable, is the greatest source of sea tang. Don't be too "Dutch-housewifish" about seafood, therefore!

Fish can be skinned most easily by dipping for a short time in boiling water. Milk overcomes excessive saltiness in cooking salt fish.

III

The Great Disputatious Chowder Family

IF ANYBODY tells you that the American people are "regimented" or "standardized", just ask quietly, *"What about clam chowder?"* Your cocksure informer will get very red in the face, for nothing is more notorious than that various sections of Eastern America come to blows over chowder. Tomatoes or milk is the crucial question, also caraway seeds and salt pork. New England is rent and torn over these dissenting practices, but Boston, Maine, and Connecticut are allied against Manhattan or Long Island chowders, while Rhode Island teeters in between.

Where did this disputatious chowder family come from? Chowder has a much more fascinating origin than most of us realize; in fact it is so "communistic" in origin that the Dies Committee at Washington is likely to get excited about it as a red invasion! It originated in the fishing villages of Brittany, France, where *faire la chaudière* (prepare the caldron) was a community enterprise of the fishermen for common use, each one contributing something to the pot, whether fish, vegetable or spices, and each receiving a proportionate quantity of the finished hodge-podge, made with fish and ship biscuits, vegetables and savory ingredients (see the first chowder recipe given in this chapter). Nothing is said of milk in these early origins in France, nor, it must be admitted, anything about tomatoes! The French fishermen, settling in Newfoundland, brought along their *faire la chaudière* habit, using the rich abundance of seafood in their new home. This name traveled to the Maritime Provinces and then into New England a very long time ago; and of course quickly also traveled across the narrow inlets of Long Island Sound to the eastern end of Long Island, thence to Manhattan. On the way *"chaudière"* naturally became anglicized to *chowder*.

In those early days, before the American Revolution, admittedly nearly all chowders were milk chowders. Some chowders, like the original one, never had either milk or tomato. The tomato, it must be recorded, had few friends in any dish made to eat in those days, being called a "love apple" by the romantic, and designated by an encyclopedia of the period as a "straggling, clammy, ill-smelling, grayish-green plant." The fruit of this plant, the tomato, was regarded as possibly poisonous, certainly objectionable, and in any event disgusting!

Since Long Island has all this time been the place where New York and New England merge (at the eastern tip) it is not surprising that the chowder controversy rages even today on Long Island, despite the fact that a majority opinion certainly sides with tomato. But a few old, gnarled eastern island baymen, and hardy old ladies, who learned the cookery arts somewhere around the Civil War period when the tomato was still an outlaw, today continue to cling to the milk basis for chowder, and will not surrender. Canceling this out is the fact that many New Englanders, even up into Maine, and particularly in Rhode Island, have acquired the tomato chowder idea and uphold it against their scandalized neighbors. Connecticut is too close to New York to be pure New England, and also is in part a renegade from the milk chowder. And, in the main, west of the Hudson, as New York goes, so goes the U. S.

The caraway seed development is a trick which has muddied the chowder waters still further. It is not approved by gourmets, who cynically believe the scheme was concocted by low-grade restaurateurs to give some flavor to their scandalously "watered" clam chowder, lacking both clams and clam flavor. It is a red herring across the clam chowder trail, meant for appeasement of the chowder-hungry who are served with a chowder so diluted that a couple of clam pieces the size of a pea are all that can be found, while the chowder is over-stuffed with potatoes to further hide its poverty. The gourmets applaud the old salt on Cape Cod who remarked with devastating satire that he was surprised that New York "didn't put in a leetle bird seed, and plug tobacker." They agree that the average chowders sold in the beaneries of New York and low-grade roadside restaurants as Manhattan clam chowder—yes, even in some of New York's more ignorant but fancy hostelries—are mere travesties on the name, and it would be a blessing if they *were* prohibited by law!

Let it be understood that the real masters of the Long Island chowder—men now past threescore and ten in their struggle to keep the milk chowder out, men like old Bob Matthews (86) of Hempstead, or others like Coles Johnson or Capt. Benj. Combes, (who, alas, have now gone where St. Peter must decide the controversy)—all these men have had very severe notions of what makes a real chowder, even a tomato chowder. Old Bob Matthews, still alive, and still peppery on the point (see his recipe) insists, like his departed comrades in arms, that the chowder pot must be kept simmering *all day;* and insists, further, that it be cooled outdoors after it is cooked. To eat a chowder within a few hours after making it—or even on the same day it was made—sounds like sacrilege to these old men of the chowder pots of Long Island. They were Long Island's praetorian gourmet guards, who snorted like whales when an hour-old chowder was offered them; and might draw their fish knives menacingly if a milk chowder was even mentioned. Kenneth B. Van de Water, elderly editor of the Hempstead *Sentinel,* is more devastating than them all because he wields a trenchant pen his clam chowder prejudices to proclaim, and he sneers heartily (with New York and Long Island gourmets sneering in chorus with him) at the average chowder recipe, whether of tomato or milk. "They aren't worth tasting," he says, loftily, and he adds, confidently, that "every Long Island clamdigger will echo a loud, throaty 'you said it.' They are nothing but vegetable soup masquerading as clam chowder." Long Island is thus a region of polyglot chowders, every kind, every style, and many individualistic ways of making. (See for example a striking one, that has a long authentic background—the Strong's Neck Chowder).

The chowder family is thus lusty and numerous, as full of surprises as it is of nourishment and savor. You can get many different fish or clam chowders in Boston or New York, in restaurants across the street from each other. The clam chowder is, like baked beans, now running amok all over America, and alas! often prejudicing people against it because badly made. The fish chowder is slowly moving from New England and Long Island and the Gulf coast to the rest of America, as inland America obtains more fish. The lobster chowder, the codfish chowder, the crab chowder, the eel chowder, the haddock chowder, the whitefish chowder, the oyster chowder, the mussel chowder, the scallop chowder and a few more, are all cousins boasting the same family traits—and all good meals in themselves. There is no way to test out your reaction to chowders except to eat them, and in all probability you will pick your particular horse and bet on it, as we all do!

What is the actual merit of this violent chowder controversy? What started it? It is admitted to be the most famous gastronomic controversy in American history, exceeding easily the strawberry shortcake controversy. In February, 1939 Assemblyman Seeder introduced into the Maine legislature a bill to make tomato in clam chowder illegal!

Long Island's tomato clam chowder first captured New York City, where it was adopted and dubbed Manhattan clam chowder, and has since spread its conquering way throughout the rest of the country. Clam chowder, to most of America, means tomato clam chowder, even in the canned varieties of it sold nationally. Long Island came very naturally by the tomato base for clam chowder because it is a great truck farm region and tomatoes are very plentifully grown there; whereas in New England with its colder climate, tomatoes are not so readily grown, and therefore not so inexpensive as on Long Island and in New York.

There are definite things to be said for tomato clam chowder which are lost sight of in the mere argumentative heat of battle. The New England clam chowder appears to have been used widely, like the New England fish chowder, as a whole meal by itself. Thus it could be, and was desired to be, particularly substantial. In New York and on Long Island, clam chowder was developed more as a soup course, which therefore was *not* desired to be so substantial as to clog the appetite for other courses. The restaurants of New York, in particular, were not patronized in earlier days by those who wanted to dine only on clam chowder. They wanted a soup which would fulfill what French masters of cookery have always allotted to soup as its proper function, namely to *whet,* rather than to completely satisfy the desire for food.

So clam chowder (Long Island or Manhattan) was made with tomato instead of milk, and thus it performed its function admirably—even though the old New Englander finds it too insubstantial, and thinks he can logically scorn it for this reason. He does not stop to consider the point that a milk clam chowder is too filling—which was a merit in the old frugal days of New England, but not now when the diner wishes to go on eagerly to several other courses. Admitting quite readily that clams, like oysters, have a nice affinity for milk and cream, the Long Islander contends that the clam's affinity for tomato is also well demonstrated. I like a milk clam chowder for the same purpose that I like a milk fish chowder—because it does so well for a whole meal! But it would be rather ill-advised and even absurd, speaking from the gourmet or the nutritive standpoint, to serve a milk clam chowder, New England style, on a five or seven course dinner menu, with hors d'œuvres before it, and fish and meat, salad and desert courses to come after! Manhattanites and others have come to like a rather thin tomato clam chowder, for precisely this reason. The same principle can be seen at work in gumbos. A gumbo as served in New Orleans is a meal in itself, and used as such; and therefore the thin chicken gumbo soup usually served elsewhere elicits the contempt of such New Orleans folk who are in the habit of dining on heavy gumbos and little else. But the tendency is perfectly understandable in a day of more ample provision and fuller menus. At an ample dinner menu served at Antoine's, New Orleans, the soup course is never a thick gumbo. Antoine's knows better, just as the New Englander should.

The New Englander also may use the soft shell clam for his clam chowder, largely (we Long Islanders suspect) because New England's soft shell clams are likely to be more succulent than their quahogs (hard shell clams). On Long Island, however, the hard shell clams come in smaller and more succulent size ("cherrystones", for example) and thus make better chowder. The soft shell clam is more perishable, losing its freshness more easily, and is harder and less sanitary to handle.

Long Islanders and New Yorkers, in their opinion, reserve for the soft shell clam its true place—for steaming and eating with melted butter. Certainly no one can deny its extra deliciousness in this form, or the succulence of clam chowder made from the smaller quahogs. Long Islanders also occasionally make clam chowder out of soft shell clams, but they prefer the others, and New Yorkers are better served with fresher clams when their chowder is made from quahogs. Thus another difference between Long Island and New England seafood is explained, not as a mere cockfight of intransigent opinion, but as fact. That the rest of the United States tends strongly, I think, to agree with Long Island and New York City, rather than New England, seems to point to the solid basis of fact behind Long Island's practice.

There is something about the chowder which is kind to all shellfish, and many other fish; something that gently entices out more savors than ordinarily found when eaten in other ways. Fishermen who won't broil or stew or bake any fish, and generally care nothing for the fish they handle, care for it nevertheless *in a chowder.* Therefore chowder may be said to be a fisherman's choice of seafood; which may be a significant hint to all of us.

The line of demarcation between a chowder, a fish stew, a fish soup, and other forms of fish mixtures, like gumbos, is not always clear. For this reason I have grouped in this chapter for convenience many types of fish chowders and soups, even bouillabaisse.

Since bouillabaisse is probably the king of all fish chowders (if we use chowder as a broad term), it should be carefully considered along with all other chowders. No one knows whether *la chaudière* or the bouillabaisse came first in history; one originated on the north coast of France, the other on the south coast; one more close to the English tradition, the other more close to the Latin; but each as a practical fisherman's dish. Those who fish for a living should surely know what good fish food is. That is why both chowder and bouillabaisse are great seafood dishes; the chowder being more nearly adapted to American taste because not so violently seasoned.

There are known to be three or four basic recipes for bouillabaisse:

(1) With mussels, eels, lobster, small flounders, sea bass and whiting

(2) Mussels, lobster, eels, kingfish, striped bass, yellow perch and mackerel

(3) Mussels, cod, red snapper, smelts, yellow perch, conger eel and lobster

(4) Mussels, soft shell clams, carp, yellow pike, striped bass, pickerel, oysters, shrimp, lobster (this is an extra special one developed by a New York chef).

Note how mussels are first and universal in all four; also eels, in three. The amount of saffron to be used is almost as great a controversy as the milk-tomato chowder controversy. Also how it shall be fried with olive oil and spices. It is not very intelligent to want, in New York, just precisely the fish that they put in a bouillabaisse at Marseilles

—for example, rascasse and rouget. In Boston or London you could replace these with bream; in New York with small flounders and sea bass, as old Mouquin's used to do. World gourmet travelers—including Thackeray (who wrote a poem about bouillabaisse, and who declared the New Orleans version he ate was as good or better than the Marseilles one) are not likely to be doctrinaire; they want the bouillabaisse *method,* not necessarily an exact duplicate of fish.

The key bouillabaisse principle is that there be *at least five kinds of varied fish.* Nor is it necessary to overload it with saffron to have really genuine bouillabaisse. It makes a splendid dish with just a pinch of saffron, and handled in this way it is a candidate for wider American use. A fairly widespread belief is current that a bouillabaisse is hard on the digestion, over-spiced, foreign, messy, etc. This is based on the bad imitations which have been served in its name.

Let us now proceed to give chowder recipes—starting with the "mother" of all chowders:

LA CHAUDIERE, BRITTANY

$\frac{1}{4}$ lb salt pork, cut thin
2 or 3 lbs fish (any fish), sliced
Salt, pepper, (as for other spices, it's "what have you?")

5 or 6 potatoes, sliced thick
Ship biscuits—"hard tack" —(or pilot crackers), broken
Water

Fry the slices of salt pork. Then put in a layer of fish which has been cut in slices and rubbed with salt and pepper. Then put in a layer of potatoes; then a layer of hard tack or pilot crackers. Then begin all over again and make another series of layers. Add water enough to cover and cook for one hour, slowly.

(This is the probable ancestor of *all* chowders; a simple fisherman's stew; and it is still made among simple fishermen almost anywhere; only the spices used indicating what country!)

BASIC CHOWDER, PECONIC BAY

2 tablespoons cubed or chopped salt pork
1 tablespoon bacon fat
1 onion, minced
1 shallot, minced
2 sprigs parsley
4 cold boiled potatoes, diced
2 cups water in which the potatoes have boiled

1 quart clam broth
Pinch of thyme
$\frac{1}{4}$ teaspoon freshly ground black pepper
$\frac{1}{2}$ teaspoon paprika
Pinch cayenne pepper
24 medium-sized hard shell Clams
3 tablespoons flour
1 pint water, lukewarm

Fry the salt pork in the bacon fat. Add the onion, shallot, parsley (put through chopper with stems), and cook until the onion is golden brown. Add the potatoes, the potato water, the seasonings and the clams. Heat through. Blend flour with lukewarm water and add to the chowder. Bring to a boil, simmer below boiling point 10 minutes before serving.

(Note: this basic chowder recipe is a good standard for all chowders. For a *tomato* chowder add only 1 cup lukewarm water and a pint of stewed tomatoes. For a *milk* chowder, add a pint of Grade A milk. For an oyster, mussel, crab or lobster chowder—whether tomato or milk—simply substitute the desired shellfish for the clams, but always use the liquor of the shellfish; in the case of crab or lobster use clam broth and always put in some *shell*).

CLAM CHOWDER, STRONG'S NECK

$\frac{1}{2}$ lb salt pork
4 or 5 onions
6 potatoes

Salt and pepper
12 large hard shell Clams

Grind the salt pork through the coarse knife of the food

chopper, and fry it in a large kettle. Grind the onions also, and fry them in the salt pork fat until yellow-brown. Grind also the raw potatoes, place them in the kettle with just enough water to float them. Season with salt and pepper and cook until potatoes are tender, stirring occasionally to prevent sticking. Open the clams and save the liquor. Grind the clams in the chopper. Just before serving, add the clams and their liquor and bring just up to a boil, remove immediately from the fire and serve.

CLAM CHOWDER, BOB MATTHEWS

$\frac{1}{4}$ lb salt pork, diced
48 hard shell Clams,
    chopped
2 cups celery, chopped
2 onions, chopped

3 large fresh tomatoes,
    coarsely chopped (or one
    large can)
Salt, freshly ground black
    pepper

Start out 12 or 24 hours before eating to make this chowder. Heat the (preferably iron) kettle in which the chowder is to be cooked, then put in the salt pork, and fry out. Then put in the clams, chopped, and all the clam liquor. Add to this the celery, onions, tomatoes and seasoning. Put on a very slow fire, never let come to a boil, and let it simmer all day long (or at least 6 or 7 hours), stirring occasionally. Then take the pot off the fire and let cool in the open air. Then reheat (but never boil) when ready to serve.

(Old Bob Matthews of Hempstead, now 86 years of age, was for many years noted for his skill with chowders. He and his friend Kenneth B. Van de Water, editor of the Hempstead *Sentinel,* agree that this is the *real* Long Island or "Manhattan" clam chowder which makes New England chowders look pale at the gills and taste like "just another soup on the menu".)

MUSSEL CHOWDER, CHRISTINE

48 Mussels
2 small onions, minced
4 tablespoons butter
1 quart light cream, Grade
  A milk (or part evapo-
  rated milk)

Salt, pepper
¼ cup fine cracker crumbs
Toasted pilot biscuits

Steam the well-scrubbed mussels to open, remove meats, and save liquor separately. Fry the onions lightly in two tablespoons of the butter and add mussel liquor; simmer 10 minutes or until onions are tender. Add cream or milk and heat. Season, add mussel meats, and heat through, but do not boil. Just before serving sprinkle with fine cracker crumbs and put a big lump of butter on top. Serve very hot, immediately; accompany with toasted pilot biscuits.

CLAM CHOWDER, BLOCK ISLAND

50 soft shell Clams
Small piece of salt pork
1 tablespoon chopped
  onion
2 or 3 potatoes, boiled and
  diced
1 quart Grade A milk

3 tablespoons butter
Pinch of thyme leaves
1 bay leaf
1 clove
1 sprig parsley
6 soda crackers

Steam the well-washed clams in a cup of water. Remove the clams from shells; separate the hard and soft parts of the clams. Chop the hard parts fine. Strain the liquor through a fine cloth. Cut the salt pork into small cubes, fry it with the onion until onion is lightly browned, in large kettle. Add the diced potatoes, the minced clams (both the hard and soft parts), the milk, the butter, the thyme, bay leaf, clove and parsley. Break the soda crackers finely into it. Bring to the boil, then simmer for 15 or 20 minutes. Just before serving add the clam liquor which has been heated separately. Remove the bay leaf and parsley, and serve with pilot crackers.

CLAM CHOWDER, GLEN COVE

50 medium-sized hard shell
    Clams
¼ lb salt pork
3 onions, thinly sliced
3 potatoes, raw, thinly
    sliced

12 Uneeda Lunch Biscuits,
    broken
Salt, pepper, paprika
1 tablespoon flour

Open the clams, saving the liquor. Cube the salt pork, place in a saucepan, then add a layer of onions, then of potatoes, then of the biscuits, then of clams. Season with salt and pepper and dredge over each layer a little flour. Add the clam liquor—adding a little water if liquor is not sufficient, just to cover, but do not make a soup out of this dish. Cook until the potatoes are soft. This dish is to be eaten with a fork, not a spoon.

OYSTER GUMBO CHOWDER, AMITYVILLE

1 quart Oysters
2 tablespoons onion,
    chopped fine
¼ cup butter
½ can okra

1 small can tomatoes
Salt, pepper, cayenne
5 cups fish stock
1 tablespoon sweet butter
Saltine crackers

Parboil the oysters in their liquor; drain. Let liquor settle for awhile. Meantime fry the chopped onion in the butter for 2 minutes, then add the okra, tomatoes, salt, pepper, few grains cayenne. Boil for 5 minutes, add the oyster liquor and the fish stock, bring to a boil again and let simmer gently for 12 minutes. Adjust the seasoning and add the sweet butter. Just before serving, add the oysters. Heat through. Put a saltine cracker in each soup plate and pour chowder over.

FISH CHOWDER, BRIDGEHAMPTON

2 lbs any white-fleshed fish
$\frac{1}{8}$ lb salt pork
3 small onions, chopped
4 pilot crackers, broken
Water

Salt, pepper, nutmeg,
allspice, cayenne
2 tablespoons tomato catsup
1 pint white wine or cooking sherry

Cut the fish into 2-inch pieces. Fry the salt pork together with the onions. Place fish into a saucepan and just cover with water. Add the onions and the salt pork, the pilot crackers and the seasonings. Cook gently for 30 minutes. Then add the catsup and wine; simmer 15 minutes more. Accompany with pilot crackers.

OYSTER CHOWDER, JOHN HOWARD PAYNE

1 quart Oysters
3 cups milk
2 cups thin cream
1 cup water
1 cup thick cream
1 bouquet garni
2 thyme leaves

$\frac{1}{4}$ teaspoon ground cloves
$\frac{1}{4}$ teaspoon onion juice
1 blade mace
1 tablespoon creamed butter
2 tablespoons parsley, minced

Parboil the oysters in their liquor, drain. Let liquor stand awhile, then pour it slowly into a double boiler, and add the milk, thin cream, water, thick cream, the bouquet garni, thyme, clove, onion juice, mace. Bring just to a boil, then strain. Separate the soft parts of the oyster. Chop the hard parts and add to the liquid and bring just to the boil again. Add the soft parts of the chopped oysters just before serving, and the creamed butter and the parsley. Pour into soup plates, and serve with water crackers.

(John Howard Payne wrote "Home Sweet Home," and his home at Easthampton, a shrine for many visitors, has been preserved as one of Long Island's treasures).

FRUIT OF THE SEA CHOWDER

12 Oysters
12 Clams, steamed, shelled
 1 quart Mussels, steamed
   and shelled
 6 Shrimp, boiled and
   shelled
 1 stalk celery, chopped
 1 medium-sized onion,
   finely chopped

2 leeks, finely chopped
$\frac{1}{4}$ lb butter
1 pint milk
$\frac{3}{4}$ lb potatoes, diced
1 cup light cream
3 egg yolks, beaten
Pilot crackers

Cook oysters in their liquor just until edges curl; drain. Prepare other shellfish as directed. Dice the celery, onion, leeks and fry gently in the butter. Add $\frac{1}{2}$ cup each of oyster and clam liquor, the milk, and the diced potatoes. Cook for 20 minutes, then press through a sieve. Heat the cream, pour over beaten egg yolks, beating constantly. Add to soup just before serving. Then place the prepared shellfish into a soup tureen, and pour the liquid over it. Serve with pilot crackers.

OYSTER AND OKRA CHOWDER

1 large onion, chopped
$\frac{1}{8}$ lb salt pork
3 tomatoes, peeled and
   chopped
4 Okra pods

2 sweet peppers, minced
$3\frac{1}{2}$ pints white stock
$\frac{1}{3}$ teaspoon curry powder
1 teaspoon arrowroot
24 Oysters

Brown the onion in the salt pork, then add the tomatoes, the okra and the peppers. Then put in the white stock and curry and simmer for 15 minutes. Add the arrowroot mixed with a little cold water. Cook 5 minutes longer. Then just before serving heat the oysters in their own liquor for 3 or 4 minutes and add to the soup.

MUSSEL SOUP, MARSEILLES

48 Mussels
1 large onion, minced
3 parsley stalks
1 small bay leaf
5½ cups water

3 leeks (white parts),
  finely minced
4 tablespoons olive oil
1 teaspoon salt
1½ cups of vermicelli or rice
Pinch saffron and pepper

Steam open the well-scrubbed mussels in a large kettle containing also the onion, parsley, bay leaf, and the water. Shell out the mussels and keep warm; reserve the broth and strain. Fry the leeks in the olive oil, add broth, bring to a boil; add salt, vermicelli or rice, and the saffron and pepper. Simmer for 30 minutes. Just before serving add the mussels. Serve with saltines.

WHALER FISH SOUP, NORWEGIAN

1 stalk celery, diced
6 carrots, diced
¼ cup butter
1½ quarts fish stock (made
  from heads, tails, trimmings of any fish)

3 egg yolks, beaten
1 cup cream
1 tablespoon sugar
1 tablespoon vinegar or
  lemon juice
2 cups scalded milk

Cook the celery and carrots in the butter add the stock and simmer for 30 minutes. Mix together the egg yolks, cream, sugar, vinegar, stir in the scalded milk, and pour into the fish stock mixture. Serve immediately with pilot crackers.

FISH HEAD OYSTER SOUP

3 or 4 fish-heads
1½ quarts cold water
1 cup milk
1 small onion, sliced
1 small carrot, sliced
4 peppercorns
Blade of mace

Salt and pepper
1 tablespoon butter
1 tablespoon flour
12 Oysters
1 tablespoon parsley,
  minced

Wash the fish heads lightly and put in a pot with cold water, the milk, the onion, carrot, peppercorns and mace, also salt and pepper. Bring to a boil, skim, and then let simmer for 2 hours. Strain the liquor into another saucepan, add the butter and 1 cup of the oyster liquor in which flour has been blended, and keep stirring until it boils. Then put in the oysters, the parsley and let cook for 4 or 5 minutes. Serve with salt crackers.

(Do not in any way deprecate this soup because it is made from fish-heads. The head produces more flavor than almost any other part).

SHRIMP CHOWDER, BABYLON

$\frac{1}{4}$ cup diced salt pork
1 large onion, chopped
1 cup diced celery
1 quart boiling water
1 quart diced cooked potatoes
2 teaspoons salt
$\frac{1}{4}$ teaspoon pepper

$\frac{1}{2}$ teaspoon celery salt
2 cups prepared Shrimp
1 pint milk
1 tablespoon flour
1 tablespoon butter
Paprika
1 teaspoon minced parsley

Fry pork in kettle in which chowder is to be made. Remove crispy bits and in the fat cook onion; when yellow add celery and boiling water. Cook 15 minutes, then add potatoes, salt, pepper and celery salt. Let all come to a boil and add shrimp. Cook 15 minutes longer and add milk. When this again comes to a boil thicken with flour and butter which have been blended together with a little cold milk. Pour into serving dishes and sprinkle with paprika and finely minced parsley. This is intended as the main dish for any meal. For the soup course, make it thinner.

FISH CHOWDER, À LA SCANDINAVIAN

1 lb fish, sliced
2 onions
2 carrots
2 outside stalks celery
1 small turnip
1 small bunch parsley
½ teaspoon salt

Vegetable left-overs,
   diced
1 cup thin cream
1 tablespoon flour
1 tablespoon butter
½ teaspoon sugar
A little mace, pepper

Wash the fish, put in a pot with 2 quarts of water. Add the onions, carrots, celery, turnip, parsley, salt. Let come to boil gradually, then simmer for 1 hour. Add any left-over vegetables, also the cream which has been blended with the flour. Cook 5 minutes. Then add the butter, sugar, mace, pepper and serve.

CODFISH CHOWDER, BLOCK ISLAND

3 lbs Codfish
Water
3 onions, chopped fine
1 carrot
3 sprigs parsley
1 bay leaf
1 clove
1½ teaspoons salt

2 lbs potatoes
2 tablespoons butter
Pepper
1 pint Grade A milk
1 tablespoon chopped parsley
½ cup broken lettuce

Remove the skin and bones from the codfish; place these trimmings in a kettle with water to cover, adding one of the onions, carrot, parsley sprigs, bay leaf and salt and clove; boil for 15 minutes. Dice the codfish fillets and potatoes into small pieces half an inch square. Melt the butter in a deep saucepan, and fry the onions until lightly browned. Then strain the fish broth over the onions, add the codfish and potatoes. Cook just below the boiling point for about 30 minutes, or until potatoes are soft. Add salt and pepper to taste, the milk, the chopped parsley and the lettuce. Heat thoroughly and serve at once.

FLOUNDER CHOWDER, BAYVILLE

2 onions, sliced
2 carrots, diced
1 parsley root, diced
½ celery root, diced
2 cups water

Salt to taste
1½ lbs Flounder
1 large potato, diced
¼ teaspoon pepper
1 cup light cream
3 tablespoons butter

Put in a kettle the onions, carrots, parsley and celery roots and water. Boil for about 15 minutes. Clean and slice fish and place in separate saucepan with potatoes, salt and pepper with just enough water to cover. Simmer just below boiling point for 25 minutes. Drain. Remove fish; bone, skin and flake. Add potatoes and fish to other vegetables in kettle. Strain water in which fish was cooked, blend with cream and butter, and pour into kettle. Bring just to a boil and serve.

OYSTER CHOWDER, STONY BROOK

⅓ cup diced salt pork
¼ cup celery, diced
1 cup potatoes, diced
1 onion, minced
¾ cup carrots, diced

½ cup water
Salt and pepper
3 cups milk
1 pint Oysters

Fry salt pork until crisp; add diced vegetables. Cook one minute. Add ½ cup oyster liquor drained from oysters, water and seasonings. Cook ten to fifteen minutes or until vegetables are tender. Add milk; bring almost to boiling point; add oysters and cook until oysters frill. Adjust seasonings to taste. Serve hot with small biscuits, crackers or melba toast.

CLAM CHOWDER, MIDDLE ISLAND

¼ lb bacon, diced
2 cans concentrated tomato soup
2 cups water
1 small bunch celery
4 medium onions
5 medium potatoes, peeled
1 bunch carrots

½ head cabbage
1 teaspoon thyme
6 parsley sprigs
1 teaspoon salt
¼ teaspoon pepper
50 medium-sized hard shell Clams, shelled

Brown the bacon in the soup kettle, then add the tomato soup, with 2 cups water. Simmer for 5 minutes. Grind the vegetables together and save the juice, adding both to the kettle, together with the clam liquor. Add seasonings. Let simmer again. Separate the hard parts of the clam from the soft; grind the hard parts, chop the soft parts and add both to kettle. Let simmer for 5 minutes more, and then let stand for 2 hours without heat. Before serving bring almost to a boil.

SEA TANG, LONG ISLAND

2 lobsters, boiled
1 lb Bay Scallops (not large deep sea kind)
1 lb crab meat
8 soft shell clams, medium size, steamed and shelled
1 lb mushrooms
1 quart Grade A milk

½ lb shrimps
2 tablespoons butter
2 tablespoons flour
1 pint cream
Pepper, salt, few grains cayenne
½ cup sherry or Chablis (white wine)

Cut the lobster meat into small pieces. Simmer the scallops and crab meat and the soft part of the clams and mushrooms in the milk, with several mussel and lobster shells. Boil the shrimps separately and shell. Melt the butter, blend in the flour; add the cream. Season. Then add the other ingredients and the milk in which they were cooked. Finally add the sherry or white wine.

CODFISH CHOWDER, GARDEN CITY

3 lbs Codfish
3 onions
1 carrot
2 teaspoons parsley, chopped
1 bay leaf
1 clove

2 tablespoons butter
2 lbs potatoes, cubed
Salt and pepper
1 pint Grade A milk
2 tablespoons chopped lettuce

Clean the fish and cut into cubes. Put the head, tail and trimmings in a pot with salted water to cover, add one onion and one carrot, a teaspoon of parsley, the bay leaf and clove. Bring to a boil and simmer for 15 minutes. Strain. Meantime cut the codfish into cubes, and cube the potatoes also. Chop the remaining two onions fine and put in the kettle with the butter; cook 2 or 3 minutes. Put the codfish and potatoes and onions into strained broth and simmer until tender (about 20-25 minutes). Season, and then add the milk, remaining teaspoon of parsley and the lettuce. Pour into soup plates on which have been laid toasted pilot crackers.

CREAM OF OYSTER AND CLAM, LONG ISLAND

1 pint Blue Points or other small Oysters
1 pint medium-size hard shell Clams
½ cup cold water
2 tablespoons cornstarch
1 quart Grade A milk

Salt, celery salt, white pepper
1 tablespoon creamed butter
3 egg yolks, beaten
1 tablespoon sweet butter
4 drops onion juice
Whipped cream

Clean the oysters and clams, separate from their liquor and chop fine. Add them to the liquor together with cold water, and bring to a boil. Let simmer gently for 5 minutes. Blend the cornstarch with a little milk, stir into the remaining milk and add to the hot mixture. Bring to a boil, season, and let simmer for 5 minutes. Then strain through a fine cloth into another pot, add the creamed butter and simmer for 10 minutes. Then add gradually also the beaten egg yolks, stirring meanwhile, and adding also the sweet butter and onion juice. Serve in cups and top with whipped cream. (The shellfish need not be strained out of this soup, if you prefer to serve them).

OYSTER SOUP, STATE PARKWAY

1 quart Oysters	1 clove
2 cups white stock or water	1 blade mace
1½ cups bread crumbs	2 tablespoons creamed but-
2 cups celery, chopped fine	ter
1 onion, chopped fine	2 cups scalded milk
2 sprigs parsley	½ cup thick cream
½ bay leaf	

Clean the oysters, drain and reserve the liquor. Cut away the soft parts of the oysters and chop the hard parts. Place in a saucepan the white stock or water, the bread crumbs, the oyster liquor, the chopped oysters, the celery, the onion, the parsley and the spices. Cook for 15 minutes. Then puree, forcing hard through a sieve; again bring to a boil, after which add the butter, the milk and cream. Simmer 3 minutes and serve piping hot.

HADDOCK CHOWDER, NATHAN HALE

2 lbs Haddock, including 2 fish heads	1 small piece salt pork, finely chopped
2 slices each of onion, carrot	1 can tomatoes
1 bay leaf	3 tablespoons butter
1 clove	⅓ cup cracker crumbs
2 thyme leaves	Salt and pepper, nutmeg
1 cup diced raw potatoes	2 tablespoons creamed
1 onion, fried in butter	butter

Make a fish stock with the 2 heads and the fish trimmings, by placing in a saucepan with enough salted water just to cover, bringing slowly to a boil, and simmering for

20 minutes with the carrots and onion slices, the bay leaf, clove and thyme. Strain. Place the fish, cut into 2-inch pieces in the strained broth in the saucepan. Add the raw potatoes, the fried onion, the salt pork, the tomatoes, the butter, cracker crumbs, salt and pepper, a few grains of nutmeg. Bring to a boil and then simmer for 25 minutes. Then add the creamed butter and cook for 5 minutes longer. Serve in soup plates in which a pilot cracker has been laid.

FISHWIFE'S STEW, GREENPORT

2 lbs fish fillets: L. I. flounder, sea bass, blackfish, mixed
1 eel, skinned and cut in pieces
1 tablespoon wine vinegar
$\frac{1}{4}$ cup olive oil
1 clove garlic, crushed
12 sorrel leaves
1 bay leaf

1 teaspoon minced parsley
1 onion, chopped
10 mussels, well scrubbed and steamed open
$1\frac{1}{2}$ cups white wine (Chablis)
2 tomatoes, peeled and sliced
Salt and pepper
Stale bread, thin slices

Place the fish fillets and eel in a saucepan. Then add the vinegar, oil, herbs, mussel meats with two mussel shells, tomatoes and wine; shake the pan so that the contents are well mixed. Season with salt and pepper, and then bring just to a boil; cover tightly and simmer for 15 minutes. Lay the stale bread slices on the bottom of a casserole, distribute the fish over them and pour in the liquid, leaving the mussel shells out. Cover tightly and bake in moderate oven for 15 minutes.

FISH-MUSSEL CHOWDER, MONTAUK POINT

50 mussels, steamed
$\frac{1}{4}$ lb salt pork, diced small
2 onions, chopped
3 cups water

4 potatoes, cubed
$1\frac{1}{2}$ lbs fish, cut in 3-inch pieces
3 cups milk

Remove the mussels from the shells, and save liquor. Fry

the salt pork cubes brown, add the onions and fry until light brown. Add water and two clean mussel shells and boil for 5 minutes. Then add the potatoes and 2 cups of the mussel liquor. When potatoes are nearly done, add the fish and the mussels and simmer 5 minutes more. Then take out the shells, add the milk, heat thoroughly; season with salt and pepper and serve hot with pilot crackers.

FISH CHOWDER, PATCHOGUE

5 or 6 lbs of almost any Long Island fish
½ lb bacon, chopped fine
2 onions, chopped fine
2 sweet peppers, chopped fine
3 cloves garlic

4 sprigs parsley, coarsely minced
3 sprigs thyme
1 quart of canned tomatoes
3 potatoes, cubed
Salt, pepper
Juice of ½ lemon

Cut the fish into small slices, bones and all; leave even the heads and tails on (but cut off tips of tails). Fry the bacon slowly, add the onion, peppers, garlic, parsley and thyme and fry until brown. Add the tomatoes, the potatoes and salt and pepper. Cook slowly for 30 minutes; add fish and cook slowly for another 30 minutes. Just before serving add lemon juice. Serve with pilot crackers as a chowder; or strain and serve as soup.

FISH CHOWDER, BELLE HARBOR

1 clove garlic, minced
2 onions, chopped
¼ lb butter
¼ lb cooked ham, chopped
2 tomatoes, chopped
10 shrimp
1 eel, skinned, sliced
1 slice each of 4 or 5 kinds of fish

5 sorrel leaves
25 mussels
1 bay leaf
Salt
¼ teaspoon freshly ground pepper
10 oysters
3 tablespoons lemon juice

Fry the garlic and onions in butter until tender but not browned. Add the ham and fry gently. Add the tomatoes, the shrimp, eel, fish and the sorrel. Stir and fry, shaking the pan, until well heated. In another saucepan steam the mussels in a little water; remove them from their shells. Add boiling water (sea water if available) enough to make nearly two quarts of liquid in the pot, and leave two or three mussel shells in it. Drop the mussel meats in also and cook for 15 minutes gently. Then strain this liquid over the fish mixture, add the bay leaf, salt and pepper. Also add the oysters, together with their liquor and simmer until the oyster edges curl. Then add the lemon juice, take out the mussels and mussel shells and throw them away. The chowder is ready to serve; each person to receive at least one of all the various seafoods in it.

FISH BISQUE, MATINICOCK

1 lb cod, haddock, salmon or other fish	Salt, pepper, few grains cayenne
1 quart cold water	$\frac{1}{4}$ cup green peas, cooked
3 bruised peppercorns	$\frac{1}{4}$ cup asparagus heads, cooked
1 bunch herbs	
2 tablespoons butter	1 tablespoon potato, cooked and cubed
3 tablespoons flour	$\frac{1}{2}$ pint cream

Clean and wash the fish, remove skin and bones, cut the fish into small pieces; place in 1 quart of cold water with the peppercorns and herbs, let simmer for 40 minutes. Press through sieve to a fine puree. Melt the butter, blend with the flour, add the hot fish puree. Bring to a boil and let simmer for 10 minutes, constantly stirring. Season with salt, pepper, cayenne, add the vegetables, and finally the cream. Heat thoroughly and serve.

CREAM OF OYSTER, BLUE POINT

1 quart Oysters	Pinch of thyme
3 cups Grade A milk	Pinch of ground clove
1 cup water	Blade of mace
1 cup thick cream	1 tablespoon creamed butter
2 cups thin cream	5 drops lemon juice
(or 3 cups milk)	3 tablespoons chopped
Bouquet garni	parsley

Parboil the oysters in their liquor; strain and let the liquor settle in deep dish, and then pour slowly into double boiler. Add the fresh milk, the water, the cream, the spices. Bring just to a boil and strain. Chop the hard parts of the oysters and add. Bring to a boil again and strain. Then add the soft parts of the oysters, the creamed butter, the lemon juice and the parsley.

SHRIMP SOUP, NORWICH

1 lb fresh Shrimp	$\frac{1}{2}$ cup tomato juice
3 tablespoons butter	6 sorrel leaves, chopped
1 tablespoon olive oil	1 tablespoon lemon juice
1 onion, chopped	$\frac{1}{8}$ teaspoon pepper
$\frac{1}{2}$ clove garlic, minced	Croutons

Cook shrimp 20 minutes in seasoned boiling water just to cover. Drain, and save the liquid. After shelling the shrimp and removing black veins, cut up the shrimp, but save the shells and heads. Melt the butter, add the oil and fry the onion and garlic slowly, but do not brown. Add the tomato juice, sorrel, the liquor in which shrimps were cooked, and the shrimps, bring to a boil. Then grind, in a mortar or with a hammer, the shrimp shells and heads as fine as possible; mix with some of the shrimp liquor and press it hard through a sieve. Add to the soup, and simmer until all is well blended. Add the lemon juice; season. Serve with croutons.

SHRIMP SOUP, BROOKVILLE

25 Shrimp
1 quart fish stock
1 tablespoon butter
1 teaspoon mixed herbs
2 tablespoons arrowroot or
  cornstarch

½ cup cream
1 egg yolk
Salt, pepper, few grains of
  cayenne
Asparagus heads

Wash the shrimp, cook in the fish stock for 10 minutes; drain off and save the stock. Shell the shrimp (saving the shells and tails, but not heads). Fry these shells and tails in the butter, together with the herbs; then pound the shells in a mortar (or with hammer). Simmer the pounded shells in the liquor in which the shrimp were boiled. Strain. Mix the arrowroot with the cream, into a paste, add to the stock and simmer for 10 minutes. Mince the shrimp, add to the soup, thicken with the beaten egg yolk, season and garnish with the asparagus heads.

LOBSTER SOUP, WATERVILLE

1 small Lobster
1 cup cold water
1 anchovy fillet, minced
4 tablespoons butter
1 quart Grade A milk

4 tablespoons flour
Salt, pepper, few grains of
  cayenne
Triangles of fried bread

Plunge the lobster in boiling water, remove pot from fire at once and let cool. Extract the meat, laying the coral and green aside. Crush claws and shell, put into the cold water with the anchovy fillet, and let simmer 30 minutes. Strain carefully, add to a white sauce made of the butter, milk and flour. Chop the lobster meat fine and add; season. Mash to a paste the coral and green; stir into the soup, reheat. Serve with triangles of fried bread.

FISH CHOWDER, NEW LONDON

1 lb Codfish
1 lb Haddock
5 cups water
2 cups raw potatoes, diced
1 onion, finely chopped
1½ inch cube salt pork, minced
Bouquet garni
Blade of mace

Pinch of thyme
Few grains cayenne
2 cups Grade A milk, scalded
Salt and pepper
2 crushed peppercorns
2 tablespoons butter
6 saltine crackers, soaked in milk

Cut fish into two-inch pieces. Place in a soup kettle with 5 cups of water, add the potatoes, the onion and the salt pork and the seasonings. Simmer the mixture just below the boil for 25 minutes. Strain off the liquid and reduce over a hot fire to 3 cups. Return to kettle in which potatoes and other ingredients have been kept warm; simmer for 5 minutes. Add the milk, bring the mixture to a boil, season with salt and pepper and cayenne, add the butter and the soaked crackers. Let stand for 10 minutes. Serve with pilot crackers.

FISH CHOWDER, SHEEPSHEAD BAY

2½ lbs any white-fleshed fish in season
5 cups cold water
1 teaspoon salt
1½ inch cube, salt pork
2 onions, finely chopped
2 cups diced, raw potatoes
Pinch of thyme
½ bay leaf

2 cups Grade A milk, scalded
1 sprig of parsley
1 clove
Few grains nutmeg
1 tablespoon butter
1 tablespoon minced parsley

Wash and wipe the fish with damp cloth, put in soup kettle with 5 cups cold water and teaspoon of salt. Bring to a boil, then let simmer gently for 25 minutes. Strain the fish out of the broth; take skin and bones from fish and set aside to keep warm. Fry the salt pork with the onions; and add to the broth together with the potatoes, the thyme and the bay leaf. Cook until potatoes are soft, then put in the fish and add the milk, the sprig of parsley and remaining seasonings. Heat well, and just before serving add butter. Put in the bottom of each soup plate a toasted pilot cracker and a bit of the minced parsley, and pour the chowder over it.

FISH BROTH, FORT POND

2 tablespoons butter	¾ teaspoon salt
2 tablespoons flour	Few grains cayenne
1 cup Chablis (white wine)	Nutmeg
4 cups water	2 lbs bones, heads and trim-
2 small onions, sliced fine	mings of any fish
2 small leeks, sliced fine	2 tablespoons creamed
1 crushed clove	butter
1 bouquet garni	Toast
2 crushed peppercorns	Grated Parmesan che

Blend the butter, melted, in the flour; pour in the wine, water, the onions and the leeks sliced fine, the clove, bouquet garni, peppercorns, salt, cayenne and nutmeg. Boil furiously for 15 minutes. Then add the fish bones, heads and trimmings which have been washed and cleaned. Let simmer for 25 minutes, and then strain through a fine sieve. Adjust the seasoning, add the creamed butter and cook for 10 minutes. Serve on soup plates on which has been placed toast topped with a spoonful of the cheese.

SCALLOP AND OYSTER STEW, POINT O' WOODS

3 quarts Grade A milk	1 quart Bay Scallops (not
1 small onion, chopped	the large deep sea kind)
6 stalks celery, chopped	2 quarts Oysters
5 tablespoons butter	Salt, pepper, cayenne,
	nutmeg

Scald the milk in a double boiler. Meanwhile fry the onion and celery in 2 tablespoons of the butter. Then fry the oysters and scallops together in remaining butter until the oyster edges curl. Season with salt and pepper and a few grains of cayenne and nutmeg. Combine with milk in double boiler. The stew is poured into soup plates containing toasted pilot crackers. It should be served immediately.

LOBSTER CHOWDER, BAYVILLE

4 Lobsters, boiled
$\frac{1}{4}$ lb salt pork
1 stalk celery
4 potatoes
1 carrot
3 onions
1 teaspoon chopped parsley
2 quarts chicken stock
  or consommé

$\frac{1}{8}$ teaspoon poultry
  seasoning
1 small can tomatoes
$\frac{1}{4}$ cup cooked rice
3 tablespoons flour
1 pint or 1 quart light
  cream or rich milk
2 tablespoons butter
Whipped cream

Pick the meat of the boiled lobsters and dice, saving the fat and coral. Dice the salt pork finely and fry out the fat. Dice the celery, potatoes, the carrot and the onions; add the parsley and fry with the salt pork. Then add $\frac{1}{2}$ cup of the liquor in which the lobster has been boiled and the chicken stock, the seasonings, also a claw and some of the lobster shell. Simmer until the vegetables are tender, add the lobster meat and let simmer for 15 minutes. Skim carefully, remove shells. Add tomatoes and rice. Thicken as follows: Blend the flour with the cream or milk and add to chowder, stirring constantly until smooth. Beat in the butter. Adjust seasonings, and use additional milk or chicken broth to bring to preferred consistency if necessary. Serve with whipped cream.

EEL CHOWDER, SMITHTOWN BAY

2 small Eels	6 tablespoons butter
3 slices onion	$\frac{1}{2}$ cup stale bread crumbs
3 leeks	3 egg yolks
1 quart boiling water	$\frac{2}{3}$ cup thick cream, warmed
1 cup fresh spinach, minced	Salt, pepper, a little
1 cup fresh lettuce, minced	nutmeg

Skin and wash the eels, and soak in salted water for 10 minutes; cut in one-inch pieces. Fry the onions and the leeks (white part only) for 4 minutes in 3 tablespoons of butter. Pour in the quart of boiling water and add the eel. Bring to a boil and then let simmer gently for 25 minutes. Remove the eel, reserve the broth. Take the bones from the eel; keep the eel meat hot. Cook the spinach and lettuce in 2 tablespoons of butter for 5 minutes, stirring occasionally. Add $\frac{1}{4}$ cup of broth in which eel was cooked and the stale bread crumbs. After this blends, add it to the remaining broth; simmer for 10 minutes. Take from fire and stir gradually into the egg yolks; add the cream. Then add eel meat, one tablespoon butter, the salt, pepper and a few grains of nutmeg. Serve with pilot crackers. The eel meat may also be served separately, as an accompaniment to the soup, if desired.

CLAM CHOWDER, CENTER ISLAND

15 uedium-sized hard shell Clams	2 green peppers, chopped fine
2 onions, chopped	8 raw potatoes, diced
1 large can of tomatoes	2 black peppercorns

The clams are opened, and the clam liquor used in the mixture. Mince clams; add with other liquor to other ingredients. Cook until potatoes are tender.

CRAB BISQUE, GREAT SOUTH BAY

8 hard shell blue Crabs cooked & picked, (or 1 can crab meat)
1 quart fish stock or clam broth
1 cup stale bread crumbs
1 onion, sliced fine
2 sprigs parsley
$\frac{1}{2}$ bay leaf

Pinch of thyme
2 tablespoons of creamed butter
1 cup thick cream
Salt and pepper
Cayenne pepper
2 tablespoons cooked, diced shrimps
1 tablespoon sweet butter

Pick the meat from the crabs, and chop finely. Place in kettle with the fish stock, the bread crumbs, onion, parsley, bay leaf and thyme; also piece of crab shell. Bring to a boil, then let simmer gently for 20 minutes. Press all through a sieve, add the creamed butter and bring just to a boil again; then add the cream and season with salt, pepper and a few grains of cayenne. Heat through. Just before serving take out crab shell, add the diced shrimps and the sweet butter. Serve with salt crackers.

CORN-OYSTER CHOWDER, GREAT SOUTH BAY

4 strips bacon
$\frac{1}{4}$ cup minced onion
$\frac{1}{4}$ cup minced green pepper
2 cups diced raw potatoes
1 cup water

2 cups canned corn
3 cups milk, scalded
Salt, pepper
1 pint Oysters

The bacon, onion and peppers are fried together, after which the potatoes and water are added. The sauce pan is covered and let simmer until the potatoes are tender. Add more water if necessary to keep from sticking. The corn and milk are added and seasoned, after which the oysters are put in and the mixture heated very slowly, only until the oyster edges begin to curl; it must not boil. Serve hot and immediately.

FISH STEW WITH DUMPLINGS

2 lbs fish, sliced
1 cup potatoes, diced
½ cup celery, diced
2 tablespoons onion, minced
1 tablespoon butter
2 slices bacon, chopped

½ cup diced carrots
1 tablespoon minced green
  pepper
4 cups stock or clam broth
Salt, pepper
2 cups stewed tomatoes
Dumpling mixture

Put all the ingredients except the dumplings in a pot and simmer for one hour; if necessary adding more stock. Then drop in the dumplings, cover closely and cook 20 minutes.

CLAM-CORN CHOWDER, BAYSIDE

24 or 36 hard shell Clams,
  minced
1 medium-sized onion,
  finely chopped
2 outside stalks celery,
  coarse threads removed;
  cut into shreds; include
  celery leaves
3 tablespoons vegetable oil
  or fat

2 cups clam liquor
3 potatoes, sliced
3 tablespoons flour
1 teaspoon salt
½ teaspoon pepper
3 tablespoons hot fat
2 cups cold milk
1½ cups Corn pulp
1 tablespoon chopped
  parsley

Cook gently the onion and celery shreds in the oil or fat, stirring occasionally. When they are soft and yellowish add the clam liquor and let cook for 30 minutes. Prepare the potato slices and parboil in boiling water 2 minutes; after which drain and pour the potatoes in the onion-celery mixture and let cook for 30 minutes more. Blend together the flour, salt, pepper in the hot fat for a few minutes, then add the cold milk and bring to a boil, stirring; then add gradually the corn pulp, also the clams, minced. Stir, and then add the onion mixture and let boil for 1 or 2 minutes.

Add more salt if necessary, sprinkle with the parsley and serve hot.

CLAM GUMBO, HUNTINGTON BEACH

48 hard-shell Clams	3 tablespoons flour
Clam liquor	1 cup canned okra
1 tablespoon minced onion	1½ cups seived tomato pulp
4 tablespoons fat	Salt, pepper

Wash the clams, open and shell, reserving their liquor. Cut away the hard parts and put these hard parts through a food chopper. Add to the clam liquor enough fish stock or clam broth to make 1 quart. Simmer the soft parts of the clams, and the chopped hard parts in this liquor for 15 minutes. Cook the minced onion in the fat until brown, then blend in the flour, and when smooth, add to the clam mixture. Stir until it boils, then add the okra and tomato pulp, salt and pepper. Serve hot in soup plates with toasted pilot crackers laid in them.

OYSTER AND GREEN CORN CHOWDER

2 slices bacon	3 tablespoons flour
1 small onion, sliced	1 teaspoon salt
3 cups fresh sweet corn cut from cob (or whole-grain canned corn)	½ teaspoon black pepper
	2 tablespoons butter
	24 Oysters
2 cooked new potatoes, diced	1 tablespoon parsley, minced
1 quart milk	Pilot crackers, toasted

Cut the bacon into cubes and fry moderately crisp. Then add the onion and brown. Next put in the corn, and the potatoes. Add the quart of milk and one cup of oyster liquor. Let come to a boil, then thicken with the flour, salt, pepper and butter rubbed together, and then add the oysters. Stir until the mixture has boiled for 2 or 3 minutes. Serve in bowls, sprinkle parsley on top, and have pilot crackers handy.

SMOKY CHOWDER, SHIP AHOY

12 hard shell clams
2 tablespoons butter
½ lb salt pork, diced
4 large onions, sliced thinly
2 large leeks, white parts, sliced

2 tablespoons flour
2 qts milk, heated
4 large potatoes, diced fine
½ lb finnan haddie, diced
Salt, pepper, cayenne

Steam clams open. Drain, reserving broth. Discard hard parts of clams; dice soft parts. Melt butter in deep kettle, fry in it the salt pork, onions and leeks. Do not brown. Blend in flour until smooth; slowly add the milk, stirring until well blended. Simmer over low heat 20 minutes. Then add diced clams, potatoes and clam liquor. Simmer five minutes, or until potatoes are almost tender. Then add finnan haddie, and simmer five minutes more. Season.

BOUILLABAISSE, SUNRISE HIGHWAY

7 lbs of 8 kinds of firm-fleshed fish—bass, porgy, haddock, lobster, codfish, pieces of eel, halibut, etc.
3 tomatoes, peeled, crushed
½ cup olive oil
2 onions, minced
2 leeks, minced, white only
Several pieces lobster, clams

4 cloves garlic, crushed
1 bay leaf
1 pinch fennel
2 pinches saffron
1 teaspoon chopped parsley
1 sprig marum savory
Salt, pepper, few grains cayenne

Cut all the fish into 3-inch pieces. Place with all the remaining ingredients, including lobster claws and at least one fish head, in a pot with cold water to cover. Add salt and pepper and the spices and cook just below the boil for 25 minutes. That is all there is to it—it remains now only to serve in the traditional bouillabaisse manner. The soupy portion is poured into a soup tureen or deep dish, into which have been laid 4 or 5 pieces of bread. The solid portion is put on a platter, arranged tastefully, after removing the fish head; the platter is decorated with red lobster claws. The soup is served first, then the other.

BOUILLABAISSE, WALT WHITMAN

½ cup olive oil
1 lobster, freshly boiled and picked
3 onions, chopped
5 leeks (white parts only), chopped
1 stalk celery, with leaves, diced
2 cloves garlic, crushed
1 eel, skinned and cut in 2-inch pieces
1 shark fin
1 striped bass, cut in 2-inch pieces

1 young mackerel, cut in 2-inch pieces
5 tomatoes, peeled and chopped
2 cups Chablis (white wine)
1 cup mussel liquor
1 cup oyster liquor
16 mussels, steamed and shelled
16 oysters, shucked
2 pinches saffron powder
1 teaspoon parsley, chopped

Put the olive oil into a saucepan, add the lobster meat and two pieces of lobster shell and two mussel shells and cook for 10 minutes. Then add the onions, leeks, celery and the garlic. Cook again for 10 minutes. Then add the eel, the shark fin, the fish pieces, the tomatoes, the wine, the mussel and oyster liquor. Cook for 15 minutes. Add the steamed mussels and oysters, also the saffron powder and the parsley. Simmer 5 minutes more. Then lift out the solid parts and put on a platter containing bread slices; serve the soup in soup plates and eat both together.

BOUILLABAISSE, SEAWANAHAKA

3 different fish—whatever is available: flounder, mackerel, snapper, weakfish, or what have you.
2 small eels
3 cups Chablis (white wine)

1 cup water
Thyme, 1 bay leaf
2 tablespoons butter
3 sticks celery
4 sprigs parsley
Bread fried in butter

Clean and trim the fish and the eels and cut into 2- or 3-inch pieces, with the bones. Cook for 15 minutes until tender in wine and water together with thyme, bay leaf, butter, celery and parsley. Drain the fish and place on a hot platter, and pour some of the broth over it. Strain the rest of the broth into a soup tureen, into which have been placed squares of bread fried in butter.

GEFUELTE FISH, ROCKAWAY BEACH

$1\frac{1}{2}$ lbs white fish
$1\frac{1}{2}$ lbs pike
3 medium-sized onions
2 medium-sized carrots
1 parsley root
1 celery root, and some leaves

$\frac{1}{3}$ cup water
1 egg
1 tablespoon cracker meal
1 teaspoon salt
1 teaspoon sugar
$\frac{1}{4}$ teaspoon pepper

For best results clean, fillet and salt fish the night before and keep in refrigerator. Keep the heads, skins and all large bones. Prepare a four-quart pot with 2 onions sliced fine, carrots cut in round slices, parsley and celery roots cut in small pieces, and 1 quart cold water. Add the fish bones and skins, and let boil about 10 minutes before adding fish patties.

Chop remaining onion fine, adding a little water, then gradually add a little fish and water at a time and chop; next add egg, crackermeal, salt, sugar and $\frac{1}{8}$ teaspoon pepper, chopping all together. Fish should feel sticky against chopper. Form into patties and place in pot carefully. When all the fish is in pot, water should just cover it. Add remainder of pepper and more salt if necessary after cooking an hour. Cook covered for 2 hours, shaking pot every once in a while. Uncover and cook $\frac{1}{2}$ hour longer so there won't be too much gravy. Set aside to cool. Heat gravy, then strain into gravy boat. Arrange fish on platter, top each piece with slice of carrot. Serve hot or cold. If serving cold let fish gravy jell.

Serve with horseradish sauce, made by placing 4 tablespoons freshly grated horseradish in a bowl and mixing with $\frac{1}{4}$ teaspoon sugar, pepper and salt to taste, 1 teaspoon vinegar, 4 tablespoons tomato catsup.

GEFUELTE FISH, LONG BEACH

1 lb fish	2 cups cracker dust
6 small onions	1 carrot, sliced thin
1 egg	Boiled potatoes
1 teaspoon salt	Horseradish, grated
1 teaspoon pepper	

Use white-fleshed fish. It is better to blend flavor by using several varieties. Carefully preserve the clean raw fish skin. Chop the fish and mix with four finely minced onions, egg, salt, pepper, and cracker dust. Mold in small balls, wrapping each with a strip of the fresh skin, tying with string or fastening with toothpicks. Drop fish balls in boiling water with two onions and carrot. Remove to back of stove, and let simmer for $1\frac{1}{2}$ hours. Lift out balls; chill in refrigerator. Serve cold with horseradish. Boil potatoes in liquid in which fish was cooked, and serve hot with fish.

FISH MULLIGAN, STEWART EDWARD WHITE

3 lbs fish (any fish)	6 pilot crackers, broken
2 quarts water	Salt, pepper
12 potatoes, peeled	$\frac{1}{8}$ teaspoon cayenne
3 onions	1 tablespoon flour
6 pieces bacon or salt pork	1 pint oysters
1 can corn (or left-over rice)	

Clean and wash fish; cut in 2-inch pieces. Place in a deep kettle with water, the potatoes, onions, bacon or pork, and bring to a boil. Then let simmer until the potatoes fall apart. Add a can of corn or left-over rice, the pilot crackers, and the seasonings. Blend the flour in a little cold water and add for thickening. Add oysters or whatever shellfish you may have, together with their liquor, and cook 4 or 5 minutes longer. Serve immediately.

LONG ISLAND BUCK STEW

$\frac{1}{4}$ lb salt pork	2 cups potatoes, finely diced
Salt, freshly ground black pepper, few grains cayenne	24 Oysters
1 quart Grade A milk	$\frac{1}{2}$ cup finely crushed crackers
2 onions, finely chopped	2 tablespoons butter

Fry out the salt pork in the kettle, mix the seasonings with the milk and add with the onions and the potatoes. Let simmer until vegetables are tender, then add the oysters with their liquor. Add also the crushed crackers. Heat through, but do not let the milk boil. Just before serving put in the butter.

EEL CHOWDER, RIVERHEAD

$6\frac{1}{4}$ lbs Eels	Salt, pepper
1 lb salt pork, sliced	2 tablespoons butter
1 lb onions, sliced thin	Pilot crackers
$6\frac{1}{4}$ lbs potatoes, sliced $\frac{1}{4}$-in. thick	Celery
	Dill pickles

Clean and skin the eels, cut into $2\frac{1}{2}$- or 3-inch pieces. In a large kettle, preferably iron, put the diced pork at the bottom and fry until well browned. Then drain out the pork pieces, and fry the onions in the pork fat until brown. Turn out, and have ready to lay upon the kettle bottom a tin pie plate punched with holes, to keep the contents from burning. Lay in a layer of eels, then a layer of potatoes, sprinkle in some of the fried pork, and onions, salt and pepper; then begin with another series of eels, potatoes, pork, onions until material is used up. Dot the top with the butter. Cook slowly, do not let burn. The chowder is finished when the eel meat begins to leave the bone. Serve hot with hardtack or pilot crackers, celery, pickles.

(This is a Long Island recipe over a century old, used by several clubs of men around Riverhead at famous annual feasts. It is usually made outdoors on the pine bluffs overlooking the salt water bays of eastern Long Island, in a large kettle, using 4 times the quantities given above, to serve 25 people.)

BROWN FISH SOUP, CAPTREE PARK

1 lb fish trimmings (head, skin, bones, tails)
1 quart cold water
1 bunch herbs
½ teaspoon salt
4 bruised peppercorns
2 carrots, finely chopped
2 onions (or 2 sticks of celery) finely chopped

4 tablespoons butter
4 tablespoons flour
Pepper, few grains cayenne
½ cup red wine
2 tablespoons cooked potatoes, diced

Place the fish trimmings in cold water, bring to a boil and simmer for one hour, with herbs, salt and peppercorns. Strain. Cook the carrots and onions until tender; press through a sieve. Melt the butter in a frying pan and brown the flour in it. Stir in the fish stock, season, add the wine, bring to a boil again, and then add the diced potatoes which have been browned in butter, and the seived vegetables.

IV

Hail the Long Island Oyster!

Just as the Romans never were quite decided whether the best oysters came from Britain or from Lake Lucrinus, so we Americans seem to be undecided as to whether the best American oysters come from Long Island (varieties such as Gardiners Bay, Robbins Island, Blue Points, Cape Cods, etc.) or Chesapeake Bay waters (Lynnhavens). Oysters from *both* sections, I think, are superior to Gulf of Mexico or Pacific or European or Japanese oysters. Incidentally these names of oysters are often used *merely* to describe size: Blue Point for small, Cape Cod for medium, Lynnhaven or Robbins Island for large. This is a confusing error; the names mean a specific *quality*.

I am for the Long Island oysters, especially as they are now cultivated with great care by the "oyster farmers" on the various shores of Long Island. The Chinese and the Romans knew thousands of years ago how to farm oysters to make them fat, saline and succulent, and gourmets in all ages and in all lands which have seawater hovering near 70°F in temperature have grown them. Instincts both of health and of flavor-loving have incited people to eat oysters, for not only are they peculiarly flavorful, but they carry a rich load of both vitamins (A, B, C, D, G) and minerals—all the minerals a healthy body needs, but particularly iron, copper, iodine. Out in the "goiter belt" in the Middle West where scarcity of iodine in the diet produces much goiter, this same instinct makes the people of St. Paul, Minn., eat more oysters than almost any other city. The new facilities for shipping fresh oysters inland bring oyster succulence to the entire country, just as today orange juice is made available everywhere. It is possible now to ignore the old Latin phrase, *Mensibus erratis vos ostrea manducatis* ("oysters should be eaten only in certain months"), because oysters are quite edible and safe to eat in summer months which do not have the letter R in them, despite the fact that New York State law still prohibits the sale of oysters between May 15 and August 31. Other states do not have such laws. Long Island oystermen eat plenty of oysters in summertime, and they know oysters well; and even U.S. government bulletins say it is all right (Fishery Circular No. 21). Quick frozen oysters are of course available everywhere in all months.

One of the greatest stumbling blocks to the wider consumption of oysters is a certain peculiar temperamental attitude on the part of many *women*. They have a special squeamishness concerning (as near as I have ever been able to figure out) the oyster's "slipperiness," "gooiness," "jelly-likeness," or the idea that they're alive. Once at a dinner organized to promote seafood, I sat next to the wife of the chairman whose daily job it was to educate the public to extend the consumption of shellfish and seafood. In an indiscreet moment, to my amazement, this worthy lady confessed that she would rather part with a $10 bill than swallow one raw oyster. A great helpmeet *she* was to her husband!

In the speech I made on that occasion, I quite pardonably placed the blame for the too limited consumption of shellfish and seafood in America, where I still think it belongs —on squeamish women, who don't like to handle, clean, cook or eat it. They will handle chicken without a murmur, but they cannot look a fish in the eye, or take an oyster in hand without shuddering and recoiling! As for serving a fish on a platter *with its head still on,* or cooking a fish's head (as the Creole cooks love to do in making their superb Courtbouillon), they usually cannot stomach it. Women who *do* love oysters and seafood and gladly cook it for their men folks, are all the more to be praised and treasured because of the widespread attitude of their sisters.

Some folks have supposed that the old "fish on Friday" Catholic tradition, or the Jewish dietary laws against shell-fish, are largely responsible for the comparatively low rate of consumption of seafood in America. But I am convinced it is the women, for restaurants sell relatively a very large quantity of it to men who do not get it at home.

The Long Island oyster encourages a much wider acquaintance with the cookery possibilities of this bivalve, because it is farmed by a highly organized industry with superb sanitary facilities, because it is developed in varied size and type, and is distributed all over the nation. So many people have too narrow an idea of oyster eating; they know *three* ways only—raw, fried and stewed! Probably three-quarters of all oysters are eaten in these three forms, whereas there are, according to my count, at least 200 separate oyster dishes! Even the professional cooks usually know only about 40 or 50 of these oyster recipes, I find. This is accounted for by the fact that only in recent years have many people cared to inquire beyond the old ways.

The truth is that oyster taste, if indulged in one or two or three ways only, tends to cloy the appetite. The most usual situation (except in great "oyster towns," like Philadelphia, Baltimore, Norfolk, New Orleans) is for a man to have a periodic "oyster hunger" which he indulges about once every fortnight or month. He eats six, or a dozen or (rarely) two dozen raw oysters, or a stew or a big mess of "fried," and then waits for his next oyster hunger (which may really be an instinctive iodine hunger). The real oyster-educated person does not "gorge" periodically, but dines on oysters in many ways at more frequent intervals; raw oysters at the start of a meal several times a week perhaps, and with oysters in new ways as a special delight at various times. It will be a surprising thing for many to learn that in Baltimore (and even in Chicago and in Oklahoma), they eat *oysters for breakfast* quite extensively!

One of the main faults I have to find with oyster eating is the unholy manner of sousing the raw oysters in a very hot sauce—catsup, chili, horseradish or tabasco. It seems to be a fact that 19 out of 20 men who eat raw oysters (and 19 out of 20 restaurants who serve them) do so with these sauces—and plenty of them! Now this is a great pity. You are dining then on sauce and not on oysters, for oyster flavor is delicate and easily smothered by strong sauces. Gourmets prefer to use only lemon; perhaps sometimes a spot of horseradish. My personal habit is to eat just one oyster with any sauce on it, the rest with only lemon on it. Do it this way, and you will be able to savor the choice oyster taste and obtain the real oyster satisfaction.

Because of the high acid-ash reaction of oysters, it is always well to use plenty of lemon on oysters—ask for more lemon if you are handed only a small piece. Also—in my judgment at least—one ought never to dine on oysters alone; always with an accompaniment of at least some starch and some relishes, like cole slaw. Some people affect to believe oysters cooked are no match at all for oysters raw. On the contrary, I believe oyster flavor comes out most delightfully in *good* oyster cookery; but the cookery must be understanding and not ignorant, or you have nothing left at all. Like coffee, oysters represent mainly a savor and an aroma, and woe to the cook who forgets them!

For this reason I present selected oyster cookery recipes which it seems to me make Long Island oysters into richly satisfactory dishes.

PANNED OYSTERS, WORLD'S FAIR

36 Oysters	Salt, pepper
2 tablespoons *paté de fois gras*	Toast
2 tablespoons butter	Wineglass of Chablis (white wine)
½ cup chopped mushrooms	

This dish is international, reputedly originating in New Orleans, then moving across the ocean, and emerging sometime later as Oysters Tipperary. With such a history its reappearance during the World's Fair is a "natural."

The oysters are shelled and laid in a baking pan, with

some of the oyster liquor and the butter, and baked in a hot oven until the oyster edges curl. Then hot toast is spread with *paté de fois gras,* and the oysters and their sauce poured over them, together with the chopped mushrooms which have been fried in a little butter, 2 additional tablespoons of the oyster liquor, and the Chablis wine.

OYSTERS, GOURMET SOCIETY

24 or 36 medium sized Oysters
1 package rock salt
Tin pie plates
1 cup raw spinach, finely minced
$\frac{1}{4}$ cup parsley, minced
$\frac{1}{4}$ cup spring onions, finely minced (white part and a little of green)
1 teaspoon salt
2 tablespoons browned, rolled breadcrumbs
3 drops tabasco sauce
$\frac{1}{4}$ lb butter

The rock salt is spread over the tin pie plates to the depth of $\frac{1}{4}$ to $\frac{1}{2}$ inch, and the opened oysters placed on them. The oysters are baked in a hot oven for 4 or 5 minutes, then removed and a tablespoon of the sauce made of the other ingredients placed on top, and the oysters put back in the oven for another 3 or 4 minutes. The idea is not to cook the oysters further than to have the edges curl.

The sauce is made by mixing the spinach, parsley and spring onions together (the spring onions to include not only the white but an inch or two of the green part). Then the salt, tabasco and breadcrumbs are added, and all this worked into a paste with the butter.

(This dish is a variation on Oysters Rockefeller, which is very 'hot," at one time made with absinthe.)

FRIED OYSTERS, À LA PRINCE OF WALES

30 Gardiners Bay, Robbins Island (or other large Oysters)
$\frac{1}{3}$ teaspoon red pepper
$\frac{1}{2}$ lemon, sliced
1 sprig thyme
1 small bay leaf
1 branch parsley
1 egg
$\frac{1}{2}$ cup cold milk
Salt and pepper
1 cup cracker dust

$\frac{1}{2}$ cup clarified butter
$\frac{1}{4}$ cup olive oil

Sauce:
Oyster liquor
$\frac{1}{8}$ teaspoon red pepper
Juice of $\frac{1}{4}$ lemon
$\frac{1}{2}$ cup Sauce Espagnole (No. 33)
1 teaspoon chopped chives

Put the oysters with their liquor in a saucepan and add the red pepper, the sliced lemon, the thyme, bay leaf, parsley. Heat for $1\frac{1}{2}$ minutes without boiling on a hot fire; then put the oysters in an earthen bowl to cool. Beat the egg into the milk, season with pinch of pepper and salt. Steep the oysters in this, one by one, roll in the cracker dust, shape each oyster with the palm of the hand. Then let the olive oil and butter get very hot in a frying pan, and fry the oysters in this for only one minute on each side. Remove the oysters from the pan with a skimmer, and place them on a hot platter with a folded napkin. Serve the following sauce separately: Strain the oyster liquor into a saucepan, reduce it to one half, add the red pepper, the lemon juice and the Espagnole Sauce. Cook for 3 minutes, add the chives and pour in a sauce boat.

RED PEPPER OYSTERS, BROOKHAVEN

1 pint Oysters
1 onion, minced
1 sweet red pepper, minced

6 toast slices, buttered
8 slices bacon, cut in 1-inch squares

Butter a shallow baking pan, lay in the oysters, side by side, all one layer. Pour in 4 tablespoons of oyster liquor, which has been reduced by boiling. Sprinkle the onion and red pepper evenly across the pan, then lay on the bacon squares at regular intervals. Broil for 6 to 10 minutes, just enough to make the oyster edges curl. Serve hot on buttered toast.

BAKED COD ROE AND OYSTERS, GREENPORT

1½ lbs Cod Roe (or any fish roe)
1 cup milk
10 Gardiner's Bay or Robbins Island or other large oysters
2 anchovy fillets

4 tablespoons bread crumbs
2 tablespoons butter
2 eggs
Salt, pepper, few grains nutmeg
1 tablespoon flour
Lemon slices

Wash the roe in several waters, then simmer for 30 minutes in the milk with one cup oyster liquor (or water). Wash the oysters and mince them fine with the anchovies; blend in the bread crumbs, butter and eggs. Season. Then cut the roe into neat slices, spread with the oyster mixture, and lay them in a buttered baking dish, sprinkle with flour and dots of additional butter. Brown gently in hot oven, and serve with lemon slices.

SAUCE (FOR OYSTERS AND CLAMS), DUMAS

1 teaspoon salt
¾ teaspoon white pepper
1 shallot, chopped
1 teaspoon chives, chopped
½ teaspoon parsley, minced

1 teaspoon olive oil
6 drops tabasco sauce
½ teaspoon worcestershire sauce
5½ tablespoons tarragon vinegar

Mix the salt, pepper, shallot, chives, parsley together, then add the olive oil, tabasco, worcestershire, vinegar and stir thoroughly. Serve in sauce cups with any shellfish appetizer.

PANNED OYSTERS ON TOAST,
MEADOWBROOK CLUB

36 medium-sized Oysters	2 tablespoons lemon juice
3 tablespoons butter	Grated Parmesan cheese
Salt, pepper	Toast

Shell the oysters, and lay them in a baking pan with some of their own liquor, and the butter. Season with salt, pepper and lemon juice, and bake in a hot oven for 5 or 6 minutes until the oyster edges curl. Then sprinkle with the cheese and heat for a minute or two. Serve hot on warm toast, with the liquor poured over it.

BAKED OYSTERS, ROBBINS ISLAND

12 Robbins Island or other large Oysters	Salt, pepper
1 tablespoon butter	1 teaspoon chopped chives

Scrub the oysters well, and place them unopened in a deep baking pan, and bake in hot oven for 2 or 3 minutes until they open. Then remove the upper half of the shell, and put a bit of butter, salt and pepper and some chopped chives on each one and put back in the oven for 3 minutes more. Serve hot.

BLUE POINT SOUFFLE

12 Blue Point Oysters (or any medium or small oysters)	$\frac{3}{4}$ cup milk
	Salt, red pepper
2 tablespoons butter	2 eggs, separated
3 tablespoons flour	Browned bread crumbs

Put the oysters in a saucepan with the oyster liquor, bring to a boil. Drain, reserving liquor. Chop each oyster into about 3 pieces. Melt the butter, stir in the flour, add the milk, and a few tablespoons of the oyster liquor, stir, and season with salt and red pepper, and then cook for

10 minutes. Strain, and then add the chopped oysters, heat and stir in the well beaten egg yolks and keep stirring for a few minutes, then remove from the fire. Meantime beat the egg whites stiffly and fold into the other ingredients. Fill into little baking dishes or ramekins, sprinkle with breadcrumbs and melted butter, and bake in a moderate oven for 30 minutes.

SCALLOPED OYSTERS, PORT JEFFERSON

6 potatoes	2 tablespoons butter
Cracker crumbs	Salt, pepper
36 Oysters	American cheese, grated
2 teaspoons minced parsley	1 pint milk
1 onion, chopped	

Cook the potatoes with their skins, in water to which has been added some of the oyster liquor. Let cool and slice. Butter a good-sized baking dish, rub its sides with garlic, sprinkle it with cracker crumbs, then put in a layer of potatoes, then a layer of oysters, then of potatoes, then oysters, topping with potatoes. At each layer sprinkle parsley, also onion and pieces of butter, pepper and salt. Sprinkle the top with the cracker crumbs and the cheese. Pour the milk, blended with 1 cup of the oyster liquor, into the dish. Bake for 30 minutes. If it appears too dry at the end of 25 minutes, add another cup of the oyster liquor

CURRY OF OYSTERS, DARMADASA

½ green pepper	1 cup coconut milk (or
1 clove garlic	cream)
4 shallots	½ teaspoon salt
2 tablespoons butter	3 tablespoons flour
1 tablespoon currypowder	12 Gardiner's Island, Rob-
Dash of turmeric	bins Island or other large
Piece of cinnamon bark	Oysters
3 bay leaves	Juice of 1 lemon
3 cloves	Boiled rice

Mince the green peppers, garlic and shallots and brown in butter, if possible in an iron pot. Then add the curry powder, turmeric, cinnamon, bay leaves, cloves. Add the coconut milk blended with salt and flour. Cook for 3 minutes. Then add the oysters and cook for 5 minutes. Take off the fire, add the lemon juice, stir it up. Serve with boiled rice arranged in a ring on a large round plate, pouring the curry into the middle. Some Major Gray chutney served as a relish goes well with it. The coconut milk can be made from fresh coconuts obtainable at the market. Chop or shred the fresh coconut, soak for 30 minutes in hot water, and then squeeze through a cloth or sieve.

(Hard or soft shell clams, mussels, shrimps or scallops can be curried with this recipe.)

OYSTERS À LA MAISON, BLUE SPRUCE INN

36 Oysters, medium size	$\frac{1}{2}$ cup cream
2 cups Chablis (white wine)	Salt, pepper, cayenne
	1 tablespoon lemon juice
1 cup fish stock	

In a double boiler steam the oysters with wine, stock, and some of the oyster liquor; cook until edges curl. Then add the cream and seasonings, heat through, add lemon juice and serve on toast.

STEAMED OYSTER LOAF, SEA CLIFF

36 Oysters	1 tablespoon tarragon vinegar
Salt, cayenne pepper, grated nutmeg	2 eggs, beaten
Juice of 1 lemon	2 tablespoons thick cream
2 tablespoons bread crumbs, rolled fine	1 can concentrated cream of celery soup
1 teaspoon meat extract	1 cup cooked celery

Cut the oysters in half and put in a saucepan with $\frac{1}{2}$ cup of oyster liquor. Add the salt, red pepper, a pinch of grated nutmeg, lemon juice, the bread crumbs, the meat extract, the vinegar. Bring to a boil; and take off the fire. Stir in the beaten eggs and the cream. Butter a mold and dust the sides with bread crumbs, then put in the mixture, covering the mold with buttered paper, and seal tightly. Steam for 1½ hours. Turn out and serve with a celery sauce made by combining the heated can of concentrated cream of celery soup with the cooked celery.

SCRAMBLED OYSTERS, WATER ISLAND

36 Oysters
 Salt, pepper
 7 eggs, beaten
 4 tablespoons cream

½ cup forked bread
1 tablespoon butter
Parsley sprigs

Chop the oysters fine, season them. Beat the eggs, stir in the cream, and work in the forked bread. Then add this to the butter melted in a frying pan. When eggs begin to get firm, stir in the oysters, and scramble. Serve garnished with parsley.

OYSTERS-MUSHROOM CASSEROLE, COLD SPRING HARBOR

½ cup chopped mush-
   rooms
1 tablespoon minced onion
4 tablespoons butter
2 tablespoons flour
1 cup light cream
2 tablespoons sherry

1 tablespoon minced pars-
   ley
Salt, cayenne pepper
18 Robbins Island or other
   large Oysters
Buttered crumbs

Fry the mushrooms and onions in butter lightly. Mix in the flour, add the cream gradually and heat slowly, not allowing to boil. Add sherry and seasonings. Arrange the opened oysters in a casserole, pour over them the sauce, and 2 tablespoons of the oyster liquor, and top with the crumbs. Bake in a hot oven (400° F) for 15 minutes until browned.

OYSTER FRY, JONES BEACH

½ cup whole wheat flour or
   finely rolled "wheaties"
½ cup milk
½ cup good catsup
½ teaspoon salt

36 Blue Points or other
   medium-sized Oysters
Cracker dust
Peanut oil, or fresh
   sweet lard
1 teaspoon butter

Mix well the flour, milk, catsup and salt, and then mix the Blue Points in it, and roll each well in the cracker dust. Then have ready a frying pan filled ½ inch or more with the boiling hot oil or lard, to which has been added the butter. Fry until brown, drain on absorbent paper laid on a piping hot platter. Serve with fresh pickled cucumbers as a relish.

DRIED OYSTERS, HAMPTON BAYS

36 Robbins Island or other
   large Oysters
1½ cup fresh mayonnaise
2 tablespoons finely
   chopped chives

¼ teaspoon salt
Pepper
1 cup cracker crumbs,
   rolled fine

Dry the oysters, without too much handling. Use a steel fork, catch the oyster in the "eye" and dip it in the mayonnaise mixture, made by mixing the mayonnaise with the chives, to which the salt and a few dashes of pepper have been added. Then roll the oyster gently in the cracker crumbs, and dip them in deep fat at 375° F until brown.

OYSTER FRY, FLUSHING BAY

36 Oysters
1 cup fine rolled brown
   bread crumbs
½ teaspoon salt

¼ teaspoon pepper
2 eggs
1 teaspoon vegetable
   sauce

Dry the oysters thoroly, and dip each one in the bread crumbs, in which the salt and pepper have been mixed. Then dip in the beaten eggs into which the vegetable sauce has been mixed well; then roll in the crumbs again. Fry in the deep fat at 375° F and drain on a hot platter on top of absorbent paper.

OYSTER HASH, FIRE ISLAND

Meat left-overs	green peppers
1 tablespoon worcester-	$\frac{1}{4}$ cup chopped cooked pi-
shire sauce	mentos
1 cup cooked celery	36 Oysters
$\frac{1}{2}$ cup chopped cooked	2 cups mashed potatoes

Use beef or other cooked meat left-overs to make a hash, and add any left-over gravy. Mix Worcestershire, celery, peppers and pimentos into the hash. In a greased baking pan put a layer of the hash, then a layer of oysters and then a layer of hash, and another layer of oysters, and cover with mashed potatoes neatly arranged. Bake in a moderate oven until thoroughly hot and serve from baking dish.

OYSTER BROWN, GREAT NECK

36 medium-sized Oysters	$\frac{1}{2}$ cup chopped celery
1 cup boiling water	$\frac{1}{4}$ cup chopped ripe olives
2 tablespoons butter	Salt, cayenne pepper
2 tablespoons flour	Buttered toast

Pour the boiling water over the oysters. Drain off and add to the raw oyster liquor. Melt the butter in a frying pan, and slowly mix with the flour until brown. Add the oyster water and celery and let boil five minutes, stirring constantly. When it thickens, pour in the oysters, and the olives, and let cook for just a minute or two. Pour over hot toast laid on hot plates and serve at once.

OYSTERS-ON-HAM-ISLANDS

1½ lbs ham, broiled
12 slices rye toast
24 Oysters, medium size
¼ cup melted butter

½ cup rolled bread crumbs
1 small can mushrooms
Lemon slices

The ham should be about ¼ inch thick, brushed with melted butter, and broiled (with care not to broil until tough). Cut into rounded pieces, 3 inches in diameter, by using a large biscuit cutter. With the same cutter, cut pieces of freshly toasted and buttered rye bread. Keep the ham and toast hot. Dip the oysters in the melted butter, then into the crumbs, and broil them brown for 5 or 6 minutes. On the toast pieces lay the ham rounds; on each ham round put two broiled oysters, with which have been mixed the small mushrooms cooked in butter. Serve hot, with lemon slices, two rounds on a plate.

OYSTER DUMPLINGS, FAR ROCKAWAY

50 Oysters
2 tablespoons lemon juice
Salt, pepper

1 recipe plain pastry
1 egg, beaten
2 tablespoons butter

Drain the oysters, keeping the oyster liquor. Pour the lemon juice, salt and pepper over the oysters and keep cool. Make a pastry dough, using some of the oyster liquor for moistening. Roll the pastry thin, cut into 5-inch squares. Brush them with the beaten egg, and lay upon each square 4 oysters and a dot of butter. Then with a toothpick bring the four ends together. Bake in a hot oven (475°F) until brown. Before serving remove picks and pour into each dumpling a spoonful of the oyster liquor brought to a boil.

DEVILED OYSTERS, WOPOWOG

½ cup butter
1 clove garlic, minced
2 tablespoons minced parsley
4 shallots or chives minced
½ cup minced celery
1 sprig thyme, minced

30 Oysters, minced
½ tablespoon flour
½ cup cracker crumbs
Salt, pepper
3 drops tabasco sauce
1 egg, beaten
1 tablespoon cream
1 tablespoon chili sauce

In the butter, fry the garlic, parsley, shallots, celery and thyme to a light brown, then add the minced oysters, the flour, crumbs, salt and pepper and tabasco sauce. Mix well and take from stove, and immediately add the beaten egg mixed with the cream. Fill mixture into cleaned oyster shells, sprinkle with the chili sauce and additional crumbs, butter, and minced parsley; brown in hot oven, serve very hot, 4 to 6 on plate.

BAKED OYSTERS, LOCUST VALLEY

½ cup butter
2 tablespoons flour
2 cups cream
½ teaspoon pepper
½ teaspoon salt
2½ teaspoons anchovy paste
Grated rind of 1 lemon

36 Robbins Island Oysters (or any large oyster)
1 cup cracker crumbs, or browned bread crust crumbs
1 cup pimento cheese, grated
1 teaspoon minced parsley

Melt the butter, blend in the flour, stirring until smooth. Add the cream and continue stirring until mixture thickens. Take from stove and add salt and pepper, the anchovy paste and grated lemon rind. Butter a casserole, place a quarter of the above mixture in the bottom, and then put in 18 oysters. Sprinkle with the crumbs and cheese and parsley, then add another quarter of the mixture, then the other 18 oysters and again sprinkle with crumbs and cheese, and then top with the other half of the mixture. Bake in oven at 375° F until brown.

OYSTER-STUFFED FISH, WUSABANNUCK

1 large fish
Salt and pepper
2 onions, chopped
1 clove garlic
½ cup olive oil or butter
3 teaspoons minced
   parsley
1 bay leaf, minced
Thyme and sage

1 teaspoon Maggi Sauce
1½ cups cracker crumbs, or
   browned, rolled bread
   crumbs
1 cup milk
24 Oysters
½ can mushrooms
1 egg
Butter

The fish is scaled and cleaned, with fin removed, but the head and tail left on. Rub with salt and pepper inside and out. For the dressing the onion and garlic are fried until tender in the butter or oil; and the seasonings then added. The cracker crumbs are soaked with the milk and squeezed, then stirred into the mixture, and fried for 3 minutes. The oysters are cut in half and added, also the mushrooms. After mixing and cooking for 3 more minutes the egg is stirred in.

The mixture is then taken from the stove and stuffed into the fish and sewed in. The fish is put into a buttered baking pan and dotted with pieces of butter. Oyster liquor is poured in two inches deep. The fish is baked in a slow oven for 1½ hours, basting occasionally.

OYSTER-CELERY-BACON TOAST, SYOSSET

36 Oysters
2 tablespoons lemon juice
½ teaspoon worcester-
   shire sauce
1 teaspoon grated horse-
   radish
Salt, pepper

½ cup sifted bread crumbs
4 tablespoons butter
4 slices buttered toast
1 cup seasoned medium
   white sauce
½ cup celery, minced
4 slices bacon, fried crisp

Wash and dry the oysters thoroly. Put them in a bowl and pour in the lemon juice, worcestershire and horseradish, and let stand 5 or 6 minutes. Then take out the oysters, sprinkle with salt and pepper, roll in the crumbs and fry in the butter until edges curl. Then arrange the oysters on the toast slices on a platter and pour on the heated white sauce, sprinkle with the minced celery and garnish with the fried bacon strips.

NESTED OYSTERS, GARDINER'S ISLAND

24 Robbin's Island, Gardiners Bay or other large Oysters
2 lbs cooked spinach
5 tablespoons butter
2 tablespoons onion, minced

1 clove garlic, minced
1 teaspoon salt
$\frac{1}{8}$ teaspoon pepper
2 tablespoons cream
1 egg yolk
1 egg
1 cup bread crumbs

Put the oysters in a pan with their liquor and bring to a boiling point and drain. Chop 12 of the oysters, leave the other 12 whole. Chop the spinach fine; brown the onion and garlic in some butter in a saucepan, then add the spinach, chopped oysters, salt, pepper, cream. Cook slowly for 5 minutes, take off and then add the yolk of one egg and another entire egg. Butter a baking dish and arrange the *whole* oysters on the bottom, cover with the spinach mixture, sprinkle with the crumbs mixed with melted butter. Bake in a moderate oven (350° F) until firm in the center. Serve from the baking dish.

OYSTER FLOATS, BAYSIDE

1 quart Oysters
1 cup thick white sauce
Salt, cayenne pepper

2 tablespoons chopped chives
Grated rind of 1 lemon
Toast slices

Warm the oysters in their own liquor until the edges

begin to curl. Drain, save the liquor, and mix the oysters with the cup of thick white sauce and heat in a double boiler, adding some of the oyster liquor. Add salt, cayenne and the chives, and the grated lemon rind. Pour the mixture over hot buttered toast slices.

HAM-OYSTER FLOAT, SAYVILLE

4 slices raw Ham
1 tablespoon butter
25 Oysters
6 tablespoons tomato
   catsup

4 tablespoons worcester-
   shire sauce
6 tablespoons white sauce
4 slices buttered toast
2 tablespoons chopped
   parsley

Fry the ham in butter until browned. Then take out and fry the oysters in the same butter, adding the catsup and worcestershire sauce. Cook for 5 minutes, then take out the oysters and add the white sauce, and cook the sauce 3 minutes more. Add the parsley. Put the oysters and sauce on the toast slices, and serve on a hot platter with the ham slices.

OYSTER PADDIES, WALT WHITMAN

1 pint mashed potatoes
1 egg, beaten
1 tablespoon minced onion
Salt
½ teaspoon freshly ground

black pepper
12 oysters
2 tablespoons milk
1 tablespoon parsley,
   minced

The mashed potatoes are mixed with the egg and the onion, salt and pepper and pressed into cakes. Then with a silver knife the cakes are split in half and 2 or 3 oysters laid in, and the other half of the cake pressed back into place. Brush with milk and bake in moderate oven (375° F) until brown. Garnish with parsley, serve very hot.

FRIED OYSTERS, BOARDWALK

18 Robbins Island or Gardiner's Bay or other large Oysters
2 eggs, separated
Salt
1 tablespoon boiling water
Cracker dust
½ cup olive oil, or sweet lard
1 teaspoon butter
3 sprigs parsley

Drain the oysters and dry thoroly. Beat two egg yolks, add a pinch of salt and the boiling water. Into this roll the oysters, using a steel fork, and spearing each oyster in the "eye" or hard part. Then roll lightly in cracker dust. Put in a frying pan in which is boiling hot olive oil (or lard) and butter. Cover the bottom with the oysters. When brown on one side, turn over. Drain on double layer of absorbent paper, serve hot, garnished with parsley and pickles or cole slaw or tartar sauce.

OYSTERS ON TOAST, TIFFANY

2 tablespoons butter
24 Robbins Island or Gardiner's Bay (or other large Oysters)
½ teaspoon worcestershire sauce
½ teaspoon salt
¼ teaspoon freshly ground black pepper
¼ teaspoon paprika
½ cup Sherry or Chablis (white wine)
4 pieces Buttered Toast
½ teaspoon chopped parsley

In a frying pan or chafing dish heat the butter very hot and put in the oysters, with 2 tablespoons of oyster liquor. Season, and as soon as the oyster edges curl, pour in the Sherry or wine. Have the hot buttered toast ready on four warm plates, and pour on each piece 6 oysters and some sauce, and sprinkle on it a bit of parsley.

OYSTERS ORIENTAL, JACK DEMPSEY

1 onion	1 tart apple
2 tablespoons butter	Salt, pepper
2 tablespoons best curry powder	1 tablespoon flour
1 cup beef stock	50 Blue Points or other small Oysters
½ cup grated coconut	

The onion is sliced thin and sautéed in one tablespoon of butter, and then the curry powder blended in slowly, adding also the other tablespoon of butter. Add then the beef stock and stir until it boils. Add then the coconut. Peel the apple and grate it in. Let simmer for 5 minutes. Dry the oysters thoroly. Blend the flour with 2 tablespoons of the oyster liquor and stir into the sauce. Put the oysters in, and let simmer for 5 minutes. Serve on slices of hot buttered toast.

OYSTERS BOSKOVITZ

48 Oysters	1 cup oyster liquor
3 tablespoons Beluga Caviar	1 cup chicken broth
	1 egg yolk
	1 tablespoon chives, chopped
Sauce:	
4 tablespoons flour	1 teaspoon lemon juice
4 tablespoons butter	Salt, pepper

Steam the oysters in the shell until they open. Arrange the oysters in half shells and then place a bit of caviar on each oyster, and on top of this put a teaspoon of sauce made as follows: melt butter, blend in the flour, add oyster liquor broth. Simmer 5 minutes. Then add the egg yolk, the chives, lemon juice, salt, pepper. Bake the oysters in a very hot oven (450° F) for 4 or 5 minutes.

SEA TANG COCKTAIL, LONG ISLAND

½ cup cooked lobster, diced
½ cup cooked Bay scallops, diced
½ cup cooked shrimp, diced

½ cup steamed soft shell clams (halved)
½ cup cooked celery, diced
Salt, pepper, cayenne

Mix all the above ingredients together and serve in 6 or 8 sherbet glasses, mixed with a dressing made of ½ teaspoon of onion juice, 1 teaspoon lemon juice, 1 tablespoon tomato catsup, ½ teaspoon fresh horseradish, 3 drops tabasco sauce, ½ teaspoon tarragon vinegar. Top with a ripe olive.

BAKED OYSTERS, QUEENSBORO BRIDGE

½ cup butter
1 onion, minced
½ teaspoon garlic, minced
2 stalks celery, chopped
2 tablespoons flour
1 small can tomatoes

Salt, pepper, few grains cayenne
1 small can mushrooms
50 Oysters
3 tablespoons worcestershire sauce
¼ cup bread crumbs

Fry the onion in the butter, then add the garlic, the celery and the flour. Strain in the tomatoes, add salt, pepper, cayenne, the mushrooms, oysters—the worcestershire sauce last. Cook until the oyster edges curl. Place in buttered baking dish, spread with bread crumbs, dot with butter, and bake for 15 minutes in moderate oven.

OYSTER PEPPERS, HORSE SHOW

50 Oysters and their liquor
3 large bell peppers
1 teaspoon salt
1 pint Grade A milk
2 tablespoons cornstarch
2 egg yolks
1 cup butter

1 teaspoon Kitchen Bouquet seasoning
Dash of tabasco
¾ teaspoon freshly ground black pepper
1 lb American Cheese, grated

Drain off the oyster liquor. Grind peppers in meat chopper, and boil in oyster liquor. Then add the oysters and the salt (watch the salting, the dish must not be oversalted). Cook for 5 minutes, then add the milk in which the cornstarch has been blended. Cream together the egg yolks and butter, add the Kitchen Bouquet and the tabasco, the black pepper. When this mixture thickens, add the cheese, and keep stirring for five minutes.

Serve this on slices of buttered toast.

MUSHROOM OYSTERS, TOMMY HITCHCOCK

45 Oysters
1 tablespoon flour
1 tablespoon butter
1 cup Grade A milk
$\frac{1}{2}$ cup cream
2 shallots
1 sprig parsley

1 teaspoon salt
$\frac{1}{2}$ teaspoon freshly ground black pepper
Few grains cayenne
$\frac{1}{2}$ cup fresh mushrooms
Buttered Toast

Stew the oysters in their own liquor until their edges curl. Then drain. Make a sauce in a double boiler with the flour, the butter, 1 cup of the oyster liquor, the milk, the cream. Simmer 5 minutes. Mince the shallots and parsley, add salt, pepper and cayenne; fry with mushrooms in a little butter and add to the sauce. Then add the oysters. Serve hot on thin slices of buttered toast.

OYSTER-NOODLES, FLATBUSH

50 Oysters
1 teaspoon salt
Additional oyster liquor to make 1 pint
1 pint Grade A milk
2 egg yolks
2 tablespoons cornstarch

1 cup butter
1 teaspoon Kitchen Bouquet sauce; dash of tabasco
1 lb egg noodles
1 lb American cheese
1 teaspoon black pepper

Use an iron pot if possible and let it get very hot while

empty. Put the oysters without their liquor in the pot so that some of them appear to scorch. Use a cake turner to remove these scorched oysters; put in the salt, and let cook five minutes. Add the oyster liquor and the milk. Cream together the egg yolks, cornstarch and butter, and add. Put in also the Kitchen Bouquet sauce and dash of tabasco. Let cook until thick. In another pot meanwhile boil the noodles in salted water and drain. Butter a baking dish or casserole and make a one-inch layer of noodles, then one-third of the oysters, then put in 1 or $1\frac{1}{2}$ cups of the sauce, then sprinkle with grated cheese, then sprinkle black pepper. Then begin another layer, and still another, with plenty of the liquid on each. Bake in a slow oven for 20 minutes.

CURRIED OYSTERS, BABYLON

$\frac{1}{3}$ cup minced onion	$1\frac{1}{2}$ teaspoon curry powder
2 tablespoons butter	$1\frac{1}{2}$ cup milk
3 tablespoons flour	2 dozen Oysters
$\frac{3}{4}$ teaspoon salt	2 eggs, hard-boiled and
Pepper	sliced

Saute onion in butter until tender. Remove from heat, add flour, salt, pepper and curry powder; blend. Add milk; and cook over boiling water, stirring constantly, until thickened. Add oysters and eggs, cook until oyster edges curl.

OYSTERS POULETTE

1 pint Oysters	$1\frac{1}{2}$ cup milk
2 tablespoons butter	$\frac{1}{4}$ cup cream
3 tablespoons flour	2 egg yolks
Pepper	2 tablespoons lemon juice
$\frac{1}{2}$ teaspoon salt	2 cups boiled rice
$\frac{1}{4}$ teaspoon nutmeg	

Drain oysters and cook in saucepan two or three minutes

until their edges curl. Melt butter, stir in flour and seasonings; and when well blended, add milk and cream. Stir over a low heat until thick; then cook one minute. Beat the eggs, add a little of the hot sauce to them, and then stir into the sauce. Add oysters and lemon juice and reheat. Serve on a platter with a rice border. Garnish with green pepper or pimento and parsley.

SCALLOPED OYSTERS, SALT-AIRE

1 quart Oysters	Pepper
2 cups bread crumbs	4 tablespoons butter
Salt	1 cup milk

Drain the oysters and save the liquor. Season bread crumbs with salt and pepper. Lay half the medium-sized oysters in a buttered baking pan; add half the crumbs; dot with half the butter; add a second layer of oysters. Mix the oyster liquor and milk; pour over the oysters. Finish with butter and crumbs. Bake in a quick oven for 35 minutes.

OYSTERS BRULOT

Embed shallow oyster cocktail glasses in crushed ice. Fill these with freshly shelled oysters which have been dried very thoroly. Just before serving, cover with light rum and set them ablaze; use enough rum ($1\frac{1}{2}$ tablespoons) to keep them blazing for about one minute. When the blaze finally flickers out, there remain six delicately-broiled oysters, fragrant with the flavor of burnt rum. Serve with lemon wedges.

OYSTERS, BRIGHTWATERS

6 Oysters	Paprika
$\frac{3}{4}$ teaspoon lemon juice	6 drops tabasco sauce
$\frac{3}{4}$ teaspoon Sauterne Wine	$\frac{1}{4}$ teaspoon chopped
$\frac{3}{4}$ tablespoon melted butter	parsley

The above is a per-person ration. For each person is required 6 oysters, opened and lying in the deep shell. Partially fill a shallow baking pan with rock salt. On the salt place the oysters so that they will not tip over. Broil until the edges curl. Rub the inside of a bowl with a cut garlic clove, place six baked oysters in it; and dress with sauce made by blending the remaining ingredients.

BAKED OYSTERS, SYOSSET

4 dozen Oysters (in half shell)
Rock salt
1 teaspoon tabasco sauce
2 tablespoons worcestershire sauce
2 tablespoons tomato catsup
2 tablespoons horseradish
2 tablespoons vinegar
4 tablespoons lemon juice
4 young onions, minced
Bacon
Bread crumbs
Butter

Partially fill glass or tin pie pans with rock salt. Arrange 6-8 oysters on top of each. Mix remaining seasonings in the order given, and place 1½ tablespoons of mixture upon each oyster in the shell. Then lay on top of each oyster a strip of bacon the length of the shell and cover with bread crumbs and ½ teaspoon of butter. Broil for 3 to 5 minutes. Serve the tin plate on top of a regular plate (the heated salt keeps the oysters hot).

OYSTERS WITH SHERRY, WESTBURY

2 tablespoons butter
½ cup finely chopped celery
2 tablespoons chopped green pepper
1 pint Oysters
½ teaspoon salt
½ teaspoon paprika
½ cup sherry
Toast slices

Melt butter in saucepan, add celery, green pepper and drained oysters. Cook until oyster edges curl. Add seasoning and sherry, reheat and serve on toast.

OYSTER BISQUE, GARDINER'S ISLAND

1 pint Oysters	Bay leaf
4 cups milk	$\frac{1}{3}$ cup butter
1 slice onion	3 tablespoons flour
2 stalks celery	Salt and pepper
1 sprig of parsley	

Drain oysters reserving liquor and chop. Heat slowly to the boiling point and press through a coarse sieve. Scald milk with oyster liquor, onion, celery, parsley, and bay leaf. Melt butter, stir in flour; add milk mixture. Stir over a low heat until mixture thickens. Add the strained oysters and season with salt and pepper to taste. If a thinner soup is desired, more milk may be added. Serve with fried croutons or toast sticks.

OYSTER ROLLS, EASTPORT

1 cup butter	Salt and pepper
24 hard rolls	2 quarts Oysters
1 quart milk	$1\frac{1}{3}$ tablespoons lemon juice
$\frac{1}{2}$ teaspoon powdered thyme	24 anchovy fillets
$\frac{1}{2}$ teaspoon nutmeg	Parsley

Melt butter. Remove inner soft part from rolls; brush crusts inside and outside with some of the melted butter, and heat in a moderate oven (350°). To the remaining. butter, add the milk, the soft part from the rolls, and the seasonings. Stir over a low heat until mixture is thick and creamy. Add drained oysters and lemon juice, and cook over low heat until edges of oysters curl. Fill hot roll shells with this mixture and garnish with anchovies and parsley.

OYSTERS, BENEDICT

6 thin slices boiled ham
1 pint Oysters
3 English Muffins or 6
slices bread

Hollandaise Sauce
6 strips pimento

Fry ham lightly in its own fat and remove from frying pan. Drain oysters and fry one minute in the ham fat. Split muffins and toast on cut side. If bread is used, toast on both sides. Arrange one slice of ham and four oysters on each split muffin. Cover with Hollandaise Sauce and garnish with pimento.

SCALLOPED OYSTERS AND TONGUE, ROSLYN

1½ cup bread crumbs
18 Oysters, halved
2 cups cooked Tongue,
chopped
2 teaspoons chopped
parsley
2 teaspoons onion juice

2 teaspoons salt
½ teaspoon black pepper
4 tablespoons butter
½ cup meat stock from
boiled tongue
½ cup oyster liquor

Butter a baking dish, and cover the bottom with one-half the bread crumbs. Then mix well the oysters, tongue, parsley, onion juice, salt, pepper. Spread into the dish, then cover with the rest of the crumbs. Dot with the butter, pour on the meat stock and oyster liquor and bake for 20 minutes in a moderate oven (375° F.).

OYSTER AND KIDNEY STEW, EAST NORWICH

24 Oysters
12 Lamb Kidneys
2 tablespoons butter
1 onion, chopped fine

3 tablespoons flour
1½ cups broth from cooking
kidneys
1½ cups oyster liquor

Drain the oysters, reserving their liquor. Wash and cut the kidneys, and simmer them for 15 minutes. Melt the butter, fry the onion in it, then blend in the flour. Pour in the kidney and oyster liquors, then add the oysters and kidneys and stew for 15 minutes on a moderate fire. Serve with potatoes.

OYSTER AND SAUSAGE LOAF, PATCHOGUE

12 Oysters, fried
1 16-inch loaf French bread
½ cup butter
1 cup diced salami and bologna
1 cup cooked green peas
¼ cup cooked celery, diced
¼ cup cooked mushrooms
2 cups Creole Sauce (No. ....)
Salt, pepper

Open the oysters, reserving liquor. Fry them in the usual way, in beaten egg and cracker crumbs. Cut open the entire loaf of bread, lengthwise, scoop out the center, making 2 crusty shells about ¾-inch thick. Butter the insides, then put into the oven until the butter melts. Meantime mix together the sausage and vegetables with the Creole Sauce. Then lay one crust in a baking dish and fill it with the mixture. Cut the oysters in half and lay on top. Pour over it ½ cup oyster liquor. Season. Lay the other shell on top and bake in a hot oven (400° F.) until browned. To serve, cut the loaf into 1-inch thick slices.

GUMBO, SANDY HOOK

1 lb raw shrimp
1½ dozen oysters
1 tin (½ lb) crabmeat
2 tablespoons butter
3 medium-sized onions, minced
1 can (No. 2½) tomatoes
2 cups water
1 tablespoon chopped parsley
1 teaspoon worcestershire sauce
¼ teaspoon celery salt
½ teaspoon salt
Dash of pepper
2 tablespoons flour

Cook and clean shrimp; pick over and drain oysters, reserving liquor. Flake crabmeat removing all bony tissues.

Melt butter, saute onions until brown, then add tomatoes, water, parsley and seasonings. Add shrimp, oyster liquor and crabmeat. Heat almost to the boiling and add flour mixed to a paste with a little cold water. Add oysters, cover and simmer 5 minutes.

OYSTERS IN MUSHROOMS, GILGO

6 very large mushrooms
3 tablespoons butter
1 cup chopped, cooked
  spinach
1 tablespoon lemon juice
6 large oysters

6 rounds of toast
2 tablespoons flour
$\frac{1}{4}$ cup heavy cream
2 tablespoons sherry
Salt and pepper
Paprika

Break stems from mushrooms and wash and peel caps. Saute caps in 1 tablespoon butter, cover and cook over low heat 5 minutes or until tender. Fill with spinach, seasoned to taste, sprinkle with lemon juice and top with an oyster. Place each on a round of toast and put under broiler until oyster is heated through. Chop and saute mushroom stems in remaining butter. Blend in flour, then add oyster liquor, cream and sherry. Cook, stirring constantly until smooth and slightly thickened. Season to taste and serve over mushroom-oyster dish.

OYSTERS AND CHICKEN LIVERS, GREAT NECK

8 chicken livers, halved
1 cup oyster liquor
$\frac{1}{2}$ teaspoon salt

2 tablespoons butter
18 Oysters
Pepper

Put the chicken livers in a saucepan with the oyster liquor to which has been added $\frac{1}{2}$ teaspoon salt; bring to a boil and cook gently for 5 minutes. In a hot frying pan put the butter, and let brown. Then add the oysters and the chicken livers. Cook for 7 or 8 minutes, turning frequently. Serve hot on toast slices and pour the liquor over them, and add a little freshly ground black pepper.

OYSTER (OR CLAM) OMELET

6 tablespoons butter
6 eggs, separated
1 cup milk
$\frac{1}{2}$ teaspoon salt

$\frac{1}{4}$ teaspoon black pepper
1 cup Oysters (or clams)
2 tablespoons melted butter

Melt the butter in an omelet pan over mild flame. Beat the yolks of the eggs, add the milk, stir together, season with salt, pepper; add the oysters (which have been cut into quarters). Add the 2 tablespoons of additional butter, melted. Beat in the stiff-beaten egg whites. Pour this mixture into the omelet pan where the butter has been heating, and then with a flexible spatula lift the omelet as it forms so that the butter may reach every part. When golden brown, fold the omelet and serve hot.

LIVER AND BACON AND OYSTERS, WESTBURY

1 lb calf's liver
12 slices bacon
1 cup sifted tomatoes
$1\frac{1}{2}$ cups thin onion slices
2 sweet peppers, minced
2 tablespoons cornstarch
$1\frac{1}{2}$ teaspoons salt

1 teaspoon paprika
1 teaspoon sugar
$\frac{1}{4}$ teaspoon dry English
   mustard
1 cup gravy, meat stock
   (or water)
18 Oysters

Cut the liver into neat slices, brown in 2 tablespoons of the bacon fat, available after frying the bacon slices crisp. Brown the liver only on the outside. Add the tomatoes, onions, green peppers, cover the pan and cook for 5 minutes. Meantime blend together the cornstarch, salt, paprika, sugar and mustard, and then add the gravy or meat stock or water; stir and bring to a boil, but do not let burn. Add the oysters to the liver and vegetable mixture, let cook 4 or 5 minutes. Serve the liver and oysters and bacon on the plate with the seasoned sauce.

OYSTER AND LIVER LOAF, GARDEN CITY

1 lb calf's liver or lamb or pork liver	$\frac{1}{2}$ teaspoon pepper, few grains cayenne
12 Oysters	$\frac{1}{2}$ teaspoon celery seed
2 cups soft bread crumbs	3 eggs, beaten
4 tablespoons bacon fat	

Parboil the liver lightly, then chop it fine, and mix with the oysters which have been broiled slightly and cut in quarters. Add the bread crumbs which have been soaked in the hot oyster liquor and pressed out; add also the bacon fat, pepper, cayenne, celery seed, and some additional salt to taste. Then blend in the eggs and pour into a greased bread tin. Lay this tin in a larger pan of hot water and bake for 1 hour at 350°F. Serve either hot with an oyster or mushroom sauce, or cold with pickles.

FLOUNDER MIGNONETTE WITH OYSTERS, WEYLIN

12 Oysters	Bouquet of herbs
2$\frac{1}{2}$ lbs Flounder fillet	$\frac{1}{2}$ cup cream sauce
2 tablespoons butter	$\frac{1}{2}$ cup cream
$\frac{1}{2}$ teaspoon salt	Whipped potatoes
1 cup Chablis (white wine)	4 tablespoons whipped cream
3 large peeled ripe tomatoes, chopped	1 egg yolk

Clean and dry fillets thoroly. Butter a baking saucepan, lay in the fillets, add salt, wine, tomatoes and herbs; let simmer for 15 minutes. Lift fillets to a hot oven platter. To the saucepan add the cream sauce, cream, salt, pepper, then add the oysters and cook until the edges curl. Lay the oysters separately on top of the fillets. Arrange the whipped potatoes around the edges; add to the sauce the whipped cream and the egg yolk, pour over the fish, and glaze in the oven for a few minutes.

OYSTER SAUSAGE PUDDING, CHESAPEAKE

1½ cups flour
3 teaspoons baking powder
½ teaspoon salt
1 tablespoon vegetable shortening

¼ cup oyster liquor
1 cup Oysters
8 small pork sausages

Sift the flour, baking powder and salt together, then add the shortening, mixing in thoroly with a fork. Drain the oysters and chop them, and add to the mixture, together with ¼ cup of oyster liquor. Butter a shallow round baking dish and lay in the mixture. Prick the sausages with a fork and lay them on top of the mixture like the spokes of a wheel. Bake in a hot oven (475° F.) for 15 minutes.

OYSTER-STUFFED STEAK, GARDEN CITY

1½ lbs round steak (or flank steak)
Stuffing:
  Oyster liquor, hot
  1 cup stale bread crumbs
  ¼ cup chopped crisp bacon
  ½ pint oysters, minced
  ¼ teaspoon black pepper,

Few grains cayenne
1 egg, beaten
2 or 3 cups meat stock
4 small carrots
3 mushrooms
2 tablespoons flour
1 tablespoon tomato catsup

Pound the meat thoroly flat with a wooden mallet or potato masher. Spread evenly on it a stuffing made as follows: Pour hot oyster liquor over the bread crumbs, press it out, and mix the bread with the bacon, the oysters, pepper, cayenne, and the egg. Roll up the steak, tie securely with string, and cook in hot stock, for 2 hours, in a very slow oven (250°F) or over low flame. In the same pan place the carrots and mushrooms. When tender, place on a hot platter, and thicken the pan juice with the flour and add the tomato catsup.

BROILED PARTRIDGE WITH OYSTERS, SOUTHAMPTON

3 Partridges
Bacon Fat
Pepper, salt
24 Oysters

2 tablespoons melted butter
2 tablespoons butter
$\frac{1}{4}$ cup rolled, sifted bread crumbs

Dress and wash the birds, and split; rub with pepper and salt on the inside; with bacon fat on the outside. Broil them, mainly from the under side, turning occasionally to skin side. When almost done, put on a platter in a warm place. Dip the oysters into the melted butter and broil them lightly and lay them around the edges of the birds on the hot platter. Heat the oyster liquor, add the 2 table-spoons of butter which have been mixed with the bread crumbs, and bring just to the boiling point. Pour this on the platter, but not on the birds.

OYSTER STUFFING (FOR FISH OR FOWL)

1 cup bread crumbs
1 teaspoon mixed dried powdered herbs
1 pinch grated nutmeg

Oyster liquor
3 tablespoons butter
1 pint Oysters
2 eggs, beaten stiff

Mix the bread crumbs with the powdered herbs and nutmeg. Bring the oyster liquor to a boil and mix into the crumbs. Blend in the butter. Heat the oysters in a double boiler until their edges curl, then mince them and mix into the bread crumbs, and bind with the beaten eggs. Fill at once into the chicken, turkey, duck or fish prepared for stuffing.

OYSTERS À LA POMPADOUR

36 Oysters
1 cup oyster liquor
2 tablespoons butter
Pinch of salt and pepper

1 cup Hollandaise Sauce Supreme (No. 31)
1 teaspoon chopped pars-ley
Juice of one lemon

Cook the oysters for 3 minutes in a saucepan with their own liquor, and the butter, salt, pepper. Then add the Hollandaise Sauce and stew together for 2 minutes, but do not let boil. Add the parsley and lemon juice, stir slightly, serve hot.

FRIED OYSTERS À LA VILLEROI

24 Gardiners Bay, Robbins Island or other large Oysters
$\frac{1}{4}$ cup chicken forcemeat

2 eggs, beaten
$\frac{1}{2}$ cup fresh bread crumbs
Fried parsley

Cook the oysters in their own liquor for 2 minutes, then drain them. Spread the chicken forcemeat over both sides of each oyster, dip in the beaten egg and then in the bread crumbs and fry in hot fat for 3 minutes. Serve with fried parsley.

DEVILED OYSTERS, EAST NORTHPORT

$\frac{1}{2}$ bunch celery
1 onion
$\frac{1}{2}$ cup butter
1 pint Oysters
1 cup bread crumbs
2 egg yolks, beaten

2 tablespoons water
$\frac{1}{4}$ teaspoon curry powder
1 tablespoon worcestershire sauce
Salt, pepper, few grains cayenne

Chop celery and onions fine. Cook in the butter, remove from fire. Add oysters and three-fourths of the bread crumbs, the beaten egg yolks to which the two tablespoons of water have been added. Add seasonings and pour into buttered baking pan and cover top with remainder of bread crumbs. Cook in a hot oven for 20 minutes.

DEVILS ON HORSEBACK, DIVINITY HILL

12 thin slices cold chicken, turkey or veal	12 slices bacon
	Toast
12 Gardiner's Island, Robbins Island or other large Oysters	Brown sauce
	Sliced tomatoes, parsley

Spear on each of six small skewers 2 pieces of the meat, 2 oysters and two pieces of bacon, fastening each together well mixed. Brush with melted butter, place under a broiler and broil; turning once or twice. Serve on toast, garnished with Brown Sauce, parsley, tomatoes.

OYSTER FRIZEE, AQUEBOGUE

2 lbs tender veal	1 teaspoon salt
3 tablespoons butter	$\frac{1}{2}$ teaspoon pepper
24 Oysters	Toast triangles
1 tablespoon flour	

Cut the veal into thin pieces 3 inches square. Fry in the butter; when brown add the oysters and their liquor in which the flour has been blended. Season and cook until the oyster edges curl. Serve in a deep platter, garnished with toast fried in butter.

OYSTERS, HASHAMOMUCK BEACH

$\frac{1}{4}$ green pepper	2 teaspoons Roquefort cheese
$\frac{1}{2}$ onion	
4 slices bacon	1 teaspoon worcestershire sauce
$1\frac{1}{2}$ teaspoons butter	
	24 Oysters (on half shell)

Remove seeds and membrane from pepper and chop very fine with the onion. Cut the bacon strips into 2-inch squares. Melt the butter, blend with cheese and the Worcestershire sauce. Put a piece of bacon on each oyster on the half shell, spread with the onion mixture, top with the cheese mixture. Broil the oysters for 10 minutes.

OYSTER SHORTCAKE, BEAUX ARTS

2 cups flour
4 teaspoons baking powder
$\frac{1}{2}$ teaspoon salt
$\frac{1}{4}$ cup shortening
$\frac{3}{4}$ cup milk
Butter

$\frac{1}{4}$ cup cream
2 tablespoons flour
1 quart Oysters
Salt, pepper, few grains of cayenne

Sift together twice the baking powder, flour and salt, then with a pastry blender, work in the shortening; add the milk, and stir quickly until a soft dough is formed. Toss on a floured baking board, separate into two parts, pat and roll out. Lay each piece in two shallow buttered baking pans and bake 15 minutes in a hot oven. Spread each with butter and lay one on hot platter. Blend the cream with the flour, place in a saucepan with the oysters and their liquor, salt and pepper and cayenne; cook for 3 or 4 minutes. Then pour half of the mixture on round of dough on the platter; place the second round on top, and pour over it the other half of the oysters. Serve hot.

OYSTER SALAD, WESTBURY

24 Oysters
2 grapefruit
4 tablespoons tomato catsup
3 drops tabasco sauce
2 tablespoons lemon juice

1 tablespoon grated horseradish
1 teaspoon powdered sugar
$\frac{1}{2}$ cup cream, whipped
4 sprigs parsley, chopped
Bunch radishes

Cook the oysters in their own liquor until their edges curl, then drain and chill. Then cut off any tough parts of oysters. Cut the grapefruits in halves, take out the pulp with a spoon, and press through a sieve. Add this pulp to the oysters. Mix seasonings into the whipped cream, blend into oyster mixture, garnish with parsley and radishes.

BAKED OYSTERS, JOHN DREW

1 tablespoon butter	Island or other large
1 cup cream	Oysters
1 teaspoon anchovy paste	2 tablespoons grated Par-
1 tablespoon grated lemon	mesan cheese
rind	2 tablespoons bread crumbs
12 Gardiner's Bay, Robbins	Salt, pepper, paprika

Melt the butter in a saucepan, blend in the cream, stir and heat, add the anchovy and lemon rind. Butter a baking dish, place half of this cream sauce in it, lay in the oysters; add 2 tablespoons of liquor drained from oysters, sprinkle on half the cheese and bread crumbs over it, and pour on the other half of the sauce. Season, sprinkle on remaining bread crumbs and cheese, bake in a hot oven until brown.

OYSTER CROQUETTES, PATTERSQUASH ISLAND

18 Oysters	1 tablespoon parsley,
1 tablespoon butter	minced
2 tablespoons flour	$\frac{1}{4}$ teaspoon onion juice
1 cup minced chicken	2 egg yolks, beaten
	$\frac{1}{2}$ cup fine bread crumbs

Cook the oysters in their own liquor for 3 minutes, drain and chop. Melt the butter, blend in the flour; add $\frac{1}{2}$ cup oyster liquor, heat and add the oysters and chicken. Bring to a boil. Remove from fire, add the parsley and onion juice; add to egg yolks, stirring constantly. Cook 2 minutes, over low fire, stirring constantly; chill. When cold, form into croquettes; roll in bread crumbs and fry in deep fat.

OYSTERS AND SPAGHETTI, OYSTER POND

½ lb Spaghetti, cooked
1 pint Oysters
1 can mushrooms and their liquor
2 tablespoons butter
2 tablespoons flour

1½ cups milk
Salt, pepper, few grains cayenne
2 tablespoons bread crumbs
2 tablespoons melted butter

In a buttered baking dish, alternate layers of hot cooked spaghetti and the oysters and mushrooms. Make a sauce with the butter, flour, milk and the oyster and mushroom liquor; pour over the layers, sprinkle with bread crumbs and the melted butter. Bake in hot oven 10 to 15 minutes or until brown.

OYSTERS, PROMISED LAND

2 tablespoons butter
2 tablespoons flour
1 cup milk
Salt, pepper, a few grains cayenne

3 tablespoons grated Parmesan cheese
1 egg yolk
36 Gardiner's Bay or Robbins Island or other large Oysters

Melt the butter, blend in flour; add milk, season with salt and pepper; cook 5 minutes. Add 1 tablespoon of the cheese and egg yolk, mix well and heat through, stirring constantly. Remove from fire. Simmer the oysters in their liquor for 10 minutes; drain, and add them to the sauce, with 2 tablespoons of their liquor. Fill ramekins with the mixture, sprinkle remaining cheese on top; brown in hot oven for 10 minutes.

STUFFED OYSTERS, WILLIAMSBURG

2 doz. Oysters, chopped
2 slices bread, crumbed
¼ onion, finely minced
1 tablespoon chopped parsley
2 tablespoons chopped celery
Few grains cayenne
1 teaspoon walnut catsup

2 tablespoons butter
1 lemon, juice and grated rind
Salt and pepper
2 eggs, beaten
2 doz. oyster shells
2 tablespoons buttered bread crumbs
1 lemon, sliced

Put the oysters, drained of their liquor and chopped, into a pan, and add the crumbed bread, onion, parsley, celery, cayenne, walnut catsup, butter, lemon juice and grated rind and salt and pepper. Cook for 15 minutes, stirring constantly. Then add the two eggs mixing in thoroly. Clean the oyster shells and fill them with the mixture. Sprinkle with the buttered bread crumbs, brown in a hot oven. Serve with lemon slices.

(This is an old colonial recipe, in use not only on Long Island but also along the Maryland and Virginia tidewater districts 200 years ago).

CURRY OF OYSTERS, EAST INDIA

2 tablespoons butter
1 onion, chopped
½ green pepper, chopped
1 clove garlic, chopped
¼ teaspoon curry powder

2 tablespoons flour
½ cup cream
1 pint Oysters
Boiled rice

Fry in the butter the onion, pepper, garlic, and curry powders; blend in the flour, then the cream. Then drop in the drained oysters and cook until the edges curl. Before removing from the fire add ½ cup of the liquor drained from oysters. Serve over rice.

V

Ho! For the Long Island Clam!

I HAPPEN to be a very great partisan of the clam, and Long Island is the world's greatest home of the clam (at least so it seems to me).

Most people, when you say clam, know only one kind, the hard shell clam, otherwise known as quahogs—or if you like the fanciful Latin name better, *Venus Mercenaria,* whatever dreadful thing that may mean! But the soft-shell clam is quite particularly worthy of attention. It is a somewhat messy object both to clean and to eat, but it has flavor that, in my opinion, is superior to all other clams; more delicate and succulent. There are no more delightful family memories on our Long Island place than the steamed soft shell clam feasts we have had—outdoors preferred, not only by me, but by the cooks and the housewife because of the mess of shells, sauce and leavings. Still I insist it is a dish to set before a king, and I pity the King of England visiting the World's Fair on Long Island without sitting down to a steamed soft shell clam feast, napkin tucked under his chin. Of course nobody will give it to him because it makes such an unkingly mess! But the Prince of Wales ate it when some years ago he visited Long Island, which he regarded as his favorite playground.

It seems to me that Long Island must literally be built of clam, oyster and mussel shells, when I think of the billions of them from its sandy shores that have been opened since the Indian first came there. Little wonder they called Long Island "the island of shells!"

The clam has a reputation for being close-mouthed, and

that is why his taste is so good. He keeps it all inside most
stingily, like a Scotchman's purse, and when he yields it
forth when cooked, it is a savor calculated to make any
half-hearted diner into a full-fledged gourmand. Even the
squeamish women often make an exception when it comes
to clams.

The most widely acclaimed clam dish is clam chowder.
America goes strong for it, so strong that it is divided into
fighting clans on the subject. Up in Maine, those on one
side of Penobscot Bay like their clam chowder made *with*
tomatoes, and those on the other side of the bay with milk
and *no* tomatoes. New York *insists* on tomatoes in its clam
chowder, and Rhode Island has still other ideas. It came to
such a pass that Maine (which has a long record of being
censorious about what goes into Maine mouths, and was the
first prohibition state) now wants to prohibit by law tomato
in clam chowder.

Clam chowder is today served a little too often and is
usually too indifferently made to rouse very special interest
in me. I like my clams best in other ways. It is time that
the splendid variety of other ways be made known more
widely. The restaurant in the Grand Central Terminal has
for years made many friends for its *clam stew,* which is a
grand dish—better, in my opinion, than oyster stew, which
is more widely known. Clams on the half shell—particularly "Cherrystone" and "Little Neck" Long Island clams—
are also very popular, and deservedly so, if one applies to
them the same caution against the use of cocktail sauces,
catsup, tabasco, etc. as I have already applied to the oyster.
A little lemon, and that's all a good fresh clam on the half
shell needs.

The other ways to serve clams of various kinds are far
less known, and here are the best of them, many original
on Long Island, some from abroad, and some adopted from
New England where they also like clams. Long Island has
done something special with clam pie, so I give it second
place (and for emphasis I repeat the recipe under Seafood

Pie). New England's clam pies are lacking, I think, in the loving extra touch which sets them apart.

Clams: preparation.—The *soft shell* variety is steamed open in a large fish kettle, after carefully picking them over to remove all open ("dead") ones, or those too small or too large. Ideal is 2 to 2½ inch length. They must be well scrubbed and washed. Put 1 cup water in the kettle, over a hot fire. When they begin to open, stir with a wooden spoon, so that those at top will get more heat. Strain the broth through cheese cloth. The soft shell clams, to eat or use, must be "bearded" after they are steamed open—that is, the long black hood removed from the neck, together with its trailing "veil."

The *hard shell* clams are prepared by selecting and scrubbing, and opening with an oyster knife, like an oyster. They have no beards.

STEAMED SOFT SHELL CLAMS, EATON'S NECK

100 soft shell Clams	1 tablespoon lemon juice
1 cup melted butter	(or onion juice)

Scrub the clams thoroughly, removing from the lot any that are imperfect, or too large or too small. (The ideal is the soft shell clam of 2 to 2½ inches in length). Then put them in a large pot with 1 cup of cold water, and a few slices of onion. Close the pot tight, but stir the clams once or twice with a big wooden spoon. Do not let come to a frothy boil, but see to it that the clams all open.

Then strain off the clam liquor, through a clean cheese-cloth, and serve in cups to drink. The opened clams are served on a big platter or deep dish, and dished out on individual plates. An oyster or dinner fork is then used to remove the clam from its shell, and take the black cap off the head. By the side of each diner is a warm soup dish containing the melted butter sauce, (mixed with the lemon or onion juice or worcestershire sauce if desired) and each diner dips the clam into the butter before eating. Some diners like to eat 30 or more clams, the average is 20. (A few go on until they lose count!)

CLAM PIE, APPLECROFT

48 soft shell Clams	2 tablespoons flour
2 cups hot boiled potatoes, sliced $\frac{1}{4}$ inch thick	Salt, pepper
	$\frac{1}{4}$ cup cream
2 onions, chopped finely	2 tablespoons parsley,
2 cups celery, diced finely	minced
5 tablespoons butter	Biscuit or pastry dough

Steam well-scrubbed clams to open; remove meats, and save liquor separately. Butter a 2-quart baking dish, and set inverted glass mixing cup in center. Line bottom and sides of casserole with potato slices. Fry onions and celery in 3 tablespoons of the butter until golden brown. Add clam liquor and simmer until tender. Make a "roux" of flour rubbed with remaining butter and add to clam liquor, stirring until smooth, making a thin gravy. Season. Combine cooked clam meats, gravy, and the cream; turn into casserole, pouring carefully so as not to disturb potatoes. Sprinkle with minced parsley. Have ready either biscuit crust or rich flaky pastry crust to fit top of casserole. Fit, trim, and prick with air holes. Make a "rose" of narrow strips of paste and set on top of pie. Bake in hot oven (450° F.) for about 15 minutes, or until browned.

(The inverted glass cup supports the crust and acts as a vacuum to hold juices in. The trick of making this pie so tasty is the cooking of onions and celery in the clam liquor.)

CLAMS CARNEGIE

48 soft shell Clams	4 slices bread soaked in milk
2 tablespoons butter	
1 onion, chopped	2 tablespoons chopped parsley
6 mushrooms, chopped	
2 tomatoes, chopped	Salt, pepper
	$\frac{1}{2}$ cup bread crumbs

Steam open the well-washed clams, beard them and replace them in their half shell. Then make a dressing by cooking in the butter for 10 or 15 minutes the onion, mushrooms, tomatoes, bread, parsley, salt, pepper. Then lay some of this mixture on top of each clam in its shell, sprinkle with bread crumbs, and brown in a hot oven for 5 minutes.

CLAM SHELLS, BAYSIDE

36 medium-sized hard shell Clams

36 soft shell clams

3 teaspoons worcestershire sauce

1 tablespoon diced cooked bacon

1 teaspoon parsley, minced

Salt, pepper

1 cup bread crumbs, rolled, browned

$\frac{1}{4}$ cup grated American cheese

1 tablespoon butter

Lemon slices

Open the clams, and chop them into pieces, and add the worcestershire sauce, the bacon, parsley, salt, pepper. Stir in the breadcrumbs to thicken. Have large clean, nicely shaped hard shell clam shells ready, fill them with the mixture. Sprinkle more breadcrumbs and some cheese over them, dot with butter, and bake in hot oven for 15 minutes. Serve hot with lemon slices.

SOFT SHELL CLAMS CASINO

48 soft shell Clams, medium size

3 slices bacon, diced

$\frac{1}{4}$ cup browned bread crumbs

1 tablespoon butter

1 teaspoon worcestershire sauce

Salt, pepper

Scrub the clams, pick them over carefully, steam them open, and shell. Cut away the hard part, using soft parts only. Select sufficient perfect single shells to serve a plate of 8 to each person; and then fill these shells with the soft parts of *two* clams, not one. On top of each shell place pieces of the diced bacon, some bread crumbs and a dot of butter, also bit of the worcestershire, salt and pepper. Bake until they are browned, and serve hot, with a relish.

STUFFED CLAMS, MANHASSET

24 good-sized, picked Cherrystone or Little Neck Clams
3 fresh mushrooms, minced
1 truffle

5 tablespoons butter
Salt and pepper
½ cup grated Parmesan cheese
3 sprigs parsley
2 lemons, halved

Open the clams, shell out, and save and wash the shells thoroly. Chop the clams, mix with the minced mushrooms, the truffle and 3 tablespoons of butter, salt and pepper; and then fill the clam shells with the mixture, sprinkle with the grated cheese and dot with remaining butter. Place in a baking pan and bake in a moderate oven for 15 minutes. Serve on a napkin, garnished with parsley and lemon halves.

SOFT CLAMS À LA MERRIL

36 medium-sized soft shell Clams
3 tablespoons butter
½ glass Madeira wine
¼ teaspoon pepper
1 shallot, chopped

½ cup Espagnole or Creole sauce
½ teaspoon parsley minced
Juice of 1 lemon
1 teaspoon butter

Steam open the clams, beard, and chop away the hard parts. Reserve the clam liquor. Put in a saucepan with 3 tablespoons butter and the wine, pepper, and shallot and 2 tablespoons clam liquor. Cook for seven minutes, then add the Espagnole or Creole Sauce, the parsley, the lemon juice, the teaspoon of butter, stirring as it simmers for 3 minutes more. Serve hot.

SOFT SHELL CLAMS, NEWBURG

30 soft shell Clams
1 tablespoon Madeira wine
Salt, pepper, few grains cayenne
1 tablespoon butter
1 tablespoon flour

1½ cups milk
2 egg yolks
½ cup cream
2 tablespoons sherry
Toast slices

Steam open the well-washed clams and shell. Cut away the hard parts and place carefully in a buttered pan with cover. Add the wine, cover the pan and let get hot for 2 or 3 minutes, but do not stir. Add then salt, pepper, cayenne and a white sauce made with a tablespoon of flour, a tablespoon of butter and 1½ cups of milk, and let simmer in a double boiler or chafing dish. The clams are then added. The yolks of the eggs are beaten with a half cup of cream, and put in the double boiler and stirred constantly until thick. Then on removing from the fire, 2 tablespoons of Sherry are added and the seasoning adjusted. Serve hot, on buttered toast slices.

CLAM, OYSTER OR MUSSEL FRITTERS

16 large Clams or Oysters or Mussels
½ cup oyster or clam liquor
2 eggs, slightly beaten
⅓ cup melted butter

½ cup milk
2 cups sifted flour
5 teaspoons baking powder
1 teaspoon salt
Dash of pepper

Wash shellfish and shuck, saving liquor. Run fish through meat grinder, or chop. Add liquor, eggs, butter and milk, mixing well. Mix and sift remaining ingredients and add to clams, mixing only until all flour is dampened. Drop by spoonfuls into deep hot fat (375° F) and fry until golden brown, about 2 to 3 minutes. Drain on unglazed paper. Serve at once.

(This recipe is carefully standardized for all fritter recipes.)

CLAM-OYSTER SPAGHETTI, MINEOLA

½ lb Italian Spaghetti
1 pint Oysters
1 pint soft shell Clams (soft
　parts only)
Salt, pepper, cayenne

1 cup white sauce
1 small can stewed tomatoes
1 cup buttered bread crumbs
Grated Parmesan cheese

Cook spaghetti just 10 minutes in salted boiling water. Drain and rinse under running cold water. Butter a baking dish and place a layer of the spaghetti in it, then a layer of mixed oysters and clams, add salt, pepper, few grains of cayenne; then add another layer of spaghetti and of clams and oysters. On top pour the white sauce, then the stewed tomatoes. Cover with the bread crumbs and bake in a moderate oven for 5 or 6 minutes. Before serving sprinkle cheese over the dish.

WATERCRESS CLAM SOUP

4 medium-sized potatoes
2 medium-sized onions,
　finely minced
2 tablespoons butter
1 qt clams, steamed
1½ cups potato water

1½ cups clam liquor
1 cup cream or rich milk
Salt, pepper
2 egg yolks, beaten
1 bunch watercress

Peel and dice potatoes, and cook in water to cover until tender. Drain and force through fine seive. Saute onions in butter. Steam clams in kettle with ¾ cup water; shell and chop very fine. Reserve clam liquor. Combine sautéed onion, potato purée and minced clams; mix thoroughly. Add potato water, clam liquor and cream and heat thoroughly. Remove coarse stems from watercress, chop leaves very fine or pound in mortar. Remove soup from fire, add to egg yolks carefully, stirring constantly; add cress.

CLAM SOUFFLE, SWAN RIVER

3 tablespoons butter
½ cup flour
1 cup milk
1 cup clam broth
1 onion, minced
½ green pepper
1 pimento

½ cup cracker crumbs
Salt, pepper, few grains cayenne
3 eggs, separated
50 soft shell Clams, minced
½ teaspoon baking powder

Make a white sauce of the butter, flour, milk and clam broth. Add the onion, pepper, pimento and cracker crumbs and seasonings. Stir in the egg yolks one by one, and the minced clams. Then fold in the egg whites which have been beaten with the baking powder until stiff. Butter a pyrex baking dish, and put in the mixture. Bake in a moderate oven (350° F.) for 40 minutes, until firm. Serve promptly.

CLAM-SHRIMP JAMBALAYA, LONG ISLAND

1 tablespoon butter
1 onion, chopped
1 tablespoon flour
1 clove garlic
1 bay leaf
6 thyme leaves
2 teaspoons beef extract
½ teaspoon sugar

1 red pepper pod
Salt, pepper, few grains cayenne
1 cup stewed tomatoes
2 cups soft shell Clams
2 cups cooked Shrimp
1 cup uncooked rice
2 drops Kitchen Bouquet

Melt the butter, cook the onion in it; as it begins to brown stir in the flour, the seasonings, the tomatoes. Let simmer for 10 minutes. Then steam the clams; reserve the clam broth. Shell and beard the clams, cut away the soft parts and lay aside. Add the clam hard parts, and the shrimp (being sure to remove the black vein), also the clam broth and the washed, drained rice. Bring to a boil, stir constantly but mildly, then reduce the heat, and set the pan in boiling water, let simmer until the rice is cooked, but do not let the mixture get too thick—use more clam broth if necessary. Add the Kitchen Bouquet, adjust the seasoning, add the soft parts of the clam, heat for a couple more minutes and then turn out upon a big deep platter, garnished with triangles of toast fried in butter.

SOFT CLAM SOUP, CENTERPORT

25 soft shell Clams	cayenne
1 pint clam broth	Leaves of celery
1 pint white stock or chicken consomme	1 cup thin white sauce
Salt, pepper, few grains	1 cup milk
	4 tablespoons butter

Steam open the well-washed clams, save the liquor, and cut away the hard parts of the clams. Put a pint of the clam liquor in a pot, with the white stock; add the clams, salt, pepper, few grains cayenne, celery leaves and cook for 2 minutes. Then add the white sauce and the milk, scalded. Heat thoroughly, add the butter and serve with crackers.

DOUBLE CLAMS, CHEQUIT

20 medium-sized hard shell Clams	1 tablespoon chives, chopped fine
20 medium-sized soft shell Clams	1 tablespoon parsley, chopped
4 tablespoons butter	Salt, pepper, few grains of cayenne
$\frac{1}{2}$ cup raw chopped celery	
2 or 3 mushroom heads, chopped fine	3 tablespoons clam liquor

Steam open the clams, shell and cut away the hard part of the soft shell clams. Place in a casserole or pyrex baking dish, into which 2 tablespoons of butter have been melted. Add the celery, the mushrooms, chives, parsley. Sprinkle over it 1 teaspoon salt, $\frac{1}{4}$ teaspoon pepper, few grains of cayenne. Then add two more tablespoons of butter, also the clam liquor, and bake in a moderate oven for 20 minutes. Serve from the casserole.

CLAM LOAF, LONG ISLAND

50 medium-sized hard or soft shell Clams
1 crusty loaf of bread
1 cup clam liquor

½ cup butter
Salt, pepper, few grains cayenne
2 tablespoons flour

Steam the clams open, save the liquor, and chop the clams (if soft-shells clams are used, cut away the hard parts). Cut the top off a loaf of bread. Scoop out the soft inside to make a shell. Place shell in baking dish. Fry the inside soft bread, after crumbling it, in 2 tablespoons of the butter. Make a thin white sauce with the flour and 2 tablespoons of butter and the clam broth which has been reduced to 1 cup by boiling for 4 minutes over a hot fire) and mix with the clams and the fried crumbs; season. The mixture should fill the inside of the breadloaf. Bake in a baking dish in a very hot oven (475° F) for 15 or 20 minutes.

CLAM-OYSTER STEW, JONES BEACH

⅓ cup butter
⅓ cup flour
1 quart Grade A milk
1 teaspoon salt
¼ teaspoon pepper
2 bay leaves
¼ teaspoon mace

1 pint soft shell Clams, steamed and shucked
1 cup clam broth
1 pint Oysters
Toasted pilot crackers
Liquor drained from Oysters

In a double boiler melt the butter, blend in the flour and then the milk and seasonings, stirring until smooth and thick. Separate the hard parts of the clams from the soft. Bring the oyster liquor and clam liquor to a boil, add the oysters and hard clam parts, let simmer until edges curl. Then add the soft clam parts and the milk sauce and heat. Before serving, remove the bay leaves. Lay toasted pilot crackers in soup plates, pour soup over them.

CLAMS AND OYSTERS, CREOLE TOAST

24 Oysters
24 soft shell Clams, medium-
    sized

Creole Sauce
Buttered Toast

Shell the oysters; steam open the clams and remove from shells. Cook both oysters and clams a few minutes in their liquor. Then add a pint of Creole Sauce made by frying for 10 minutes in 2 tablespoons of cooking fat on pimiento pepper and one onion diced, together with ½ cup of un-cooked ham, diced. Then add 2 minced cloves of garlic, and brown; then also add 1 cup of tomato pulp, ½ table-spoon sugar, ½ teaspoon of salt, and ¼ teaspoon black pep-per, ¼ teaspoon paprika, and a few grains of cayenne. Cook the sauce gently for 30 minutes.

The clams and oysters in the hot Creole Sauce are poured over buttered toast.

PANNED SOFT SHELL CLAMS, HUNTINGTON BAY

8 thin pieces toast, buttered
50 soft shell Clams, medium-
    sized
2 tablespoons butter

Salt, pepper.
Few grains of cayenne
½ cup clam liquor

Fill the bottom of a buttered baking pan with the pieces of buttered toast. Arrange on these little heaps of the steamed and shelled clams, and dot each with butter, salt, white pepper and a grain or two of cayenne. Add to the pan ½ cup of the clam liquor. Bake for a few minutes and serve hot.

GREEN PEPPER CLAMS, LITTLE NECK

50 hard shell Clams, me-
    dium-sized
2 small green peppers, par-
    boiled

½ cup cream
2 tablespoons butter
½ teaspoon salt
6 thin slices buttered toast

Stew the shucked clams in their own liquor until the edges curl, then chop them, and add the green peppers parboiled and chopped. Add the cream and butter and salt. Pour on toast rounds with the sauce.

BROILED OYSTERS AND CLAMS, LONG ISLAND

24 Oysters
24 Cherrystone, or medium-sized hard shell Clams
$\frac{1}{2}$ cup melted butter
1 cup fresh bread crumbs
2 tablespoons olive oil
4 pieces buttered toast

4 tablespoons maitre d'hotel butter (lemon juice, butter, parsley)
Salt and pepper
4 strips of bacon, broiled
4 sprigs of parsley
2 lemons (halves)

Open the oysters and clams, remove from liquor, dry thoroly, roll in melted butter, then in the breadcrumbs. Sprinkle a bit of olive oil on them and broil on a close-meshed broiling grid. Have ready four hot pieces of buttered toast on warm plates, and put on each 6 oysters and 6 clams. Drop a tablespoon of the maitre d'hotel butter on each pile, season with salt and pepper, and lay the freshly broiled bacon strips on top, plus a sprig of parsley. Serve with the lemon halves.

CLAM FRAPPE, BUSTANOBY

50 Cherrystone Clams
1 teaspoon lemon juice
1 cup cold water
4 slices onion

Freshly ground black pepper, few grains cayenne
6 tablespoons whipped cream
Nutmeg

Scrub the clams, changing water several times, and put in cooking pot with the lemon juice, 1 cup cold water and a few slices onion. Steam until the clams open. Then shell the clams and season with the pepper and cayenne. Chill them, and then shake up well. Fill 6 sherbet glasses with the clams, and top with a tablespoon of whipped cream on each, and sprinkle with a little nutmeg.

SOFT CLAM SOUP, FISHERMAN'S SPECIAL

1 peck soft shell Clams, medium sized
1 tablespoon butter
1 tablespoon flour
2 cups scalded milk
Salt, pepper, few grains of
cayenne, few grains of nutmeg
1 tablespoon creamed butter
1 tablespoon chopped parsley
2 cups crumbled pilot crackers

Steam open the clams, and save the broth. Melt butter, blend in flour, add milk and 2 cups clam broth. Separate the hard from the soft parts of the clams; add the hard parts to the milk mixture. Add also 2 well-scrubbed clam shells for each person to be served. Season and bring to a boil, after which let simmer for 15 minutes. Then strain through cloth, bring to a boil after adding the creamed butter. Now add the soft parts of the clams while the soup boils, also the parsley, also the crumbed pilot crackers. Have 2 clam shells in each plate.

BATTER CLAMS, LITTLE NECK

36 medium-sized hard Clams
2 eggs, beaten
1½ cups flour
½ teaspoon salt
Pinch cayenne pepper
½ cup butter
Tartare Sauce (No. 1)

Dry the raw clams thoroly. Dip them in a batter made with the eggs, flour, salt, cayenne, thinned into the right consistency with a little of the clam liquor, if needed. Melt 2 tablespoons of butter in a frying pan and when sizzling hot begin to fry, lifting with a large cooking spoon one clam at a time, into the pan, together with all the batter the spoon will hold. Keep adding more butter in the frying pan as needed. Lift finished clams to a hot platter and keep covered. Serve with Tartare sauce.

CLAM OR OYSTER SOUFFLE, NORTHPORT

36 soft shell Clams or small quahogs, or oysters
$\frac{1}{2}$ cup water
2 tablespoons butter
2 tablespoons flour
$\frac{1}{2}$ cup milk
3 eggs, separated

$\frac{1}{2}$ teaspoon salt
$\frac{1}{8}$ teaspoon pepper
$\frac{1}{8}$ teaspoon paprika
$\frac{1}{2}$ cup grated Parmesan Cheese
$\frac{1}{2}$ teaspoon minced parsley

Shell the clams or oysters. Place them in a saucepan with their liquor, and $\frac{1}{2}$ cup of water. Bring to boil and simmer 5 minutes. Drain well, reserving the liquor. Press the clams or oysters through a sieve. Heat the butter and flour together for 2 minutes, stirring constantly, then add the sieved clams or oysters, the liquor and the milk. When mixture comes to boil, remove from fire; add to slightly beaten yolks together with the salt, pepper, paprika. Mix well, fold in the stiffly beaten egg whites. Place this mixture in 6 buttered ramekins, and sprinkle with cheese. Set the ramekins in a pan of boiling hot water and bake in a moderate oven for 25 minutes. Sprinkle with minced parsley and serve at once.

MUSTARD CLAMS, ISLAND PARK

36 medium-sized hard or soft shell Clams
3 tablespoons butter
2 tablespoons flour

1 teaspoon Colman's dry mustard
1 cup milk
Salt, pepper

Steam open the well-washed clams. Shell and beard them, and place in warm covered dish. Reserve the clam liquor. Then make a sauce by melting butter in top of a double boiler, blending in flour and mustard and adding milk. Beat this into a creamy mixture, season with salt and pepper, and then cook for 3 minutes. Pour this over the clams and serve piping hot on toasted pilot crackers.

SOFT CLAMS À LA NEWBURG

42 medium-sized soft shell Clams
2 tablespoons butter
Pepper
1 glass Madeira wine
2 truffles, finely minced
3 egg yolks
1 pint cream

Scrub and steam open the clams, beard and carefully cut away the hard parts. Reserve the liquor. Cook clams gently in a covered saucepan with the butter, pepper, wine and truffles, for 8 minutes, adding 3 tablespoons of the clam broth at the end of 4 minutes. Beat the egg yolks with the cream for 3 minutes; pour over the clams. Heat the mixture just until it thickens, stirring constantly; do not let come to a boil or mixture will curdle.

CLAM CURRY, NORTHERN BOULEVARD

36 soft shell Clams, medium sized
2 tablespoons chopped onion
2 tablespoons butter
1 lime (peel only)
2 tablespoons grated coconut
A few cardamom seeds (or small piece crystallized ginger)
1 tablespoon good curry powder
1 quart clam broth
Boiled rice

Steam open the well-washed clams. Beard the clams, separating the hard parts of the clam from the soft. Reserve the broth. Brown the onion in the butter, add the chopped peel of the lime and let simmer a few minutes. Then add the coconut, the cardamom seeds (or ginger in very small cubes), the curry powder and let simmer 3 or 4 minutes. Strain the mixture and then add the clam broth, also strained, the hard parts of the clams plus two well-washed clam shells. Let simmer very gently for 4 or 5 minutes, then add the soft parts of the clams and let simmer 4 or 5 minutes. Arrange the rice in a ring on a round platter, pour the clam curry in the center of ring. Serve with the chutney or some other Indian relishes, or fresh cucumber pickles. (Hard shell clams or mussels can also be used instead of the soft shell clams.)

FRIED CLAMS, BRIDGEHAMPTON

36 soft shell Clams
3 cups thick white sauce
1 cup cooked ham, minced
Celery salt
Few grains of cayenne

1 teaspoon lemon juice
$\frac{1}{2}$ cup bread crumbs
2 eggs, beaten with 2 table-spoons water

Steam open the well-washed clams, beard them; save the broth. In making the white sauce, use some of the clam broth. Mix the white sauce with the ham and season with the celery salt, cayenne and lemon juice. Drop the clams into this sauce. Let them stand for two hours. Then roll them in the breadcrumbs, then in the egg, then in the breadcrumbs again. Fry in deep fat (at 375° F) until brown.

DEEP FAT CLAM FRY, FORT SALONGA

40 medium-sized hard shell Clams
1 egg
1 cup cream or evaporated milk

2 cups cracker crumbs
$\frac{1}{2}$ cup flour
Salt, pepper

Steam open the clams, wipe them thoroly. Beat together the egg and cream. Mix together the cracker crumbs, flour, salt and pepper. Dip the clams in the egg mixture, then in the crumbs and place in the wire basket of a deep-fat fryer and fry at 375° F until brown. Serve with Tartare sauce.

CLAMS WITH EGG NOODLES, SUPREME

48 soft shell Clams
1 package wide egg noo-
 dles
3 tablespoons butter
5 tablespoons flour
2 cups Grade A milk

1½ cups clam broth
Salt, pepper, few grains cayenne
1 cup grated American
 cheese

Steam open the well-washed clams, shell and beard them, reserving the broth. Cut the clams into halves, discarding the neck parts of some of the larger clams. Cook the noodles; then melt the butter in a saucepan, stir in the flour, add the milk and 1 cup clam broth. When thickened add the noodles and the clams, salt, pepper, cayenne. Mix, heat through, and then put into a buttered casserole. Pour in another ½ cup of clam broth, sprinkle with the cheese and bake in a moderate oven (375° F.) until brown.

CLAMS ON TOAST, EAST NORWICH

1 pint Clams
1 tablespoon butter
2 tablespoons flour
½ cup milk
2 egg yolks, slightly beaten

½ teaspoon salt
Paprika
1 tablespoon lemon juice
6 toast triangles

Pour off juice of clams. Bring to boil and skim. Add clams, chopped. Melt butter. Blend in flour. Add milk gradually, stirring constantly. Add clams and cook 5 minutes. Add slowly to egg yolks, stirring until blended. Add salt, paprika and lemon juice. Serve very hot on toast.

CLAM RAMEKINS, CRAB MEADOW

¼ cup butter
3 small onions, minced
1 pint Clams, finely chopped
2 cups boiling water
2 large potatoes, diced

1 tablespoon salt
⅛ teaspoon black pepper
1 quart milk
3 tablespoons flour
½ cup button mushrooms

Melt butter and saute onions in it until light yellow. Add clams and simmer for 7 minutes. Add boiling water, potatoes, salt and pepper, and cook 30 minutes. Blend ¼ cup milk with the flour, then add remaining milk gradually, stirring until smooth. Combine with the clam mixture and mushrooms. Pour into greased ramekins, and bake in a moderate oven (350° F.) until tops are brown, about 25 minutes.

FLOUNDER WITH SHRIMP-CLAM SAUCE

3½ lbs Flounder
2 cups fish stock
4 tablespoons butter
3 or 4 shallots, minced
½ yellow onion, minced
½ cup mushrooms, chopped
3 tablespoons flour
2 cups Grade A milk

3 tablespoons Chablis (white wine)
1 egg yolk
White pepper, nutmeg, allspice, cloves
20 soft shell Clams, chopped
12 cooked Shrimps, chopped

Fillet the fish and poach in fish stock. Butter a baking dish, spread the fillets and add shallots, onions, and mushrooms and the fish stock. Cover with buttered paper and let simmer for 12 minutes. Meantime prepare a sauce with 2 tablespoons butter, the flour, milk, wine, egg yolk, spices, and then add the clams and shrimps. Pour over the fish and brown in oven. Serve with potatoes.

CLAMS THERMIDOR

1 pint hard or soft shell Clams
2 tablespoons butter
2 tablespoons flour
½ teaspoon salt
½ teaspoon paprika
½ teaspoon Kitchen Bouquet

¾ cup light cream
2 tablespoons onion juice
1 tablespoon lemon juice
1 tablespoon minced parsley
1 egg, beaten
2 tablespoons buttered bread crumbs
Scallop shells

Open the clams, shell, reserve the liquor, and chop the clams. Make a white sauce by blending the butter with the flour, salt, paprika and kitchen bouquet. Then add the cream, stir until it begins to boil, then add the onion juice and the clams. Stir over the fire for 1 minute, then add the lemon juice and parsley. Take from fire and blend in the egg. Then arrange the mixture into the buttered cleaned scallop shells, spread with the breadcrumbs and bake in a hot oven for 2 minutes, or until lightly browned.

CLAM-STUFFED ONIONS, BABYLON

24 hard-shell Clams	1 cup clam liquor
6 or 8 good-sized Onions, alike in size	2 cups cooked spinach
	1 bacon slice, crisped

Open the clams and stew 5 minutes in their liquor. Cut off the top of the onions and bake in their skins in a slow oven (300° F) with the clam liquor in the bottom of the baking pan. When they are tender, pick off the outer skins and cut cavities half an inch deep into the tops. Fill these cavities with 3 or 4 clams each and some of the spinach, hot, drained; and pour over each one a little of the juice from the pan. Lay on top of each onion a square of crisped bacon. Serve the onions on a hot platter, each onion resting on a little nest of spinach.

CLAM BELLY BROIL, GAGE & TOLNER'S

9 large soft clams	1 tablespoon cracker dust
1 egg, beaten	1 tablespoon melted butter

Steam open the well-washed clams, beard them, and cut away the hard parts. Dip them in the freshly beaten egg, and roll lightly in the cracker dust. Lay them on a close-meshed broiling rack and broil them (if possible over live coals or charcoal). Broil until the egg and crumbs become crisp. Lay on hot platter, sprinkle some hot melted butter over them and serve quickly.

CLAM-STUFFED BAKED POTATOES

4 large Long Island or Idaho Potatoes	2 slices of onion
1 cup milk	2 tablespoons flour
½ cup clam liquor	2 tablespoons butter
2 stalks celery	Salt, pepper, paprika
	36 soft shell Clams

Bake the potatoes, cut and hollow out the centers, but leave some potato in the shells, which is to be flaked with a fork. Scald the milk and clam broth in the top of a double boiler, putting in also the celery and onion, and cook for 15 minutes. Then remove the celery and onion and add the butter and flour creamed together. Add salt and pepper to taste. Stir until it thickens, then add the clams which have been steamed open, bearded and minced. Let stand while it heats, then stuff into potatoes, sprinkle with paprika. Serve very hot.

(This recipe can be used for stuffing potatoes with oysters, mussels, or halibut or haddock or other fish.)

CLAM ROAST, NATHAN HALE

48 medium-sized hard shell Clams	2 grated onions
Salt, red pepper	Juice of 2 lemons
2 tablespoons butter	Tomato catsup

Open the clams, leave the clam in the lower shell and save top shell to match. Season each clam with a shake of salt, red pepper, a dot of butter, and some grated onion. Replace the top shell and tie together with a piece of string. Bake in a quick oven for 15 minutes. Discard the upper shell; serve hot, 8 on a plate, sprinkled with a bit of lemon juice and tomato catsup.

FROZEN CLAMS, NORTHPORT

48 medium-size hard shell or soft shell Clams	6 grapefruit shells
	Paprika, salt, pepper

Steam open the well-washed clams in tightly covered kettle, with $\frac{1}{2}$ cup of water. Skim out the clams, shell and beard them, and chop them coarsely. Let the juice settle, strain through cheese cloth, put the chopped clams in the broth and freeze. Break in pieces, serve in the grapefruit shells, sprinkled with paprika, salt and pepper to taste.

OYSTER AND CLAM PIE, LINDENHURST

Pastry crust	Salt, pepper, few grains cayenne
18 Oysters	enne
18 soft shell Clams	2 tablespoons bacon,
1 tablespoon butter	chopped

Line sides of a shallow casserole with pastry crust. Put in the drained oysters and clams, and the butter, seasonings and bacon. Season, cover with a pie crust; cut a small hole in top of crust. Bake for 30 minutes in hot oven. Five minutes before taking out add, through hole in crust, $\frac{1}{2}$ cup of the clam broth and oyster liquor which have been mixed and heated.

OYSTER (OR CLAM) AND SWEETBREAD PIE, RANDOLPH

1 pint Sweetbreads	seasoned with black pepper
1 pint Oysters or Clams	per
$1\frac{1}{2}$ cups cream sauce, well	Rich pie crust
	1 tablespoon cream

Wash and parboil the sweetbreads. Cut in cubes. Heat the oysters in their liquor for 3 minutes, then drain, retaining 2 tablespoons liquor. Chop the oysters into quarters. Butter a baking dish, lay in the sweetbreads and oysters in layers, and add the cream sauce, to which the 2 tablespoons oyster liquor has been added. Cover with a thick pie crust, brush the top with the cream and bake for 40 minutes.

(This recipe stems back to old Virginia, Mrs. Mary Randolph having put it down in 1831.)

EGGPLANT OYSTER (OR CLAM) PIE, GARDEN CITY

1 Eggplant, cubed	$\frac{1}{2}$ cup cracker crumbs
Biscuit dough	1 tablespoon butter
12 Oysters or Clams, drained	1 teaspoon salt
$\frac{1}{2}$ cup milk	$\frac{1}{4}$ teaspoon pepper

Cook eggplant cubes until tender in water just to cover. Drain. Roll out the biscuit dough one-quarter inch thick, line sides of baking dish with it. Arrange in the baking dish the eggplant cubes, the oysters, the milk, cracker crumbs, butter, salt, pepper, also $\frac{1}{2}$ cup liquor drained from oysters. Cover with the biscuit dough, vented, and bake 25 minutes in a moderate oven.

GIBLET AND OYSTER (OR CLAM) PIE, RIVERHEAD

12 chicken, turkey or goose Giblets	Salt, pepper
	1 sprig thyme
$\frac{1}{2}$ cup celery, diced	1 teaspoon parsley
Pastry crust	$1\frac{1}{2}$ tablespoons flour
24 Oysters or Clams, drained	

Cut the giblets into inch-square pieces, and cook in water just to cover until nearly tender. Cook celery in liquor drained from oysters. Line sides of a pie dish with pastry dough. Turn in giblets, celery, oysters, oyster liquor, seasoning, parsley. Mix flour with a little cold water and add, stirring until smooth. Cover with vented pastry crust. Bake 15 minutes in a moderately hot oven ($400°$ F).

RABBIT-OYSTER (OR CLAM) PIE, SMITHTOWN

2 Rabbits	$\frac{1}{4}$ lb salt pork, finely chopped
$\frac{1}{2}$ cup flour	
Salt, freshly ground black pepper	1 bay leaf
	1 sprig thyme
Puff Pastry	4 parsley sprigs
24 Oysters or Clams, drained	1 glass red wine
1 onion, finely chopped	

Skin, clean and sponge the rabbits carefully with a damp cloth. Cut the meat into small pieces and roll in the flour, which has been mixed with the salt and pepper. Line sides of a deep baking dish with pastry, and arrange the rabbit meat, oysters, onion, and salt pork in it. Tie together the bay leaf and thyme and parsley and place in casserole. Add 1 cup of liquor drained from oysters, and the wine. Top with a puff pastry crust, vented. Bake in a moderate oven for 45 minutes.

PARTRIDGE AND OYSTER (OR CLAM) PIE

4 slices bacon	1 tablespoon parsley,
½ cup shallots, chopped	minced
fine	3 hard-cooked egg yolks
3 Partridges	18 Oysters
Salt, pepper	Pastry crust

In a deep baking dish lay the slices of bacon, and sprinkle bottom and sides with the shallots. Lay in the partridges, each skinned and cut into 4 pieces; season with salt, pepper, parsley. Add the egg yolks, cut in two. Add ¼ cup liquor drained from oysters, also ¼ cup of game stock made from the partridge trimmings. Bake, covered, in moderate oven (350° F.) for 1 hour. Remove from oven, add oysters, more liquor or stock if required. Cover with pastry crust, cutting gashes in crust to permit escape of steam. Bake in a hot oven (450° F.) 15 minutes.

CHICKEN AND CLAMS, VALENCIENA

½ Chicken	½ cup green peas
3 tablespoons butter	10 thin slices Spanish (or
12 hard shell Clams	other spiced) sausage
6 shrimp	2 cups chicken (or beef or
½ cup uncooked rice	clam) broth
2 tablespoons green pepper, chopped	

Fry the chicken in butter, then lay it in a buttered baking dish. Put the clams and shrimp on top of it, then add the rice. Scatter over this the green pepper, the peas and the sausage. Add the broth. Cook, covered, on stove until the rice is soft, occasionally stirring. Then bake, uncovered, in a slow oven for 20 minutes.

CLAM (OR OYSTER) AND MUSHROOM SHORTCAKE

4 tablespoons butter
4 tablespoons flour
2 cans ready-to-serve cream of mushroom soup
$\frac{1}{2}$ cup clam broth
36 soft shell clams
3 hard-cooked eggs, sliced
2 tablespoons minced green pepper
1 teaspoon minced chives

Shortcake:
3 cups flour
$4\frac{1}{2}$ teaspoons baking powder
1 teaspoon salt
$\frac{3}{4}$ cup butter
1 cup milk
6 sprigs parsley
18 mushrooms
2 tablespoons grated cheese

Blend the butter, melted, and the flour together in a double boiler, then pour in gradually the soup, and the broth, stirring. Cook until thick, then add the clams (which have been washed, steamed open, shelled and bearded, and the necks cut off of some of the larger, tougher ones). Mix in also the egg slices and minced pepper and chines.

For the shortcake sift the flour, add the baking powder and salt, and sift once more. Blend in the butter, add the milk, stir and make a soft dough. Roll out on a floured baking board to $\frac{1}{2}$-inch thickness, then cut it into 3-inch squares. Bake a greased cooking sheet for 12 minutes in a hot oven (450° F.). When brown, split the shortcakes in half, arrange the lower halves on individual plates, pour half the clam mixture over them; then lay on top the other halves, and pour over them the rest of the mixture. Garnish with parsley and mushrooms which have been filled with grated cheese and broiled.

MINCED CLAMS AND RICE, CAROLINE CHURCH

24 medium-size soft shell Clams
1 cup celery, chopped
1 tablespoon butter
1 teaspoon good curry powder
Salt, pepper, paprika
1 teaspoon parsley, minced
Boiled rice

Steam open the well-washed clams, save the liquor. Separate the hard from the soft parts of the clams; then simmer the hard parts in the liquor, with the celery, for 10 minutes. Strain and throw away the necks. Chop the soft parts of the clams into medium pieces, cook for 2 minutes in butter in which has been blended the curry powder. Then add the clam liquor, salt, pepper, paprika, parsley, and beat together gently without cooking. Serve hot on a mound of boiled rice.

CLAM ASPIC, CENTERPORT

36 soft shell Clams
Lemon juice
Salt, pepper
2 tablespoons gelatin (approximate)
Lettuce, pimiento
Radishes, olives

Steam the well-washed clams to open, remove meats; and save liquor separately and measure to determine number of cupsful. Chop or mince clams, discarding hard portion. Combine with measured clam liquor, seasoning to taste with lemon juice, salt and pepper, and heat. Allow one tablespoon granulated gelatin to 2 cups liquor. Soak gelatin in $\frac{1}{4}$ cup cold water 5 minutes, dissolve in hot clam liquid. Pour into large mold, or small individual molds, which have been rubbed lightly with olive oil. Chill until firm. Unmold on lettuce, and garnish with pimento, olives, radishes. Pass highly seasoned lemon mayonnaise, or Russian dressing. (Excellent for the summer buffet or hot weather luncheon.)

CLAM BROTH, TOPPED WITH PIMENTO CREAM

Scrub 1 quart hard shell or soft shell clams, place in kettle with 1 quart water, cover and simmer 20 minutes. Strain settled liquor. Use as is or add milk or water to dilute strength if desired. Season with celery salt, and heat. Serve hot in bouillon cups, topped with garnish of pureed pimiento blended into whipped cream. Serve immediately with lightest sprinkle of minced parsley on top of cream.

SPAGHETTI, MUSSEL (OR CLAM) SAUCE

20 Mussels or Clams, minced
2 tablespoons olive oil
1 onion, chopped
1 garlic clove, chopped
3 tablespoons minced ham
½ cup tomato paste, or 1 cup concentrated tomato soup, or purée
1 cup clam or mussel broth
3 tablespoons olives, chopped
1 tablespoon green pepper
1 teaspoon parsley, minced
Salt, pepper
1 lb Italian Spaghetti (or Linguini), cooked *"al dente"* 9-10 minutes

Steam open the clams, reserving broth; mince the clams. Heat the olive oil in frying pan, lightly brown the onion in it, add garlic and simmer 5 minutes. Add the ham, simmer 5 more minutes. Then add the tomato and clam or mussel broth, cook, stirring constantly, until thickened. Add olives, green pepper and minced clams or mussels, let simmer for 5 minutes. Add parsley, salt, pepper. Cook the spaghetti separately in rapidly boiling salted water for 9-10 minutes for *"al dente"* effect of slight hardness. If softer spaghetti is desired cook additional 3-4 minutes. Remove to hot platter and pour the hot sauce over it and serve promptly. (Linguini is one type of Italian spaghetti often preferred by gourmets for this mussel or clam sauce).

VI
A Bow to the Long Island Flounder

Everyone has heard about Filet of Sole, Marguery; and in my introduction I have recalled that sole was the toast of the Greek epicures, as it is today the toast of France and the Mediterranean chefs. The sole has been elevated very high; I have myself, on occasion, raised a quizzical eyebrow when I learned that my order for filet of sole brought me instead Long Island flounder, even in good hotels and restaurants. Is flounder then a mere upstart substitute?

Let us understand each other and end this international culinary crisis! Flounder is really a family name for a certain group of fish, and it is no excessive wrenching of the truth to say that flounder is sole, or sole flounder. In the flounder family group authentically belong Lemon Sole, Gray sole, Blackbacks, Dabs, Yellowtails and a lot more. The family trait, like the Hapsburg chin, is *flatness*. The family inter-relationships between all these flatfish is intricate (again like the hapless Hapsburgs).

But, gastronomically speaking, flatness and delicate texture are the regal crowns of the flounder—sole to you if you like. Flatness usually means lean meat, tender and delicious, flaky and fine in texture—and has the advantage of being in season all year. The European sole, let us admit, since the argument is difficult, may have some little extra taste value. Still, I would like to face the issue down sometime, and make extended comparisons; it is a little like the tradition that the pompano is the queen of all fish for the table. These things "go by favor," usually—a more experienced gourmet hesitates about "comparing horses and apples," as the professor says!

The flounder in Long Island waters is sometimes caught in a truly sportsmanlike manner, as my friend Joe, the Long Island Robinson Crusoe, does. Joe, an Italian ex-pugilist, ex-army cook, and ex- a lot of things, lives for 6 or 8 months on the sandy shore of Long Island in a shack, and what he doesn't know about either the fish or the game of Long Island, or their cookery, is not greatly worth while knowing. I admit my debt to Joe. He goes out in a boat with his eel-catching equipment of a three-tined spear, and comes in with flounder. His sharp eyes watch for the flounders' up-turned eyes on the bay-bottom. (The flounder hides his body in sand, and only his eyes, located on his top, protrude.) Down comes Joe's spear into Mr. Flounder's rear, and the flounder is Joe's. Other more prosaic people fish for flounder with rod and line.

Flounder is deservedly popular, and all snootiness or deception about sole is out of place. (An Englishman might think I was perpetrating a pun here, because the English call flounder "plaice.") Long Island flounder can hold its own quite well indeed. It can satisfy all but the most academically exacting gourmet. The flounder, like the sole, is popular with ambitious chefs because it is so perfect a background for good sauces. There are in the neighborhood of 200 sauces used with sole or flounder, and it seems that no chef in Europe can qualify for his profession without inventing a new sauce for sole! In fact, I am too narrow in my scope, for the Chinese cooks also do unique things with flounder! But here one must cry a warning, for as with the pompano, the enthusiastic chefs sometimes overlook and overwhelm the fish in their emphasis on the sauce. Flounder is modest, but it has its rights!

FLOUNDER, CAPTAIN KIDD

1 lb Flounder	1 carrot, chopped
1 sprig parsley	1 tablespoon butter
1 onion, chopped	Salt, pepper

Fillet the fish, saving head and bones, and wash and wipe thoroly dry. Then put the head, bones and trimmings in a saucepan, together with the parsley, the onion and carrot; cover with cold water, bring to a boil and let simmer 45 minutes. Then strain and reduce the liquid to 1 cup over a hot fire. Butter a shallow covered baking dish, place in the fillets and pour the broth over it. Dot with the butter, season with salt and pepper. Close cover tight and bake in a medium oven (350° F) for 20 to 25 minutes.

FILLET OF FLOUNDER, CLIPPER SHIP

6 fillets of Flounder
Salt
1 teaspoon curry powder
¼ cup Chablis (white wine)
2 cups white wine sauce
1 shallot, chopped

1 fresh tomato
1 strip red pepper, finely minced
2 fresh mushrooms, chopped and sautéed in 1 tablespoon butter

Wash the fillets and dry thoroly. Arrange them in a buttered baking dish, sprinkle with salt, the curry powder and the wine. Cover with buttered paper and bake in oven until tender. Take out the fish and lay on hot platter. Strain the broth into white wine sauce, and add the shallot, the tomato cut into large cubes, the red pepper and the mushrooms. Mix well, season and pour over the fish.

FLOUNDER AND OYSTERS, FORT POND BEACH

4 fillets of Flounder
Salt, pepper, few grains of cayenne
1 cup oyster liquor
5 tablespoons Chablis (white wine)

1 cup white wine sauce
1 egg yolk, slightly beaten
12 oysters
1 can small mushrooms

Clean and wash the fillets, dry thoroly. Place in a buttered baking dish, season with salt, pepper, cayenne, and pour over it 1 cup of the oyster liquor, and the wine. Cover with the buttered paper and bake in oven until tender. Take out the fish and lay on heated platter. Strain the broth in baking pan into the white wine sauce and boil for 10 minutes. Remove from fire; stir in the egg yolk. Cook the dozen oysters for a few minutes in some of their own liquor, add the mushrooms; blend into wine sauce mixture and pour over the fish.

NESTED FLOUNDER, VALLEY STREAM

2 Flounders (or kingfish or halibut)	Salt, pepper
1 lb cooked spinach	1 cup medium white sauce
Few grains nutmeg	$\frac{1}{2}$ cup American cheese, grated

Fillet the flounder. Butter a baking dish and put in the bottom a layer of the spinach, to which has been added the nutmeg. Then lay in the fillets, season with salt and pepper, and cover with the white sauce to which the cheese has been added. Bake 20 minutes in a hot oven (450° F). Serve very hot.

CEBICHE (MEXICAN FLOUNDER COCKTAIL)

2 lbs fresh flounder	$\frac{1}{4}$ cup lemon juice
4 large red peppers	Salt
2 cloves garlic	1 large onion
$\frac{3}{4}$ cup orange juice	2 long light green peppers

Dice the fish into a deep earthenware dish. Seed the red peppers and boil until tender, then grind with the garlic. Add the strained orange and lemon juice and pour over fish. Add salt to taste. Slice the onion and green peppers and add to fish. Place mixture in refrigerator. Stir every few hours. Serve the following day in individual shells or cocktail glasses. Serve with anchovy sticks.

FISHERMAN'S STEW

2 doz small flounder
1 lb bacon
3 onions, chopped
1 cup butter

1 cup catsup
1 teaspoon worcestershire
   sauce
1 cup water

Clean fish. Saute onions and bacon until browned. Place alternate layers of fish and onion mixture in deep kettle, dotting each layer with butter. Add remaining ingredients and cook over moderate heat until fish are done. Serve with crisp bread rice or potatoes boiled in their jackets.

FLOUNDER À LA CREME

2 lbs fillet of Flounder
Salt and pepper to taste
2 cups milk
1 blade mace
2 peppercorns

3 tablespoons butter
4 tablespoons flour
Lemon juice
1 tablespoon cream

Cut each fillet in half lengthways, sprinkle with little salt and pepper; set aside. Wash skin and bones of fish, put them into a small saucepan with milk, mace and peppercorns, and simmer for half hour. Strain into clean saucepan, add fillets, and allow to simmer for ten minutes. Lift out fillets. Add to milk the butter and flour which have been blended together; cook, stir constantly until it becomes quite smooth. Add salt, pepper and lemon juice to taste, and cream. Reheat fillets in this sauce. Arrange fillets on hot platter and pour the sauce over them. Serve very hot.

BREADED FLOUNDER, SUFFOLK DOWNS

3 or 4 lbs L. I. Flounder
1 egg beaten with 1 tablespoon water
½ cup sifted bread crumbs
2 tablespoons olive oil
5 tablespoons butter
3 peeled tomatoes
1 small can mushrooms,
 sliced

1 teaspoon shallots, minced
1 tablespoon minced par-
 sley
3 tablespoons flour
1¼ cups meat stock
1 tablespoon tomato puree
Pinch of thyme
Salt and pepper

Make fillets of the flounder, cut each fillet in half and dip in beaten egg and bread crumbs and let stand for 5 minutes. Then fry to golden brown in olive oil and 2 tablespoons of the butter. Then cut the tomatoes in half lengthwise; set the fillets in buttered baking pan, spread with the tomatoes, sliced mushrooms, shallots, parsley. Bake in moderate oven until tender. Serve with a sauce made as follows: melt the remaining 3 tablespoons of butter, blend in the flour, add the meat stock, mushroom liquor, tomato puree, pinch of thyme, and salt and pepper. Serve with boiled potatoes.

FILLET OF FLOUNDER, LOUIS XIII

6 green onions
2 tablespoons butter
1 cup fresh mushrooms,
 finely chopped
½ cup Chablis (white wine)
1 Flounder

Salt and pepper
Thyme, bay leaf, celery leaf
½ cup oyster water
¼ cup thick cream
2 tablespoons Parmesan
 cheese, grated

The green onions are chopped very fine and fried in the butter. Add the mushrooms, cook for 5 minutes; add the wine, and cook for 5 minutes more, then strain out the mushrooms. Fillet the flounder and cook in the wine sauce; season with salt, pepper, thyme, bay leaf, celery leaf and add the oyster water. Cook until fish is tender. In an oven-proof serving dish lay the mushrooms, and on top of them the fillets. Then add the cream to the sauce; simmer 3 minutes, and pour over the fish. Sprinkle the cheese on top. Glaze in a quick oven for a few minutes, then garnish the sides of the dish with Duchess potatoes, sprinkled with chopped pistachio nuts.

(This is a dish originated by the famous Antoine's of New Orleans.)

FLOUNDER WITH SAUERKRAUT

2 lbs Flounder fillets
White wine courtbouillon
1½ lbs Sauerkraut

1 cup Mornay Sauce (No. 7)
2 tablespoons grated Parmesan Cheese

Poach the fillets in the white wine Courtbouillon (see foot of page 21). Then braise the sauerkrat in a covered baking dish, for 20 minutes, after which lay the fillets upon the sauerkraut, cover with the Mornay Sauce, sprinkle with the cheese and brown quickly in a hot oven. Serve with boiled potatoes.

FLOUNDER, OLD WESTBURY

3 lbs L. I. Flounder, filleted
1½ cups water
½ cup white wine
1 cup sliced lobster, or crab-meat

Truffles
White sauce
Parmesan cheese, grated

Poach the fillets for 10 minutes in water and white wine. In the bottom of a buttered baking dish arrange the sliced lobster pieces or crabmeat; sprinkle with a few truffles. On top of this lay the poached fillets. Pour white sauce over all and sprinkle top with cheese. Glaze in a hot oven or under a broiler for five minutes.

FILLET OF FLOUNDER, FÉCAMPOISE

4 lbs L. I. Flounder, filleted
2 tablespoons onion, finely chopped
2 tablespoons carrots, finely chopped
½ cup butter
3 tablespoons of flour

1 cup milk
Salt, pepper
1 cup shrimp
4 tablespoons cream
Cayenne pepper
25 mussels, steamed and shelled
Puff pastry

Poach fillets in salted water for 3 minutes. Arrange on a hot serving dish, and cover with a Bechamel sauce made as follows sauté the chopped onion and carrots together in 2 tablespoons of the butter for 10 minutes. Remove from saucepan, and then melt in the same saucepan 2 tablespoons of butter; blend in the flour, add the milk and keep stirring to blend smoothly. Add salt and pepper and then stir in the carrots and onions; simmer all gently for 15 minutes. Pound the shrimp to a paste, add 4 tablespoons of butter and press through a sieve. Strain the Bechamel sauce into a saucepan and add the cream, stirring until well blended. Remove from the stove and stir in gradually the pounded shrimp mixture. Then add a dash of cayenne and pour sauce over the fish. Garnish with the mussels and small pieces of the puff pastry.

CIDER FLOUNDER, SEA ISLAND

6 fillets of Flounder
Salt, pepper
3 tablespoons shallots, chopped

2 or 3 cups cider
3 tablespoons butter
2 tablespoons flour
1 teaspoon chopped parsley

Wash and clean the flounder fillets and dry thoroly; rub with salt and pepper. Butter a baking dish and lay in the fillets, sprinkle with the shallots, and just cover with the cider. Bake in a moderate oven (375° F.) for 20 minutes. Take out the flounder and put on a hot platter. Pour the sauce into a saucepan, add the butter, heat, blend in the flour. Stir until it begins to thicken, and cook 5 minutes. Add the parsley and pour the sauce over the fish.

SHRIMP-FLOUNDER ROLLS, PORT WASHINGTON

6 Flounder fillets	1 lb Shrimps, cooked
Salt, pepper	1 can tomatoes
1 tablespoon mayonnaise	½ cup buttered bread crumbs
1 teaspoon prepared mustard	Butter
2 tablespoons softened butter	3 potatoes, boiled
	1 tablespoon minced parsley

Cut each fillet in half lengthwise, rub with salt and pepper. Blend together the mayonnaise and mustard and softened butter; spread this mixture over the fillets. Place 2 shrimps on each fillet, then roll up the fillets like a jelly roll, with the shrimp inside. Fasten with a toothpick. Arrange these rolls in a buttered baking dish, and place around them the remainder of the shrimp, and pour the tomatoes over all. Sprinkle with bread crumbs, dot with butter, cover with waxed paper and bake slowly in a moderate oven (350° F) for 25 minutes; remove the paper and cook 10 minutes longer or until brown. Cut potatoes into balls, roll them first in melted butter and then in the minced parsley and use to garnish the fish.

BAKED FLOUNDER, CAPTAIN KIDD

1 large Flounder	Olive oil
Salt and pepper	Bouquet garni, salt, pepper
Clove of garlic	1 crushed clove (head removed)
1 medium-sized eggplant	
1½ lbs fresh tomatoes	3 tablespoons butter
2 large Bermuda onions	¼ cup buttered crumbs

Rub the cleaned, washed flounder with salt and pepper and a bit of garlic. Peel and cut the eggplant into thin slices. Cut the tomatoes and onions into thick slices. Fry the eggplant on both sides in the olive oil, then place the slices, drained, in a buttered baking dish or casserole; lay the flounder on top. Add the garni, the clove, and then a layer of tomatoes, then a layer of onions. Dot with butter, sprinkle with crumbs, pouring over the top the rest of the butter, melted. Cover tightly and bake in very hot oven (450° F.) for 25 minutes. Remove lid, and bake 10 minutes more to brown. Serve from the baking dish.

BAKED FLOUNDER, RONKONKOMA

1 large Flounder, filleted	3 tablespoons butter
Pepper, salt	1 tablespoon creamed butter
1 tablespoon chopped parsley	ter
½ cup fresh mushrooms	Juice of 1 lemon
1 can of tomatoes	Rice or mashed potatoes

Cut each of the fillets into 3 pieces. Rub them with pepper and salt. Butter a casserole or baking dish, sprinkle half of the parsley over the bottom, then half of the mushrooms, mixed with half the tomatoes. Then lay in the fillets and add another layer of parsley, mushrooms and tomatoes. Put pieces of butter around the top. Cover the dish and put in a particularly hot oven (450° F.) for 20 minutes. Then lift out the fish separately, and arrange in the middle of a hot, round platter. Then heat the sauce in the baking dish, adding the creamed butter, and the lemon juice. Boil for a minute or two, season to taste and pour over the fish. Arrange rice or mashed potatoes around the platter.

LONG ISLAND FLOUNDER, SHRIMP SAUCE

1 Long Island Flounder	Nutmeg, salt, pepper
½ lb shrimp	1 tablespoon lemon juice
¼ cup butter	Buttered crumbs
1 tablespoon flour	

Remove head of the flounder, also the skin on the dark (upper) side. Shell the shrimp, cook in boiling water 15 minutes; take out the shrimp, and reduce the liquid to 2 cups. Melt 2 tablespoons of the butter, fry the shrimp in it slowly. Add the flour, shrimp liquor, seasonings and lemon juice. Then let come to a boil, while stirring. Rub the flounder fillets with salt and pepper, and arrange them in a baking dish, skin side down. Place on them dots of butter, bake in moderate oven for 10 minutes, basting occasionally. Then pour on the boiling hot shrimp sauce and continue basting. When almost done sprinkle with bread crumbs and brown.

FILLET OF FLOUNDER, MARGUERY

4 fillets of Flounder	6 mushroom buttons
Salt, pepper, few grains of cayenne	1 tablespoon white wine sauce
2 tablespoons Chablis (white wine)	2 egg yolks
24 mussels, steamed and shelled	2 tablespoons butter
	2 tablespoons grated bread crusts

Wash and clean the fillets, dry thoroly. Rub with salt and pepper and cayenne. Lay in a buttered pan, add the wine and cover the pan with buttered paper. Put in a hot oven for six minutes. Then remove the fillets to a warmed and buttered oven-proof platter and place on each fillet six steamed mussels and one mushroom button. Strain the sauce left in baking pan into a saucepan, add the white wine sauce and bring to a boil; remove from fire. Stir in the egg yolks one at a time; beat in the butter. Pour this sauce over the fish. Sprinkle with the grated bread crust and brown a few minutes in a very hot oven (450° F.).

SHRIMP AND FLOUNDER, SHELTER ISLAND

1 lb L. I. Flounder fillets
Salt, pepper
Juice of 3 lemons
24 Shrimp
½ teaspoon pimpernel, minced
1 teaspoon minced parsley
1 head of lettuce

1½ cups fresh mayonnaise
24 olives, stoned
Mixed pickles
6 slices pickled beets
3 eggs, hard-cooked, halved
6 capers
6 anchovy fillets

Arrange fillets in a buttered baking dish, sprinkle with salt, pepper and the juice of 1½ lemons. Bake in a moderate oven, basting occasionally, for 10 minutes; cover dish and bake for 10 minutes longer. Drain the fish and cool. Cook the shrimp separately in salted water for 20 minutes; shell. Combine the shrimp, the fish, and season with the juice of 1½ lemons, the pimpernel and parsley. Chill the mixture. Meantime mince together two shrimps and two lettuce leaves, mix with a bit of mayonnaise. Put a little of this mixture on each of the fish fillet portions which have been cut into pieces for serving and arrange on platter; dress with mayonnaise. Garnish platter with lettuce, olives, mixed pickles, pickled beets, and with the egg halves each of which is topped with a bit of mayonnaise and a caper wrapped in a curled anchovy fillet.

FLOUNDER WITH GRAPES, SYOSSET

6 Flounder fillets
1 glass Chablis (white wine)
¼ cup fish stock
Salt and pepper

4 tablespoons butter
1 tablespoon flour
½ cup white stock (or milk)
2 egg yolks
1 cup peeled white Grapes

Wash and dry fillets thoroly, roll up each one like a jelly roll and fasten with white cotton thread, or small skewers. Lay these in a buttered pyrex baking dish, add the wine, ¼ cup fish stock; sprinkle with salt. Cover with lid or

buttered paper, and cook in moderate oven for 15 minutes.
Prepare a sauce as follows: melt the butter, blend in flour;
stir in slowly the white stock or milk. Season with pepper
and salt, and let simmer 15 minutes. Cook slightly, stir
into egg yolks, adding a little sauce from baking dish.
Remove the skewers from the fish, arrange the grapes in
the baking dish with fish. Pour the sauce over all and
brown quickly in hot oven.

CRISS-CROSS FLOUNDER, LATTINGTOWN

1 large Flounder	$\frac{1}{2}$ lb smoked salmon
1 tablespoon butter	Salt, pepper
12 button mushrooms	Capers
$\frac{1}{2}$ cup milk	

Clean and skin the flounder. Lay in an oven-proof covered serving dish, dot with butter and bake in a moderate
oven for 30 minutes, or until tender. Cook the mushrooms
in milk until tender. Warm the smoked salmon slices in
butter; then cut into long thin strips. Remove the flounder
to a hot platter, pour the melted butter on it, sprinkle with
salt and pepper, lay the mushrooms around the edge of the
platter. Arrange the strips of smoked salmon into a crisscross pattern across the entire flounder; dot with capers.
Heat in the oven gently before serving.

FLOUNDER À LA GREQUE

2 lbs Flounder, filleted	Thyme
Salt, pepper	2 tablespoons parsley
Juice of 1 lemon	1 lb cucumbers
2 tablespoons olive oil	2 tablespoons butter
$\frac{1}{2}$ pint Chablis (white wine)	$\frac{1}{2}$ lb tomatoes
	1 tablespoon pimento
1 tablespoon chopped onion	

Sprinkle fillets with salt and lemon juice, and let stand
for an hour. Heat the olive oil in a baking dish or cas-

serole, lay in the fillets, add the wine, onion, thyme, parsley. Bake for 15 minutes in moderate oven. Cut the cucumber into thick slices and stew in butter; add the tomatoes, halved, and the pimento. Arrange the cooked fillets on a hot platter, lay the cucumbers and tomatoes around it. Add the butter in which the vegetables were cooked to the juices in the baking dish, season, heat, and pour over the fish on the platter.

FLOUNDER AND VEGETABLES, FLOWERFIELD

2 lbs Flounder or any white-fleshed fish
Salt, pepper
Juice of 1 lemon
1 lb potatoes
2 celery roots

8 tablespoons butter
1¼ cups Grade A milk
2 tablespoons flour
1 teaspoon chopped onion
    mixed with sage
Few grains cayenne

Clean, fillet and wash the fish, sprinkle with salt and lemon juice; let stand for one hour. Peel the potatoes, slice the celery root, cook both in boiling salted water. Then drain and press through a sieve. Season with salt and pepper; beat until light with 4 tablespoons of the butter and ¼ cup of the milk added. Heap this upon the middle of a hot platter in an attractive mound. Saute the fish fillets in the remaining 2 tablespoons of butter. Arrange around mashed vegetables on platter. Make a white sauce with remaining 2 tablespoons of butter, flour and remaining milk; season with the onion and sage mixture and cayenne pepper. Pour sauce over the fillets and serve.

FLOUNDER IN CIDER, DEER PARK

2 lbs Flounder, filleted
Salt and pepper
Juice of 1 lemon
3 tablespoons butter
2 onions, finely chopped
2 tablespoons carrots, finely chopped

3 bruised peppercorns
2 cloves
½ cup bread crumbs
1 quart cider
1 teaspoon sugar
Cooked noodles

Rub fillets with salt, sprinkle with lemon juice. Let stand for one hour. Melt the butter, fry in it the onion and the carrot, add the peppercorns, cloves and bread crumbs. Then put in the cider and bring to a boil. Now put in the fillets, let simmer gently for 15 minutes. Take out fillets and keep warm. Strain the liquor through a sieve, reduce over hot fire; season with salt, sugar and remaining lemon juice; pour over the fish. Serve with cooked noodles.

FLOUNDER, MUSTARD SAUCE, SHAGWONG POINT

2 or 3 Flounders
½ cup wine vinegar
1 teaspoon salt
2 tablespoons butter
1 teaspoon parsley, chopped

1 teaspoon lemon juice
2 teaspoons prepared mustard
1 egg yolk
Lemon slices

Clean and wash the fish. Place in a kettle with warm water to which the vinegar and salt have been added. Simmer gently for 15 minutes. Drain and lay on hot plate. Melt the butter, brown slightly, add 2 tablespoons of the liquid in which the fish has been boiled, also the parsley, lemon juice and mustard. Remove from fire and stir in the beaten egg yolk. Return to low heat, stirring constantly for 3 minutes; do not let boil. Serve the sauce with the fish; garnish with lemon slices.

FLOUNDER AND POTATO HASH, SAGAPONACK

4 tablespoons butter, or olive oil
½ lb raw potatoes, diced
1 lb Flounder fillets
Salt, pepper

½ cup flour
¼ cup tomato sauce
1 tablespoon parsley, chopped

Heat the butter or oil in a large frying pan; then fry the potatoes in it until brown. Push them to one side of the pan, and place into the fat the flounder fillets, which have been salted and peppered and rolled into flour and cut into one-inch squares. Reduce heat, fry until tender. Then lift out the fish and potatoes together (hash style, or if preferred, fish in the middle, potatoes around). In the pan mix the tomato sauce, parsley, heat and pour over the fish hash.

FLOUNDER CURRY, NORTH HAVEN

4 Flounder fillets	$\frac{1}{4}$ cup cold milk
$1\frac{1}{2}$ teaspoons good curry	$\frac{1}{4}$ cup fish stock
2 tablespoons butter	Boiled rice
1 tablespoon flour	India chutney

Wash and dry the fillets thoroly. Lay in a buttered dish or casserole. Mix the curry powder with one tablespoon of melted butter, and spread this mixture over each fillet. Cover the casserole with lid or buttered paper and bake in moderate oven for 30 minutes. Mix the flour with the milk and fish stock. When fillets are tender, drain the stock from the baking dish into the milk mixture, and simmer 5 minutes. Pour sauce over fillets. Serve from the dish, with boiled rice and India chutney.

PICKLED FLOUNDER, PARADISE POINT

1 (2-pound) flounder	Deep hot fat
Salt	2 cups vinegar
Pepper	$\frac{1}{2}$ teaspoon salt
1 egg well beaten	1 bay leaf
$1\frac{1}{2}$ cups bread crumbs	Pinch thyme

Clean flounder. Sprinkle with salt and pepper. Brush with egg. Roll in $\frac{1}{2}$ cup breadcrumbs. Fry until golden brown in hot fat (375° F.). Place in shallow pan. Combine vinegar and seasonings and heat. Pour over fish. Top with breadcrumbs. Broil until crumbs are brown. Serve very hot or very cold.

FRIED FLOUNDER, HAWAIIAN STYLE

6 fillets of Flounder (or any white-fleshed fish)
2 eggs, beaten
½ cup cornmeal
2 tablespoons butter
Salt, pepper
½ cup bottled soy sauce

1 teaspoon lemon juice
1 teaspoon worcestershire sauce
1 teaspoon tarragon vinegar
1 tablespoon sugar
1 tablespoon onion juice
1 tablespoon catsup

Wash the fillets and dry thoroly. Dip in the egg and the cornmeal; fry in butter. Make a sauce by blending in and heating all the other ingredients, thickening with some flour if necessary. Serve the fillets with the sauce poured over them. Accompany with French fried potatoes.

FLOUNDER AU GRATIN, CHARPENTIER

1 good-sized Flounder
4 tablespoons butter
1 tablespoon chives, minced fine
1 clove garlic
1 teaspoon chopped parsley
1 tablespoon minced shallots

1 tablespoon chopped mushrooms
¼ cup water
⅜ cup Chablis (white wine)
1 teaspoon lemon juice
1 tablespoon white wine vinegar
½ cup sliced mushrooms
½ cup sifted breadcrumbs

Wash and trim the fish, removing head, tail, etc. Melt 2 tablespoons of butter and fry in it the chives, garlic, parsley, shallots, and then the chopped mushrooms. Let cook until almost dry. Then add ¼ cup of the wine and the same amount of water, the lemon juice and vinegar. Let cook until sauce is reduced one-half. Butter a baking dish or casserole and into it pour half the sauce, lay in the flounder, cover with the sliced mushrooms, then the remaining sauce. Add remaining (2 tablespoons) white wine; sprinkle top with breadcrumbs. Dot with butter. Bake for 20

to 30 minutes in a moderate oven, then brown quickly
under the broiler, if it has not browned in the oven.

TOMATO SURPRISE WITH FLOUNDER, ISLIP

6 Flounder fillets	2 tablespoons onion, minced
1 cup Chablis (white wine)	Salt, pepper, few grains
$\frac{1}{2}$ cup mushroom liquor	cayenne
6 medium-sized tomatoes	Sauce Bercy

Poach the fillets in the white wine and mushroom liquor.
Scoop out the tomatoes, bake them in a moderate oven for
15 minutes. Roll up the fillets, and place one roll in each
tomato. Garnish with the minced onion, season with salt,
pepper and cayenne and cover with Sauce Bercy. Brown
quickly in a hot oven. Sauce Bercy is made of 3 shallots
(or 1 small onion) chopped, $1\frac{1}{2}$ cups of white wine, $\frac{1}{4}$ cup
melted butter, 1 teaspoon minced parsley and the juice of
half a lemon. The shallots are simmered in the wine, the
melted butter added, the mixture well beaten, and the
parsley and lemon stirred in.

FILLET OF FLOUNDER, L'AMIRAL

6 fillets of Flounder	1 tablespoon lobster butter
$\frac{1}{2}$ cup Chablis (white wine)	2 tablespoons minced mush-
$\frac{1}{4}$ cup water	rooms
2 teaspoons onions, chopped	2 cups shrimps and mus-
2 tablespoons butter	sels, minced
$\frac{1}{2}$ cup fish stock	

Poach the fillets in white wine and water for 10 minutes.
Fry onions in the butter, add the fish stock. Place the
fillets in a buttered casserole; bake for ten or fifteen minutes in a moderate oven, adding the white wine in which
fish was poached. When tender, lay on platter and make a
sauce of the juices in the pan, blending in the lobster butter,
the mushrooms and the shrimps and mussels, minced.

FLOUNDER EN BROCHETTE, PERE MONBIOT

1 lb Flounder fillets
Salt, pepper
1 onion, sliced very thin
2 bay leaves
2 tablespoons butter melted

3 tablespoons fine bread crumbs
1 tablespoon parsley, minced
Hollandaise sauce, moutardée

Wash the fillets and dry thoroly. Cut into pieces about the size of a dollar. Rub with salt and pepper. Thread on small skewers, alternating a very thin slice of onion and a little piece of bay leaf with the fish. Dip into the melted butter and then roll in the breadcrumbs into which the parsley has been mixed. Put under a broiler for 8 minutes, turning once or twice. Serve with the Hollandaise moutardee (made by adding ½ teaspoon dry mustard just before removing the Hollandaise Sauce No. 6 from the fire).

FLOUNDER, BLUE POINT

2 or 3 lbs Flounder
Salt, pepper
2 tablespoons butter
1 lime, very thinly sliced
25 Blue Points (or other small oysters)

¼ lb raw shrimps, shelled
¼ cup Chablis (white wine)
½ cup tomato catsup
2 tablespoons bread crumbs

Wash and clean fish and rub with salt and pepper. Lay it in a buttered baking dish, dot with half the butter and cover with the lime slices. Bake in hot oven (450°) for 10 minutes. Cook oysters and the shrimps in the oyster liquor and wine and turn the mixture over fish in pan. Pour in the catsup. Sprinkle with bread crumbs and remaining butter; reduce oven to 375° and bake another 20 minutes. Serve from the baking dish.

FLOUNDER PUDDING, OTTO KAHN

2 lbs Flounder fillet
4 egg whites, slightly
   beaten
1½ pints cream
Salt, pepper, few grains of

cayenne, few grains of
   nutmeg
Lobster or oyster sauce
   (No. 15 or 8)

Run the fish through a food chopper using the finest knife. Mix with salt and pepper, then gradually add the egg whites, mixing thoroly. Force the mixture through a fine sieve. Chill thoroly in refrigerator. Blend in the cream. Fill a buttered casserole or individual ramekins with this mixture and set in a pan of boiling water. Cook slowly in a slow oven (325° F.) for 20 to 30 minutes. Serve with Lobster or Oyster Sauce.

FLOUNDER, NEW ORLEANS

3 lbs Flounder
1 tablespoon melted butter
Salt, pepper
1 tablespoon butter
2 tablespoons flour
6 allspice

1 sprig thyme
1 sprig sweet basil
2 sprigs parsley
1 can mushrooms, chopped,
   with their liquor
Croutons

Clean the fish, rub with melted butter and salt, and then parboil 5 minutes in boiling water. Drain. Lay it in buttered baking dish, and bake in moderate oven for 10 minutes. Melt the butter, and blend in the flour and seasonings; add the mushrooms and their liquor with enough water to make 1 cup. Cook for 5 minutes. Score the fish on the top, then pour the sauce over the fish. Let bake for 15 minutes. Garnish with croutons fried in butter.

VII
Give the Long Island Mussel its Due!

IT IS perennially astounding to me how, even in a depression when people need cheap food, the mussel is neglected in America, although millions of them lie untouched at low tide! In Europe they are actually regarded as a delicacy; in America, as a rule, they go to waste, unnoticed and unsung. They are truly, here, deserving of the name they have in Europe, "the oysters of the poor." In a few North Atlantic places they are esteemed by persons of discrimination. On Long Island, where they are particularly plentiful, they are becoming more and more appreciated.

But not according to their just deserts! I believe it may be a prejudice, but others feel as I do—that *no* shellfish is quite so flavorful as the mussel. My method of testing is the *stew*, which always brings out the maximum flavor of shellfish. The mussel stew is something very enticing; I predict it will develop a strong following, just as clam stew has done in the past dozen years or more.

Pickled mussels are highly esteemed in Europe, and were in America in colonial days. A mussel sauce is my idea of a big help to many fish which are a bit low in flavor. The two types of mussels, one large, one small, are both abundant on Long Island, and if you take a pot, a match, a can of evaporated milk, some pepper, salt, onions, pilot crackers and go to an open Long Island shore, near a mussel bed at low tide, you can, in no time, have a dinner that fairly throbs with salt sea tang. Build a fire with a few little pieces of driftwood, set your pot over it, and make your stew. You will want little else! The diners at the

Plaza or the Pierre in New York would sniff hungrily with you, if they were near. (See Mussel Chowder, page 35).

New Yorkers can buy mussels at various places around town because some of the foreign groups know them well. The Italians in particular relish the mussel, for Italy, like Long Island, is surrounded by many miles of tidal flats in which mussels abound. The Italians make a mussel soup (served with some shells in the soup on the soup plate) which is a noted specialty in some New York Italian restaurants. Mussels are therefore sold at most New York and Long Island fish shops.

Mussels: preparation.—Freshness is absolutely essential. They must be "alive". They require both scraping with a knife to eliminate encrustations, and scrubbing. Inspect each one carefully—reject all that are open—they are dead. Put into a closed fish kettle over a hot fire, then steam open, like clams, and make a broth. Shell them and "beard" the meats, removing with a fork the black beard on the neck. In the kettle in which they are steamed is usually put $\frac{1}{2}$ cup water, also some flavorings, such as for example 1 chopped onion, small bunch parsley, thyme, bay leaf, crushed peppercorns, perhaps a glass of white wine.

MUSSELS MARINATE, KEW GARDENS

60 Mussels	$\frac{3}{4}$ cup Chablis (white wine)
1 cup water	$1\frac{1}{2}$ cups mussel liquor
1 yellow onion	$1\frac{1}{2}$ tablespoons flour
1 sprig thyme	3 tablespoons butter
$\frac{1}{2}$ bay leaf	1 teaspoon lemon juice
10 peppercorns	1 tablespoon lemon butter
1 tablespoon minced onion	3 teaspoons minced parsley

Clean the mussels and place in a kettle with the water, the yellow onion, the thyme, bay leaf and peppercorns.

Cover tightly, cook for 2 minutes on hot fire; watch carefully; do not boil into a froth. Stir and cook 2 more minutes; repeat. While lifting out the mussels, see that all possible juice drops into the kettle with the other broth. Keep mussels warm.

Cook the minced onions in the wine until reduced to one-half, then add the mussel liquor. Make a paste of the flour and the 3 tablespoons butter, add to the liquid, stirring until smooth. Remove from fire, add the lemon juice, butter and parsley, adjust the seasoning. Add the mussels (still in their shells). Cook for 2 minutes. Then serve in a large covered soup tureen, the mussels in their shells in the soup. Serve with pilot crackers; and use oyster forks for picking out mussel seats.

(This is Frances favorite way of appreciating mussels. There are a number of variations of the recipe.)

MUSSEL SAUCE, CRAB MEADOW

40 Mussels	Salt, pepper, cayenne
2 tablespoons flour	Nutmeg
3 tablespoons butter	1 teaspoon lemon juice
1 cup scalded milk	1 teaspoon parsley, minced

Steam the well-scrubbed mussels open, in a pot with 1 cup water. Shell and beard the mussels, and then mince them. Reduce the mussel liquor to 1 cup, over a hot fire. Blend 2 tablespoons flour with 2 tablespoons of the butter. Add to this slowly the milk and the mussel broth. Season with salt, pepper, a few grains of cayenne, nutmeg and the lemon juice. Add the mussels. Bring to a boil for just a moment, sprinkle with parsley and then blend in remaining tablespoon of butter.

MUSSEL SOUP, FRESH POND

50 Mussels
1 quart water
1 onion
2 bay leaves
3 tablespoons olive oil

1 leek
$\frac{1}{2}$ lb rice
$\frac{1}{4}$ teaspoon saffron
1 tomato, chopped

Put the well-scrubbed mussels in a pot with 1 quart water, 1 chopped onion, 2 bay leaves. Cook until the shells open, and save the broth. Then shell the mussels into a soup plate. In a saucepan put the olive oil, heat and then add the white part of the leek, finely chopped, and cook until golden brown. Then add the mussel broth, the rice, the saffron, and simmer until the rice is tender. Add the mussels now, and the tomato, and let boil one minute more.

MUSSELS AND RICE, LLOYD'S NECK

48 Mussels
1 cup water
3 egg yolks
Salt, pepper, paprika

1 tablespoon butter
Boiled rice
1 teaspoon minced parsley

Steam the well-scrubbed mussels in water; drain out and shell. Strain off the liquor through a fine cloth. Place one cup of this liquor in a sauce pan and let come to a boil. Take off the fire and stir carefully into it the egg yolks, seasonings and the butter. Place the mussels in this sauce and let stand. Dress a hot platter with a ring of boiled rice, place the mussel mixture inside and sprinkle with parsley.

MUSSELS POULETTE

48 Mussels
1 cup butter
1 tablespoon parsley, minced
1 tablespoon chives, minced

1 tablespoon flour
1 cup Chablis (white wine)
Sauce Poulette
Bread triangles fried in butter

Steam open the scrubbed mussels and shell them into a saucepan. Add to them the butter, parsley and chives, and cook over low flame, while stirring. As soon as the butter melts, sprinkle in the flour, also the wine and one cup of the strained mussel liquor. Continue to simmer very slowly for 20 minutes. Let the mussels stand for a few minutes in the Sauce Poulette, and then place on a hot platter garnished with triangles of bread fried in butter.

Prepare Sauce Poulette by reducing the remainder of the mussel broth to 1 cup over a hot fire, and then add, one at a time, four egg yolks and keep stirring. Cook gently over very low flame, and add the juice of a lemon. Beat in gradually 2 tablespoons of butter and one tablespoon minced parsley.

MUSSELS AND CRABMEAT, GLEN COVE

48 Mussels   1 teaspoon dry mustard
2 cups crabmeat, cooked   1 cup mayonnaise
1 can mushroom buttons

Steam open the mussels, reserve the broth and shell them into a saucepan; mix with the crabmeat and the mushrooms. Blend the mustard with the mayonnaise, and thin with some of the mussel broth which has been boiled down and strained; stir into fish mixture and cook until all is well heated. Serve with fresh cucumber pickles and French fried potatoes.

BROILED MUSSELS, RIVERHEAD

60 Mussels $\frac{1}{4}$ teaspoon lemon juice
4 tablespoons butter   Paprika, salt, pepper
1 tablespoon finely
  chopped onion

Steam open the carefully scrubbed mussels. Lift out of kettle and shell. Save the shells. Strain the broth through a fine cloth, and reduce to about 1 cup over a hot fire. Then stir in slowly 3 tablespoons of butter. Lightly brown the onion in remaining tablespoon of butter; add with lemon juice to broth. Season mixture with salt and pepper, then dip each mussel in it and place in selected half shells which have been washed again carefully. Glaze these under the broiler for a few minutes, sprinkle with paprika. Serve with French fried potatoes.

FRIED MUSSELS, ROCKY POINT

100 Mussels	2 cups flour
$\frac{1}{2}$ cup milk	1 teaspoon salt
3 eggs, beaten	$\frac{1}{4}$ teaspoon cayenne
$1\frac{1}{4}$ cups mussel liquor	pepper

Wash and scrub mussels well and steam open. Shell and beard them and dry thoroly. Reserve mussel broth. Spear five or six mussels on a toothpick, and then dip into a batter made by combining the milk and eggs with mussel liquor, then beating in the flour sifted with salt and cayenne. Add more milk if needed to bring batter to right consistency. Fry in a frying pan half full of boiling fat, until brown. Tell the diners to remove the toothpick with their forks.

LOBSTER-MUSSEL STEW, SETAUKET

2 Lobsters	1 clove garlic, minced
2 onions	40 Mussels, cleaned and
1 bay leaf	shelled
1 stalk celery	1 quart milk
1 teaspoon salt	$1\frac{1}{2}$ teaspoons curry powder
$\frac{1}{2}$ teaspoon pepper	1 egg, slightly beaten
3 tablespoons butter	2 tablespoons cream
$\frac{1}{2}$ tablespoon flour	Boiled rice

Plunge lobsters in boiling salted water to cover. Add to the water one of the onions, the bay leaf, the celery and the salt and pepper. Cook until tender (20-25 minutes). Reserve cooking water. When lobster is cool, cut meat into 1-inch pieces, and include the coral. Melt the butter, brown the flour in it slightly; add remaining onion finely minced and the garlic. Put the lobster meat and the cleaned shelled mussels in this and add a pint of the water in which lobster was cooked; add the milk. Put also two lobster claw shells and four mussel shells in the pot. Let simmer for 20 minutes. Mix the curry powder with some of the sauce and blend smoothly into mixture in pot; simmer 10 minutes more. Remove from fire and add the egg and the cream, and stir several times. Serve at once, very hot, accompanied by a separate dish of rice.

FRIED MUSSELS, SUNKEN MEADOW

48 medium-sized Mussels	Watercress
2 eggs, slightly beaten	1 lemon, sliced
$\frac{1}{2}$ cup bread crumbs	

Steam the well-washed mussels, shell them and beard them. Reserve some of their liquor and chill. Dry the mussels thoroly, then dip in the eggs, which have been beaten with two tablespoons of the (cold) mussel broth. Roll in the bread crumbs and fry in deep fat at 375° F. until brown. Serve hot, with watercress and lemon slices.

MUSSEL FLOATS, MIDDLEVILLE

48 medium-sized Mussels	$\frac{1}{4}$ cup Chablis (white wine)
4 tablespoons cooked celery	
1 tablespoon chives, chopped	Pepper, nutmeg
2 tablespoons shallots, chopped	$\frac{1}{4}$ cup bread crumbs
2 tablespoons mushrooms, chopped	2 tablespoons butter, melted
	6 buttered toast slices

Steam the well-washed mussels open; shell and beard them. Reduce liquor to ½ cup by boiling over hot fire. Place the mussels in a buttered baking dish, sprinkle over them the celery, chives, shallots, mushrooms, and the wine, and the mussel liquor; sprinkle with pepper and nutmeg, and distribute over this the bread crumbs and the melted butter. Brown in a moderate oven. Serve hot, on hot buttered toast.

MUSSEL SOUP, SMITHTOWN BAY

48 medium-sized Mussels	1 bay leaf
1 onion, chopped	Pinch saffron
1 leek, white portion only	3 cloves
3 tablespoons butter	Pinch pepper
Boiling water	¼ cup rice
1 small bunch parsley	

Steam the well-washed mussels, shell and beard them. Reserve the liquor. Fry the chopped onion and leek in 1 tablespoon butter in a heavy saucepan; add the mussel liquor to which enough boiling water has been added to make 1 quart liquid. Bring to a boil, add the parsley, bay leaf, saffron, cloves and pepper. Put in the rice, let simmer until rice is tender. Remove the parsley and bay leaf; add the mussels, let simmer for 5 to 6 minutes. Just before serving add remaining 2 tablespoons of butter. Serve hot, with salt crackers.

SCRAMBLED EGGS WITH MUSSELS, NESCONSET

30 Mussels, steamed	1 tablespoon cream
Salt and pepper	½ cup soft bread crumbs
6 eggs	1 tablespoon butter

Remove mussels from their shells, cut off the beards, drain well and chop fine; season with salt and pepper. Beat the eggs lightly, add cream and bread crumbs. Melt butter in pan, put in egg mixture and when it begins to cook, stir in mussels and scramble well.

SPICED PICKLED MUSSELS, MACIVER

1 peck Mussels	1 teaspoon mace
1 tablespoon ground ginger	1 tablespoon black pepper

Wash the mussels, steam open; beard and shell them and let cool. Pour the broth into another bowl and let the sediment gather on the bottom; then strain out clear. Put the ginger, mace and pepper into the broth, bring to a boil, then put in the mussel meats and let simmer for 10 minutes. Then drain off the broth, let the mussels grow quite cold. Then place them in a mason jar, seal them and keep for use.

(This recipe follows closely a very old Scotch recipe in a cook book by Mrs. Maciver in Edinburgh, in 1783, a copy of the original of which is in the author's special collection of cook books.)

OYSTERS AND MUSSELS IN JELLY

12 Mussels	1 tablespoon parsley,
12 Oysters	minced
1 tablespoon gelatine	Few grains cayenne
2 tablespoons cold water	Pepper, salt
1 cup boiling water	

Steam open the mussels, preserving their liquor. Open the oysters and heat in their liquor until the edges curl. Soften the gelatine in cold water; dissolve in hot water; add ¾ cup mixed oyster and mussel liquor, parsley, cayenne, pepper and salt. Rinse six egg-cups in cold water, lay in each cup one or two oysters and two mussels, then pour in the gelatine. Chill. When gelatine is firm, set, turn out onto a platter on which has been laid some chopped lettuce or watercress. Garnish with boiled egg slices and mayonnaise or salad dressing.

PICKLED MUSSELS

3 or 4 quarts mussels
Sliced onion
Garlic buds
Mixed pickling spices

Salt
Freshly ground black pepper
Cider vinegar (or white
 wine vinegar)

Wash and scrub mussels carefully. Steam them open in large kettle with 1 cup water. Lift out mussels and shell, removing the beard. Reserve the mussel broth. In a crock or glass jar arrange layers of shelled mussels, onion slices, garlic, spices, salt and pepper. Add strained mussel broth to one third the depth of mussels, then pour on vinegar to cover. Let stand open, at least three days before using, stirring once or twice. Serve as a relish or appetizer.

FRIED MUSSELS À LA COLBERT

2 lbs Mussels
$\frac{1}{2}$ cup seasoned flour
$\frac{1}{4}$ cup Grade A milk
$\frac{1}{2}$ cup sifted bread crumbs
Sauce:
1 cup brown sauce

1 bouillon cube
$\frac{1}{4}$ cup butter
2 tablespoons lemon juice
1 tablespoon parsley,
 chopped

Scrub the mussels, steam open and shell; save the liquor. Dry the mussels thoroly, roll in flour, then dip in milk combined with $\frac{1}{4}$ cup mussel broth, then roll in the bread crumbs. Fry in hot fat until brown. Make the sauce by combining the given ingredients; add 2 tablespoons of mussel liquor and simmer for 5 minutes. Serve hot on the mussels.

MUSSELS, GUSTAV

4 lbs Mussels
1 stalk celery, chopped
4 or 5 shallots, chopped
$\frac{1}{4}$ teaspoon white pepper

1 pint Chablis (white
 wine)
1 cup Hollandaise sauce
 (No. 16)
Swedish bread

Scrub the mussels well, place in a large saucepan together with the celery, shallots, pepper and white wine. Bring to a boil over a slow fire, let simmer for 5 minutes. Then strain ⅔ cup broth slowly into Hollandaise Sauce. Serve the mussels on the half shell on soup plates, pouring the hot sauce over them. Accompany with the hard flat Swedish bread-biscuits. The mussels are to be eaten with fingers.

MUSSELS À LA MARINIÈRE, HERALD TRIBUNE

42 Mussels
½ small onion
2 branches parsley
1 stalk celery
1 branch thyme

1½ tablespoons tarragon vinegar
1 tablespoon butter
Salt, few drops of tabasco sauce

Scrub the mussels in several waters and cut away the heavy beard. Throw away any that are open. Put the mussels in a saucepan, together with the onion, parsley, celery and thyme. Cook covered 20 minutes. Fill soup plates with the mussels from each of which has been detached the empty half shell. Add the vinegar, butter, salt and tabasco to the broth and cook one minute. Then strain and serve in small bowls or ramekins by each diner's plate. The shelled mussels are to be dipped in the juice and eaten.

MUSSELS À LA BORDELAISE

48 Mussels
½ tablespoon flour
½ tablespoon butter
1 cup mussel liquor
2 shallots, finely minced
1 tablespoon bread soaked in 2 tablespoons milk

1 tablespoon chopped parsley
2 tablespoons Italian tomato puree
Salt, pepper
Buttered toast

Steam open the well-washed mussels; shell and beard, reserving liquor. Blend the flour and the butter together in a saucepan, adding gradually 1 cup of the mussel liquor, the shallots, bread, parsley, tomato puree, salt and pepper. Mix well and let simmer for 10 minutes, thinning it if necessary with more mussel liquor; add the mussels and stir for 10 minutes. Serve on hot buttered toast.

MUSSELS (OR CLAMS) WITH RISOTTO

48 Mussels (or soft shell clams)
2 tablespoons butter
2 tablespoons beef marrow
2 onions, chopped
1 cup rice
$\frac{1}{2}$ cup Chablis (white wine)

Pinch of saffron
Salt, pepper
$\frac{1}{2}$ cup grated Parmesan cheese
4 tablespoons melted butter

Steam open the well-washed mussels, shell and beard; reserve liquor. Melt the butter and the beef marrow in a deep frying pan, and add the onions and brown. Put in the rice, add 1 cup liquor drained from mussels, stir well, cook for 15 minutes. Then add remaining liquor drained from mussels, adding water if necessary to make 2 cups, the wine, saffron, salt, pepper. Mix well, and let simmer for 20 minutes, stirring occasionally. Then add the mussels, and let simmer 10 minutes more. When ready to serve, sprinkle with the cheese and the butter.

OYSTER-MUSSEL CURRY WITH RICE

1 onion, grated
$\frac{1}{4}$ cup butter
1 apple, chopped
2 tablespoons curry powder
2 tablespoons flour
$\frac{1}{2}$ cup thin cream

Salt and pepper
1 pint Oysters
$\frac{1}{2}$ pint shelled Mussels
Boiled Rice, watercress, strips of sweet red pepper

Fry the onion in the butter, also the chopped apple and curry powder, until the onion is brown. Then blend in the flour and the liquor drained from oysters and mussels, stir until thick; and then add the cream, and salt to taste, keep stirring while it comes to a boil. Then add the oysters and mussels, cook for 4 or 5 minutes, and then pour the mixture inside a rice ring on a platter. Garnish with the watercress, and strips of pepper.

STUFFED MUSSELS, CONSTANTINOPLE

36 good-sized Mussels
½ cup seedless currants, chopped
½ onion, finely chopped
1 tablespoon parsley, minced

1 tablespoon finely chopped pignolia nuts
2 tablespoons olive oil
1 teaspoon dill, finely chopped
Boiled rice

Steam open the well-washed mussels, shell, reserving the liquor and the shells. Mince the mussels, and mix with the currants, onion, parsley, nuts, olive oil, a little dill, and moisten with some of the mussel liquor to make a paste. Wash the mussel shells again and fill them on the half shell with the paste. Broil under a hot flame for a few minutes. Serve with rice.

VIII

The Misunderstood Long Island Eel

ALL eel, everywhere, I suspect, is misunderstood, and far short of the appreciation it deserves. But it is especially true in our own country. It would appear that for many people the idea of eating eel is at present at the stage in America where tomatoes were about 1850, when, believe it or not, most people thought they were repulsive, inedible, possibly poisonous! Or where tuna fish was a few decades ago (when nobody thought it edible!)

Inquiries I have made indicate that the "snakiness" of the eel is the factor that makes it unappealing to many people, especially women. (Since the Garden of Eden episode women have apparently had a horror of anything snake-like!) The "slitheryness", slipperiness, smoothness, of the eel stops some people's appetite—but of course it's only an idea. Eel is as delicately delicious as the best turtle or chicken meat. Again it is also apparent that the skinning and cleaning of eel run counter to feminine emotions. She will dodge the task nine times out of ten. But so will many men! From the way the Chinese talk about eels I assume that only the Chinese really have an unrepressed fondness for them. The Chinese say that eating eels imparts wisdom. Chao Tsao, a Chinese sage of 200 years before Christ— called the Wisdom-Bag of the East—adored eels.

There are vast quantities of excellent eel in Long Island waters, and they are succulent and delightful to anyone who rids himself or herself of the purely subjective, imaginary notions about eel. Such people grow in number by the thousand each year, and many Long Island roadside stands now sell *smoked* eel. (Somehow *smoked* eel does not set

163

so many people's feelings at edge as live eel, and it is easier to handle, keeps better.)

Since eels should be alive as near to cooking as possible, and since the eel is the world's most slippery customer, many a schoolboy wonders how he is caught. Usually in traps; but the spearing of eel is quite a sport in the bays and by-waters of Long Island. On a dark night you will see boats on the shallow waters, each with a powerful calcium, gasoline or electric light directed downward into the water. Standing by, like a grim oarsman on the Styx, is the spearer, arm and weapon poised. The floodlight glaring over an eel lying on the bottom of the bay blinds the eel, and he "sits tight", unmindful of his danger. Then down come the tines of the Neptune-like fork of the spearer, and the slippery customer is caught. The eel, because of the extreme muscular flexibility, carries meat which is as tender as anyone could hope for. Its fibre is composed of many delicate interwoven strands, not one big clumsy muscle. The skin is extraordinarily thick, but is rather easily peeled off.

Once you taste eel on its merits you become its permanent friend, especially if it is intelligently prepa ed. Even those who know and like eel are too often unaware of the many ways in which eel may be served. Sometimes, in fact, they handicap themselves by the very way they habitually cook it—usually by frying it in too much grease. Eel is a fatty fish and you should avoid too much greasiness.

I have assembled here not only all the various ways in which good Long Island cooks serve eel, but also some eel recipes I have gathered from various parts of the world. Many foreign peoples eat eel, and have made delightful dishes with it. Long Island eel, I am sure, is destined to achieve a wider place in the American diet. The eel himself is such an astounding internationalist, traveling thousands of miles in the ocean and back, that it is fitting that his cooking should be internationally studied!

Eels: preparation.—To skin an eel, tie a string around the head, hang up on a nail and cut off the skin, at the head, then peel skin off with a downward pull, toward the tail. Various methods of preparation are used; one of the best is to rub with salt and sprinkle with hot vinegar and let stand for 10 minutes in the open air. To bone the eel cut with a sharp knife along the bone, from head to tail. Then take hold with a clean towel and pull the flesh off the bone.

EEL, WORLD'S FAIR

2 Eels	$\frac{1}{2}$ teaspoon salt
$\frac{1}{2}$ cup onions, sliced	3 tablespoons butter
Herb bouquet	3 tablespoons flour
$\frac{1}{2}$ clove garlic	$\frac{1}{4}$ lb mushrooms, stewed
1 cup fish stock or clam broth	Triangles of bread fried in butter
2 cups red wine	12 pickled onions

Skin and wash the eels, let stand in salted water for 10 minutes. Cut into $2\frac{1}{2}$-inch pieces and put in saucepan with half the sliced onions, herbs, garlic, the fish stock and red wine, salt. Bring to a boil and keep simmering just below the boiling point for 12 minutes. Take out the eel, strain the sauce through a sieve into another pot, and let boil until well reduced. Melt the butter and cook in it the rest of the onions, blend in the flour and the cooked mushrooms. Add the reduced broth gradually. Let cook for 4 minutes. Place eel in center of a round, hot platter, pour the sauce over it; garnish with triangles of fried bread and the pickled onions.

EEL À LA DANUBE

2 Eels	2 hard-cooked egg yolks
Salt, pepper	1 tablespoon vinegar
$\frac{3}{4}$ cup Chablis (white wine)	1 teaspoon English mustard
2 tablespoons parsley, minced	1 teaspoon sugar
1 tablespoon butter	1 cup fish stock, or clam broth

Clean, skin and wash the eels, dry thoroly, cut into 2-inch pieces. Lay in casserole or baking dish, sprinkle with salt and let stand 3 or 4 hours. Then put the eel in a saucepan, pieces close together, pour in the wine, sprinkle with 1 tablespoon parsley, cover and let simmer until eel is tender.

Make a sauce by melting the butter, stirring in the chopped yolks of the eggs, and then the vinegar, mustard, sugar and fish stock or broth, and remaining parsley, seasoning. Serve separately in a sauceboat, to accompany eel.

EEL AND MACARONI, À LA ITALIENNE

1 large Eel	1 sprig celery
¼ cup olive oil	2 whole cloves
1½ tablespoons wine vinegar	1 blade mace
1 small onion, chopped	1 cup Marsala wine
1 small carrot, chopped	Boiling water
1 garlic clove, chopped	¾ lb any macaroni, or
1 sprig parsley	spaghetti

Clean, skin and wash the eel, cut in 3-inch lengths; rub with salt, cover with water and let stand 30 minutes. Rinse and dry thoroly. Place the pieces in a deep dish. Mix the oil, vinegar, vegetables, spices and herbs, and pour over the eel, and let marinate for one hour. Then transfer eel and liquor to saucepan, add the wine, boiling water enough to cover; simmer until tender. Meantime cook the macaroni for just 10 minutes in salted boiling water, drain and arrange on platter. Drain the eel, split and remove bones, lay the fillets on top of the macaroni. Strain the sauce through a coarse sieve and pour over the macaroni.

EEL IN WINE, FISHERMAN'S HOLIDAY

3 Eels	1 bouquet garni
2 tablespoons salt	2 thyme leaves
1 quart cold water	2 cups white wine
2 small carrots, sliced	12 bruised peppercorns
2 small onions, sliced	

Skin the eel, wash it in several waters, rub with 1 table-spoon salt and let stand for an hour; wash again. Cut into $2\frac{1}{2}$-inch pieces and drop in a wine courtbouillon, made as follows: combine 1 quart of cold water with the remaining tablespoon salt, carrots, onions, the garni, thyme and the wine. Simmer 20 minutes before adding eel; add eel and simmer 20 minutes longer. The peppercorns are added just before the eel is done. Lift out eel and arrange on platter; garnish with parsley. (By substituting $\frac{1}{3}$ cup vinegar for the wine and adding 1 quart more of water, a vinegar courtbouillon is made, which is also suitable.)

BAKED EEL, BRENTWOOD

1 large Eel	Salt, pepper
$\frac{1}{2}$ lemon	Sharp sauce

Skin and wash the eel, rub a tablespoon of salt on it and let stand several hours. Drip the juice of the lemon on it. If eel is very long cut in two; then place in a greased baking pan, season with salt and pepper, add a little hot water to the pan and bake in hot oven (450° F.) for 20-25 minutes. Then arrange eel on platter and serve with a Sharp Sauce, made as follows: press the cooked yolk of an egg through a sieve and mix with a raw yolk; gradually whip in 1 cup of olive or peanut or other oil, then add 1 teaspoon of French mustard, $1\frac{1}{2}$ tablespoon wine vinegar, $\frac{1}{4}$ teaspoon worcestershire sauce, $\frac{1}{4}$ teaspoon white pepper, $\frac{1}{2}$ teaspoon salt, $\frac{1}{2}$ teaspoon sugar. Just before serving add the $\frac{1}{2}$ cup thick cream, whipped, and 1 tablespoon chopped dill. Serve in separate sauceboat.

EEL, COMMACK

3 small Eels	2 cups Chablis (white
3 tablespoons butter	wine)
Salt and pepper	4 egg yolks, beaten
3 tablespoons chopped herbs	Juice of 2 lemons
—mint, sage, garlic, pars-	$\frac{1}{2}$ cup cold water
ley, sorrel, savory	

Wash and skin the eels, let stand in salted water for 10 minutes. Then cut into 3-inch lengths and put in a saucepan with 2 tablespoons of the butter, salt, pepper and the chopped herbs. Cook over low heat for 15 minutes, then add the wine and enough water to cover eels. Cook just below the boiling point for 12 minutes. Remove from fire. Stir a portion of the liquid gradually into the egg yolks, add lemon juice, water, and remaining butter. Return to remaining liquid in saucepan, stirring constantly. Put the eel and sauce in a baking dish or casserole and let stand till cold.

EEL SOUP, SUNKEN MEADOW

1 small Eel	3 tablespoons butter
2 tablespoons capers	3 tablespoons flour
5 sprigs parsley	

Skin and cut up eel. Simmer in 3 pints of salted water until tender. Drain. Add capers and parsley to the water in which eel is cooked; bring to a boil. Melt butter, blend in flour, add carefully to liquid, stirring constantly; let simmer for 10 minutes. Return the eel to the soup. Serve with croutons.

SHRIMP-EEL PIE, MASSAPEQUA

1 large Eel or two smaller ones	1 level tablespoon creamed butter
1 lb Shrimp, cooked and diced	1 cup clear fish stock or clam broth
$\frac{1}{4}$ cup butter, melted	1 tablespoon lemon juice
Creole sauce (No. 34), or as directed below	

Skin and wash eel; parboil in salted water for 10 minutes. Then cut in $1\frac{1}{2}$-inch pieces. Butter a deep baking dish, and place in the bottom the diced shrimp which have been dipped in melted butter. Add a layer of eel. Pour over this some celery sauce or Creole Sauce, then repeat with another layer of shrimp and eel. Dot with pieces of creamed butter, and then pour the fish stock and the lemon juice over all. Cover with pie crust, vented, and bake in a moderate oven (350° F.) for 35 minutes.

One type of Creole Sauce is made as follows: In 4 tablespoons butter, cook gently for 5 minutes 8 tablespoons of sliced green pepper and 4 tablespoons of sliced onions. Add ½ cup of sliced mushrooms and 15 quartered, stoned green olives and cook for 5 or 6 more minutes. Blend in 2 tablespoons flour. Add 1 cup of strained fish stock and 1 large can of tomatoes. Season with freshly ground black pepper and salt, a few grains of cayenne pepper, a pinch of thyme, a half bay leaf, a crushed clove. Simmer for 20 minutes. A Celery Sauce is also acceptable; quickly made with a can of ready-to-serve celery soup with a cup of cooked celery added.

BROWNED EEL, PINE-AIRE

1 large Eel or two smaller ones	Salt, pepper
1 cup flour	Tartare sauce (No. 1)

Skin and wash the eel, soak in vinegar and water for 10 minutes. Then cut in 3-inch pieces, and carefully bone them, taking care not to tear the eel meat. Roll each piece in the flour which has been mixed with pepper and salt. Have ready deep fat boiling (375° F.). Place the eel pieces in the frying basket and dip them in the deep fat for just one or two minutes. Drain on absorbent paper. Keep hot. Serve with Tartare Sauce.

EEL SOUP, OCEANSIDE

1 Eel	Bouquet garni
4 tablespoons butter	½ bay leaf
2 onions	Salt, pepper
4 tablespoons tomato juice	4 potatoes, diced
1 clove garlic	

Skin and wash the eel and let stand over night in vinegar water. Wash and dry and cook gently for 10 minutes in 2 tablespoons butter. Slice the onions and fry brown in remaining butter in a deep heavy saucepan. Add nearly 2 quarts of water, the eel, tomato juice and seasonings. Bring to a boil and simmer for an hour. Add the potatoes 30 minutes before the hour is up.

FRIED EEL, NORTH SHORE

2 Eels	1 cup whole wheat or plain
Juice of 2 lemons	flour
	Salt, pepper

Skin and wash the eel and let stand for 10 minutes in water to which the lemon juice has been added. Then cut into 2½-inch pieces, and roll in the flour which has been seasoned with pepper and salt. Fry very hot in oil or other cooking fat in frying pan, allowing 3-4 minutes for each side, depending on size of eel.

BAKED EEL, KINGS PARK

1 large Eel	Pinch of basil
6 strips bacon or salt pork	4 bruised peppercorns
1 onion, chopped	Salt and pepper
3 tablespoons butter	2 cups fish stock
1 carrot	1 tablespoon lemon juice
Bouquet garni	Spinach, hard boiled eggs

Skin and wash the eel in 2 waters, rub with salt and pepper. Then lard the thickest part of the eel with the strips of pork, and place the eel in a circle in a buttered baking dish. Then fry the onion in the butter, add 5 or 6 thin slices of the carrot, the bouquet garni, small pinch of basil and the peppercorns, also salt and pepper. Cook slowly, for about 15 minutes. Add the fish stock and lemon juice and cook for 20 minutes to reduce the liquid to half. Strain, rectify seasoning and pour over the fish, cover tightly and bake in a hot oven (400° F.) for 30 minutes. Place on a platter and garnish with hot spinach, topped by slices of hard-boiled eggs.

EEL PIE, OZONE PARK

1 large Eel	1 teaspoon chopped parsley
Pie crust	½ cup Chablis (white
Salt and pepper	wine)
Grated nutmeg	½ cup cream sauce
6 eggs, hard-cooked	Creamed butter

Skin the eel and let stand in salted water for 10 minutes. Then cut into 1½-inch pieces. Line a deep pie dish with a pie crust. Lay in it half of the eel. Sprinkle salt, pepper and a bit of grated nutmeg on the eel, then add a layer of sliced hard-cooked eggs; sprinkle with the parsley. Repeat with another layer of eel and eggs. Dot with pieces of creamed butter; add the wine (or ½ cup water with 1 table-spoon of lemon juice). Place a thin pie crust over the top, make a few vents, and bake in a moderate oven (350° F.) for one hour. Before serving open the crust and add ½ cup cream sauce.

BROILED EEL, SPEONK

1 large Eel	½ cup finely rolled bread
Marinade	crumbs
3 tablespoons butter	Mustard sauce (No. 7), or
Melted butter	as directed below
Salt and pepper	Lemon and sweet pickles

After skinning and washing the eel in 2 waters, dry thoroly. Cut it into 2½-inch pieces and place for an hour in a bowl with a marinade composed of these ingredients: wine vinegar, red wine, thyme, parsley, bay leaf, bruised shallot, slice of carrot, slice of onion, bit of garlic, piece of parsnip, salt and peppercorn. Lift out the pieces after an hour and fry in the butter on a slow fire, for 10 minutes, frequently turning. Then roll in melted butter mixed with salt and pepper, then in the bread crumbs; broil under mild flame, basting with melted butter. Serve with freshly made Mustard Sauce prepared as follows: melt 3 tablespoons butter and blend in 3 tablespoons flour, ½ teaspoon salt, ¼ teaspoon pepper; add gradually 1½ cups of hot water and boil for 5 minutes; beat in 3 tablespoons more of butter bit by bit; add 1 teaspoon of lemon juice and one tablespoon of prepared mustard. Serve sauce in separate sauceboat. Accompany dish with sweet pickles and lemon slices.

EEL, SMITHTOWN

1 good-sized Eel	¼ teaspoon each of cloves,
2 cups boiling water	cinnamon, saffron, pepper
3 tablespoons vinegar	¼ teaspoon salt
2 cloves garlic	1 cup roasted almonds
1 teaspoon minced parsley	Juice of ½ lemon
2 tablespoons olive oil	1 egg yolk, slightly beaten

Skin and clean the eel; let stand for 10 minutes in boiling water to which the vinegar has been added. Then cut into two-inch lengths and dry. Fry the garlic and parsley in oil, adding ¼ cup of the broth in which the eel has stood. Mix together the spices and salt and stir in. Bring to the boil. Put the pieces of eel in a baking pan, cover with the spiced liquid, and bake in moderate oven until tender. Remove the eel to a hot platter. Stir in egg yolk to the liquid in the pan. Add the roasted almonds, cut into shavings, and the lemon juice. Serve separately as a sauce.

GRILLED SMOKED EEL, JERICHO

1 smoked Eel	Mustard sauce (No. 17), or
	as directed below

Skin the eel, wash and dry thoroly. Cut into 2-inch pieces. Arrange pieces on a double broiler rack and broil over a charcoal or coal fire—or under an electric grid. Serve with a Mustard Sauce, made by blending a tablespoon of prepared mustard to a cup of drawn butter sauce.

CURRIED EEL, SMITHTOWN

1 large Eel	3 cloves
1 large onion	2 cardamom seeds, broken
1 ounce green ginger	1 teaspoon curry powder
2 red chillies	Boiled rice
2 shallots, minced	1 cup fish stock or water
1 tablespoon butter	

Skin, wash and bone the eel; cut into 2-inch pieces. Peel and slice the onion; cut the ginger and chillies into small pieces, thread all three on wooden toothpick skewers. Mince the shallots, fry them with the butter, add the cloves and cardamom. Roll the little skewers in the curry powder, and place on top of the fried shallots. Add the fish stock and water, and the eel pieces; cook lightly until tender. Remove the skewers, serve eel with the remaining sauce, and boiled rice.

SMOKED EEL, HORSERADISH SAUCE

1 or 2 smoked Eels	1 tablespoon tarragon vine-
4 tablespoons freshly grated	gar
horseradish	4 tablespoons tomato catsup
$\frac{1}{4}$ teaspoon sugar	

Skin the smoked eel and cut into 2-inch pieces. Arrange on platter, and serve with the sauce made by blending horseradish, sugar, vinegar and catsup.

EEL-IN-BEER, CUTCHOQUE

$1\frac{1}{2}$ lbs Eel	1 pint Lager Beer
1 onion, chopped	$\frac{1}{2}$ tablespoon butter
1 sage leaf	1 tablespoon flour

Skin, clean and wash the eel; cut into 2-inch pieces. Put these in a pot with the onion, sage and beer; cook gently until tender. Lift out the eel to a hot plate. Blend butter and flour and add carefully to the liquid left in pan, stirring until smooth. Boil 3 minutes. Strain through a sieve and pour over the eel pieces.

EELS AND GREEN PEAS, FLANDERS BAY

1½ lbs Eel
5 tablespoons butter
1 pint Green Peas (fresh or quick-frozen)
1 head lettuce, shredded
½ cup Chablis (white wine)
1 tablespoon flour
Salt, pepper, few grains of cayenne

Skin, clean and wash the eel; cut into 2-inch slices. Salt each piece and cook in the butter for one minute. Add the peas, the shredded lettuce, the wine. Sprinkle with the flour, season and simmer for 30 minutes or until tender.

EELS-IN-A-GARDEN, FLORAL PARK

3 lbs Eel
½ lb spinach
¼ lb sorrel
¼ lb nettle or lettuce leaves
3 tablespoons butter
Small clove garlic
Sprig tarragon
Thyme
Sage
Salt, pepper
2 cups Chablis (white wine)
2 tablespoons lemon juice
3 egg yolks, slightly beaten

Wash, skin and clean the eels, cut into 3-inch pieces, and rub with salt and pepper. Let stand one hour. Chop the spinach, sorrel and the nettle or lettuce leaves, cook them gently in the butter, together with the seasonings. Add the eels, the wine and lemon juice. Bring to a boil, cover and let simmer for 20 minutes. Strain off the juice and add it to the beaten egg yolks. Do not boil. Pour this sauce over the eel and vegetables and serve hot.

EELS AND OYSTERS, NORMANDE

2 Eels
2 tablespoons butter
6 tablespoons Chablis (white wine)
3 tablespoons mushroom liquor
Pinch salt, pepper, nutmeg
1 cup chicken stock, or velouté

6 mushrooms, sliced
12 Robbins Island or Gardiner's Bay or other large Oysters
6 fish quenelles
6 lobster tails
3 egg yolks
Fried croutons

Skin and clean the eels; cut in 2-inch pieces. Fry them in the butter for 2 minutes, then add the wine and mushroom liquor. Add salt, pepper, nutmeg and cook for ten minutes. Add the velouté or chicken stock, the mushrooms, oysters, fish quenelles and lobster tails. Cook for 5 minutes; then lift fish to hot platter. Beat sauce left in pan into egg yolks; when thickened pour over fish and garnish with the croutons.

EEL AND ONIONS, PARISIENNE

1 Eel
Salt and pepper
1 cup cold water
1 cup red wine
½ clove garlic

1 onion, minced
Bouquet garni
1 cup green Onions, sliced
2 tablespoons butter
6 squares of fried bread

Wash, skin the eel, rub with salt and let stand in water for 1 hour. Then cut into 2-inch pieces. Place in a saucepan, with a cup of water and the red wine, pepper, salt, the garlic, the minced onion and garni. Cook until eel is tender. Fry green onions in butter; add to eel; cook 5 minutes. Arrange the eel on a platter, with the squares of fried bread, and pour over them the sauce left in pan.

SHORE-STEWED EEL, HITHER HILLS

2 Eels

4 teaspoons tarragon vinegar (or lemon juice)

1 cup cream (or can of
evaporated milk)

Salt, pepper, few grains
cayenne

Slices of toast or pilot
crackers

Wash and skin the eels, remove backbone, cut the eel into 2-inch pieces. Put in a saucepan, barely cover with water and add 2 teaspoons of the vinegar. Simmer for 20 minutes. Remove from fire and drain. Put in fresh water and add the other 2 teaspoons of vinegar. Let simmer until tender, about 10 minutes more; drain off the liquid, add to it the cream and seasonings; boil for 2 minutes. Arrange eel on the hot toast or hot pilot crackers and pour sauce over.

SMOKED EEL, ORIENT HARBOR

1 or 2 smoked Eels

2 tablespoons butter

1 onion, finely chopped

4 tomatoes, skinned and
quartered

Salt, pepper, few grains
cayenne

1 teaspoon parsley, chopped

Hot boiled rice

Skin the eels, carefully take out bones; flake the flesh with a silver fork. Melt the butter in a saucepan, sprinkle the onion in it, add the tomatoes. Cook until soft. Stir in the smoked eel flakes, salt, pepper, cayenne, parsley and heat. Cook the rice meanwhile, and serve the eel mixture bordered with the rice.

(This recipe can also be used with smoked salmon, smoked whitefish, finnan haddie or other smoked fish.)

EELS AND OYSTERS IN CIDER SAUCE, SYOSSET

1½ lbs Eels
2 tablespoons butter
12 Oysters
12 fresh mushrooms
1 cup sweet Cider
1 cup Oyster liquor
1 tablespoon flour

1 tablespoon mushroom
   catsup
¼ teaspoon salt
¼ teaspoon white pepper
Dash of grated nutmeg
2 eggs, well beaten

Skin, clean and wash the eels in salted water, dry thoroly; cut into 1-inch slices. Fry them in the butter until brown. Put on a hot platter and keep warm. Add the oysters and mushrooms to the pan and fry until brown (6 or 8 minutes), using more butter if necessary. Lay these over the eel slices. Into the same frying pan put the cider, oyster liquor in which the flour has been blended, mushroom catsup, salt, pepper, nutmeg. Stir and let come to a boil, then carefully add the beaten eggs, and stir constantly until thickened. Pour over the platter.

SPITCHCOCKED EEL, SOUTHAMPTON

2 Eels
4 tablespoons butter
1 teaspoon parsley, chopped
Pinch sage
1 shallot, finely chopped

Salt, pepper
2 egg yolks, lightly beaten
½ cup fine bread crumbs
Melted butter

Clean and skin the eels, wash in 2 waters, dry thoroly and cut into 3-inch lengths. Melt the 4 tablespoons of butter and add the parsley, sage, shallot, salt, pepper. Mix, remove from fire, and then carefully blend in the egg yolks, stirring constantly. Into this mixture dip the pieces of eel, coating them evenly, then roll in the bread crumbs. Lay on a broiling rack and broil for 6 or 8 minutes. Serve with melted butter in a sauceboat.

(This is a dish eaten for centuries in England, and known to a few here.)

COLD COLLARED EEL, SMITHTOWN

1 large Eel
1 tablespoon parsley, minced
1 teaspoon thyme
1 teaspoon marjoram
2 sage leaves

6 allspice berries
2 cloves
1 teaspoon ground peppercorns
1 cup water
1 cup vinegar

Skin and wash the eel, dry thoroly. Remove the backbone. Lay the eel meat on a baking board and spread on it the following mixture: the parsley pounded together with thyme, marjoram, sage, allspice, cloves and the ground peppercorns. Coil the eel meat into a roll and tie or skewer it in that position. Put in a saucepan with water and vinegar; simmer gently for 45 minutes. Lift out and put the eel in a deep jar, and pour the liquid over it. If it doesn't cover the eel, add more vinegar. Chill in refrigerator. Serve cold with baked potatoes.

BAKED EEL, SAGAMORE HILL

1 Eel
Salt, pepper
Few grains cayenne
3 tablespoons olive oil
Parsley sprigs

1 clove garlic
1 pinch thyme
Juice of 1 lemon
1 lemon, sliced

Skin and wash the eel, sprinkle with salt, pepper, cayenne; let stand 30 minutes. Cut into 2-inch lengths. Put the olive oil in a baking dish, add the garlic cut into 3 pieces, and the thyme. Put the eel in the baking dish, squeeze the lemon juice over and bake in a moderate oven (375° F.) for 25 minutes. Serve garnished with the lemon slices and parsley.

IX
Long Island Crab Delights

THE millions who have visited Coney Island, Manhattan Beach, Sheepshead Bay, Jones Beach, Rockaway and other resorts are as familiar with fried crabs as they are with the hot dog. They have been long a fixture, but they are becoming more rare everywhere, especially the fried soft shell crab. The enormous increase in sale of canned crabmeat shows how popular crab taste still is, but if we don't watch out the Japs will be supplying our crab altogether, and the delight of our own fried soft shell crabs will be a thing of the past! There is rather a shortage now, and Chesapeake Bay, which also has a scarcity, has sometimes had to supply the increasing Long Island appetite. Certainly during the World's Fair, Long Island alone could not supply the demand.

The crab leads a very interesting life, and goes through more evolutions than a butterfly! He starts as a "hardshell", during the time he fattens without growing. Then he shifts to a "peeler" because he is growing another skin under his shell. Then he becomes a "buster" when he breaks out of his shell; and after this he turns into the most delectable of his phases (from the gourmet point of view!) —the soft shell crab, when he is in his nudist phase. Following this he becomes a "buckram" crab when his skin toughens, and finally he again turns into a hardshell. He is even blue-blooded, the "blue crab" being the most delicately flavored and sought after. You can see that there's a special time when the soft shell crab is at his best for us who eat him—for fried soft shell crab is superb food. That is, if you just fry it in butter and do not use a thick baking powder batter in an effort to make the crab look like a larger morsel than it is. This is an old Coney Island and Atlantic City trick, but, as the gourmet knows, is not the best crab feast.

It is remarkable how many things we can do with crabmeat; but nothing dims the sheer delight of very fresh soft shell crab fried in plenty of butter and nothing else.

Crabs: preparation.—Use only actively alive, medium-sized crabs. Plunge hardshell crabs into rapidly boiling water until they turn red; then place them in boiling stock together with 1 onion, 1 bay leaf, 1 tablespoon vinegar, salt and pepper. Simmer for 15 minutes; drain and dry. To serve cold, pick the meat from the shells, discarding the "apron" by holding the crab in both hands, with thumbs at tail end, and pulling the upper and lower shells apart. Remove all matter sticking to upper shell, also all orange waxy skin and white spongy matter between the halves and at side. Break claws with hammer. Soft shell crabs need only be washed, being cooked whole.

BROILED SOFT SHELL CRABS, CHERRY GROVE

6 live soft shell Crabs	Cayenne
½ cup butter	Salt, pepper
2 tablespoons lemon juice	½ cup flour

Wash the crab in cold water and dry well. Melt the butter, add the lemon juice, and cayenne pepper. Sprinkle the crabs with salt and pepper, roll in the butter sauce; dredge with flour, then shake off excess flour. Lay the crabs in a fine-meshed double broiler rack and grill under a hot fire for 8 minutes, turning frequently.

Serve very hot with a sauce made as follows: melt 1½ tablespoons of butter, blend in 1 teaspoon of flour, stir in 1 cup of fish stock or water. Simmer for 10 minutes; season with salt and pepper. Remove from fire. Add the slightly beaten yolks of 2 eggs and ¼ cup cream. Cook over hot water, stirring constantly, for 3 minutes; add 1 tablespoon of lemon juice. Serve immediately over the crabs.

CRAB CURRY, HEMPSTEAD

2 fresh Crabs, or 1 cup Crabmeat
$\frac{1}{4}$ teaspoon dry mustard
4 tablespoons butter
1 onion, chopped

$\frac{1}{2}$ cooking apple, peeled, chopped
1 cup Curry sauce (No. 37)
2 cups boiled rice

Boil crab, remove meat and flake it, sprinkle with the dry mustard. Melt the butter and fry in it the onion and apple for 2 or 3 minutes. Then add the Curry Sauce and the crabmeat, and heat thoroly. Pour the mixture into the center of a ring of rice.

OYSTER AND CRAB RAREBIT ON TOAST, WATER MILL

4 tablespoons butter
1 tablespoon flour
$\frac{1}{2}$ cup milk
4 tablespoons tomato catsup
2 teaspoons worcestershire sauce
Salt and pepper

$\frac{1}{2}$ lb Crabmeat
18 Oysters
6 tablespoons cream
4 tablespoons grated American cheese
6 slices buttered Toast
Parsley or watercress

Melt the butter, add the flour and stir, then pour in the milk, catsup, sauce, pepper and salt. Blend well; simmer 3 minutes. Add the crabmeat and oysters and cook for 2 minutes; add the cream and cheese and cook until the oyster edges begin to curl. Pour at once on the toast and serve, garnished with parsley or watercress.

CRAB CANAPE, BLUE SPRUCE INN

1 cup Crabmeat
$\frac{1}{2}$ teaspoon dry mustard
2 tablespoons cream

Salt, pepper
Toast
Parmesan cheese, grated

Mix the crabmeat with the mustard; blend in the cream,

salt and pepper. Arrange upon thin slices of toast, sprinkle with the cheese, and brown in a quick oven about 6-8 minutes.

SAVORY CRAB, ROCKAWAY BEACH

$\frac{1}{4}$ loaf stale white bread
2 cups warm water
1 tablespoon vegetable fat
1 tablespoon butter
2 tablespoons chopped celery
1 tablespoon minced parsley
6 shallots or chives
4 cloves garlic, washed
1 onion, minced
1 sweet pepper, finely chopped
1 lb Crabmeat, picked
$\frac{1}{2}$ teaspoon salt
$\frac{1}{8}$ teaspoon pepper
$\frac{1}{2}$ cup toasted rolled cracker or bread crumbs

Cut up the bread and soak in 2 cups of water until soft, and then squeeze dry. Fry bread in the fat and butter, together with the celery, parsley, shallots, garlic, onion and sweet pepper. Add the crabmeat and cook slowly for 15 minutes. Season with salt and pepper. Place the mixture in a buttered casserole, sprinkle top with crumbs; bake 20-25 minutes until brown in a moderately hot oven. The same mixture may be placed in crab shells and browned quickly, 12-15 minutes in a hot oven.

CRAB DELIGHT

2 tablespoons green peppers, chopped
2 tablespoons butter
2 tablespoons flour
$\frac{1}{2}$ teaspoon mustard
$\frac{1}{4}$ teaspoon salt
Dash of cayenne pepper
$\frac{1}{2}$ teaspoon worcestershire sauce
$\frac{1}{2}$ cup stewed tomatoes
1 cup grated cheese
$\frac{3}{4}$ cup milk
1 egg, slightly beaten
1 cup Crabmeat
Pastry or toast

Cook the green pepper in butter five minutes. Blend in

the flour. Add mustard, salt, cayenne, worcestershire sauce, tomatoes and cheese. Cook 4 minutes. Heat milk, add mixture to it, blend in egg, then the crabmeat. Serve immediately in pastry shells or on toast.

BLUE POINT CRAB-OYSTER SPECIAL

2 tablespoons butter	$\frac{1}{2}$ teaspoon salt
2 tablespoons grated Edam cheese	Pinch cayenne
$\frac{1}{2}$ cup cream	$\frac{1}{2}$ cup Crabmeat
4 tablespoons tomato catsup	24 Blue Point or other medium-sized Oysters
1 teaspoon worcestershire sauce	6 slices buttered toast

Melt the butter in a double boiler or chafing dish; add the grated cheese, stirring constantly. Add the cream, the catsup, worcestershire sauce, salt, cayenne, crab meat, keeping stirring meantime. The oysters are dropped into the mixture for 4 or 5 minutes, and then the dish is served quickly on toast.

BAKED CRAB, MANHATTAN BEACH

4 soda crackers	Celery salt
1 cup milk	White pepper
2 cups Crabmeat, shredded	$\frac{1}{4}$ cup buttered cracker crumbs
3 tablespoons melted butter	
3 hard-cooked eggs	

Let soda crackers stand in a flat dish for 2 hours with the milk poured over them. Place crab meat in a bowl. Lift moistened crackers gently out of the milk and place in the bowl with the crab meat. Add the melted butter and mix all well. Grate the egg yolks and add, with the celery salt and pepper. Chop the egg whites and add. Place mixture in a buttered baking dish, dust the top with cracker crumbs. Bake until brown.

CRAB STEW, EASTPORT

2 tablespoons butter
2 tablespoons flour
2 cups Grade A milk
$\frac{1}{2}$ teaspoon salt
1 lemon, chopped
$\frac{1}{4}$ teaspoon freshly ground black pepper
$\frac{1}{4}$ teaspoon paprika
3 cups Crabmeat (canned or from fresh Crabs)
1 tablespoon worcestershire sauce
1 tablespoon Chablis (white wine)

Melt butter, blend in flour; gradually stir in milk; add salt. Bring to a boil, stir in one entire lemon, chopped very fine, rind and all. Season with pepper and paprika. Let simmer 2 or 3 minutes, then add the crabmeat, the worcestershire sauce and the wine. Heat through and serve immediately.

BAKED CRABMEAT, OLD FIELD POINT

2 tablespoons butter
2 tablespoons flour
2 cups Grade A milk
Salt, pepper
1 cup cheese, grated
1 lb Crabmeat

Melt the butter; blend in the flour; add the milk, salt and pepper. Then blend in the grated cheese and the crabmeat. Put in a buttered baking dish and bake in a moderate oven for 15 minutes.

CRAB-OYSTER STUFFED PEPPERS, EASTPORT

$1\frac{1}{2}$ cups cooked Crabmeat
1 cup Oysters, chopped
$\frac{1}{4}$ teaspoon salt
$\frac{1}{8}$ teaspoon pepper
1 teaspoon grated lemon rind
$\frac{1}{2}$ cup stale bread crumbs
4 tablespoons melted butter
1 teaspoon parsley, minced
1 cup Oyster liquor
6 medium-sized peppers

Mix the crabmeat with the chopped oysters, salt, pepper, lemon rind, bread crumbs, butter and parsley, using the oyster liquor to moisten. Cut a slice crosswise from the stem

end of the peppers, remove fibre and seeds. Parboil, uncovered, in a large amount of boiling salted water 5 to 10
minutes. Drain. Fill peppers with the crab mixture, arrange the peppers in a baking pan and pour remaining
oyster liquor in the pan. Bake in a moderate oven (350°
F.) for 30 minutes.

CRAB SOUP, GULF STREAM

3 tablespoons butter	1 teaspoon salt
1 small onion, finely chopped	$\frac{1}{8}$ teaspoon pepper
3 stalks celery, finely chopped	2 cups water
	$1\frac{1}{4}$ cups (1 can) Crabmeat
3 mushrooms, finely chopped	3 cups milk
	1 cup heavy cream
$1\frac{1}{2}$ tablespoons flour	paprika

Melt butter, add onions, celery and mushrooms and cook
5 minutes without browning. Blend flour and seasonings
with the water and add with crabmeat to the vegetables.
Simmer 30 minutes. Combine milk and cream, scald and
add to soup. Let stand 5 minutes. Sprinkle with paprika
before serving.

SEA ISLAND CRAB SHELLS

3 slices bread	1 teaspoon chili pepper, chopped
1 cup milk	
3 strips bacon, chopped fine	2 cups cooked Crabmeat, flaked
2 tablespoons butter	
1 clove garlic, chopped	3 tablespoons bread crumbs
1 tablespoon chives, chopped	

Soak the bread in the milk, squeeze out; mix with the
chopped bacon. Put in a frying pan with the butter and
brown it, add the garlic, chives, chili pepper. Mix in well
the flaked crabmeat, then stuff crab or scallop shells with

it, sprinkle with bread crumbs, and brown in a hot oven (450° F.) for 15 to 20 minutes, or until nicely browned.

BAKED CRAB SHELLS, GREAT NECK

1 large onion, chopped
1 tablespoon butter
1 tablespoon cornstarch
½ cup cream
½ teaspoon mustard
Pinch nutmeg, paprika

1 teaspoon   worcestershire or other table sauce
1 cup stewed tomatoes, drained
1 cup Crabmeat
½ cup bread crumbs

Fry the onion in the butter, then add the other ingredients and mix well. Clean some crab shells and fill them with the mixture. Sprinkle with bread crumbs and bake in a moderately hot oven (400° F.) for 20 minutes or until brown.

CRABMEAT, NORFOLK

1 lb Crabmeat, flaked
⅔ cup butter

3 teaspoons cider vinegar
Boiled rice

Lay the crabmeat in a buttered casserole, drop over it the butter in pieces, add the vinegar. Bake in a very hot oven (500° F.) for 15 minutes; serve on platter inside a ring of rice.

CRAB-STUFFED HADDOCK

1 (3-lb) Haddock
1½ cups Crabmeat, flaked
¼ cup celery, chopped fine
½ cup tart apple, chopped fine
1 tablespoon green pepper
1 tablespoon minced pimento

1 cup soft bread crumbs
1 egg, slightly beaten
2 tablespoons melted butter
1 lime, sliced
4 sprigs parsley

Clean and wash the haddock, dry thoroly. Make a mixture of the crabmeat, celery, apple, pepper, pimento and bread crumbs, and egg; stuff haddock with it. Tie with skewers and twine. Lay in a baking pan, brush with melted butter. Bake 35 minutes in a moderately hot oven (375°-400° F.). Garnish with the parsley and lime slices.

X

Lobster and Shrimp in Long Island Ways

MANY people regard the lobster as the aristocrat of seafoods, as would be indicated by the phrase "lobster palace" left over from the "gay Nineties"; meaning a restaurant for high livers, such as Rector's once had the reputation of being. Quite the same thing happened, at about the same time, to champagne; in fact the two were usually linked together during that rococco period of false gourmet standards (which were really show-off, *gourmand* standards).

Both lobster and champagne, excellent food and drink, therefore had the misfortune to be romantically over-rated, and have never since quite settled down to their own intrinsic merits. The "lowly" crab and the common shrimp are good equal gastronomical companions to the lobster, and the threat to the lobster supply and its consequent high price are what really keep lobster in the "precious" class. You can actually do more things to shrimp and crab than to the lobster, whose cuisine is considerably more limited, and therefore somewhat more monotonous.

Nobody, however, denies the succulence in a good Maine lobster (which ranks tops), or a Long Island lobster. The lobster chowders made by knowing lobster fishermen (who always place the broken lobster shells in the kettle) have a bouquet that is one of the sea's best.

Many people have weird notions about lobster. For one thing, about eating lobster with ice cream or creamed desserts at night. The idea is that this is "poisonous". It is a wrong idea; the indigestion, if any, will arise from overloading the stomach, not from a peculiar "combination". Lobster and cream are constantly used in combination. For another thing, many believe the bigger the lobster the better. Not so. Lobsters weighing as high as 25 pounds have been known on American coast, but seem now to be extinct (and no gourmet regrets it). The tenderest, most delicious lobster meat comes from specimens of $1\frac{1}{4}$ to $1\frac{3}{4}$ lbs weight; the average today is 2 lbs. No seafood shrinks so much in preparation as lobster; half a lobster is rarely an ample enough meal for a man. The North Atlantic coast is blessed with the best lobster known; the French *langouste,* the African rock lobster or the other lobster-like shellfish in other American waters are no match for the North Atlantic lobster. The supply however is limited. Lobster Diavolo, Lobster Curry and a broiled lobster with a little garlic in the dressing are to my mind tops.

As for shrimp, it is a curious paradox that although the lobster feeds at the very bottom of the ocean—sometimes at 35 or 40 fathoms of water in winter, the shrimp lives and feeds mostly near the surface. Thus the Chinese say that the shrimp "walks on stilts." The quaintly imaginative and yet practical Chinese, who are very fond of shrimps, talk about "shrimps punished with bamboo", by which they mean an efficiency method they use to shell shrimp. They put the cooked shrimp in a bag and whip it with a bamboo rod, which loosens the shells from the shrimp in jig time. Shrimps come from southern waters, although some have been found in the North Atlantic, off of Maine. River shrimp from the lower Mississippi are a particular delicacy in season.

Shrimp has a very wide cooking range, from merely a border decoration on a platter to the (for me, delightful) Shrimps, Sweet and Pungent—a Chinese dish. Next to this, for my appetite, is a Crab and Shrimp Gumbo, New Orleans style. And next to that is Fried Shrimp, Japanese style. These three foods seem to me to be among the greatest of all gourmet delights. Yet vast numbers of people know shrimp only in a badly made salad or as a cocktail appetizer with a crude tomato dressing.

Lobster: preparation.—Choose medium-sized actively alive lobsters, weighty for their bulk. For boiled lobster, plunge into rapidly boiling water, with 1 tablespoon of salt. Boil 15-20 minutes (larger size longer). Leave in hot water 10 minutes, then plunge into cold water. Dry; rub shell with butter or olive oil; separate body from tail; chop off claws; remove stomach (small sac at back of head), together with intestines. To open a boiled lobster take large claws off first, then small ones, then tail. A can opener or scissors may be needed to reach meat from tail.

For *broiling* or *baking,* a live lobster is killed by inserting large sharp knife at the back (between the body and the shell tails) and severing the spinal cord. Split the lobster with the knife, from head to tail, remove stomach and intestine, crack the large claws, brush shell and meat with melted butter or olive oil.

Shrimps: preparation.—Freshness is important. They should be boiled in rapidly boiling salted water for 5 to 6 minutes, not more, to avoid toughness. In removing the shell be sure also to remove the black vein down the back.

SHRIMPS, SWEET AND PUNGENT, LUM FONG

1 lb fresh Shrimp
½ cup flour
2 eggs, beaten
2 slices canned pineapple
1 green pepper
1 cup vinegar
½ teaspoon salt
Pinch of pepper
1 cup sugar

½ teaspoon gourmet powder (Chinese name: Mei Jing)
3 teaspoons cornstarch
½ cup water
1 teaspoon black sauce (Chinese name: Gee Yeou)

Boil and shell the shrimp, remove the veins, wash in cold water, dry thoroly. Blend the flour in the eggs, and dip the shrimp in the mixture, then fry them in deep fat until golden brown. Cut the pineapple into small wedges, cut the peppers into slices. Heat together in an iron skillet the vinegar, pineapple, green pepper, salt, pepper, sugar, Gourmet Powder. Bring to a boil, stir in the cornstarch (which has been made into a paste with water). Cook until clear, about 15 minutes; add the black sauce and shrimp, and cook for 2 minutes.

(In the author's opinion this is one of the great gourmet dishes of the world. The Chinese have about 700 restaurants in New York and Long Island, and are nowadays making America acquainted with the real Chinese cookery which ranks next to the French. Chop suey, a dish which is not Chinese food, is being replaced with true Chinese dishes. Lum Fong, one of Chinatown's leading restauranteurs, has a delightful Chinese restaurant at Long Beach and serves many of China's seafood dishes. The two Chinese ingredients mentioned are usually obtainable at well-stocked fancy grocery stores, or at Chinese stores, and may be ordered by mail.)

BROILED LIVE LOBSTER À LA GOURMET SOCIETY

Split the live lobster lengthwise and crack the claws. Brush the lobster with olive oil or melted butter (even to the claws, to keep the meat inside from drying out). Sprinkle with paprika. Lay some buttered bread crumbs over the exposed meat. Broil under a fairly hot flame, preferably charcoal or coal, until just rosy and soft, taking care not to over-broil or under-broil, and broiling about two minutes less on the shell side than on the meat side.

Baste frequently with a sauce made by blending: one clove of garlic with $\frac{1}{2}$ teaspoonful of parsley and $\frac{1}{2}$ lb of butter. The remainder of the sauce is then mixed with and boiled up with the lobster liver, and served in a sauceboat at the table. The lobsters positively must be served very hot.

LOBSTER À LA AMERICAINE, SCOTTO

1 Lobster
Salt, pepper
$\frac{1}{3}$ cup olive oil
2 tablespoons butter
2 shallots, chopped
1 clove garlic, crushed
2 tablespoons Chablis
　(white wine)
2 tablespoons fish stock

$\frac{1}{4}$ cup burnt-off brandy
1 tablespoon meat glacé
3 small fresh tomatoes,
　chopped and pressed
Pinch of minced parsley
Few grains cayenne
$\frac{1}{4}$ lb butter
2 or 3 sprigs fried parsley
Boiled rice

Plunge the lobster into rapidly boiling water for 5 minutes. Remove and drain. Sever and slightly crush the claws, cut the tail into sections; split in half lengthwise, remove the green. Remove intestines and coral, and season the lobster with salt and pepper. Then place meat in a saucepan with the olive oil and butter, melted and hot. Fry covered until meat has stiffened, then tilt the pan to empty the grease, while holding the lid. Sprinkle the lobster with the shallots and garlic, add the wine, the fish stock, burnt-off brandy, meat glacé, tomatoes, parsley and cayenne. Cover and cook in the oven for 18 to 20 minutes. Then turn out the lobster pieces onto a dish; take the meat from the section of the tail and claws, and put it in a timbal, set upright thereon the 2 halves of the lobster and let them lie against each other. Keep hot. Now reduce the cooking sauce of the lobster to $\frac{1}{3}$ pint, add intestines and chopped coral together with a tablespoon of butter, cook for a moment and strain. Put this into a pan, heat it without letting it boil, and add, away from the fire, 3 oz. butter cut into small pieces. Pour sauce over pieces of lobster and sprinkle with fried parsley. Serve with rice.

(Charles Scotto, of Pierre's, was the leading French chef in America, until his death in 1937. He was Escoffier's favorite pupil, and he headed the Société Culinaire. He was especially fond of seafood cookery.)

FRIED SHRIMP À LA JAPANESE

36 raw jumbo Shrimp	Salt, pepper
1 pint milk	½ cup soy sauce
½ cup rice flour	2 teaspoons horseradish,
2 eggs, lightly beaten	grated

Shell the shrimp, which should be as large as possible, but keep the top tuft on. With a sharp pointed steel knife cut each shrimp half through along the back. Let stand for 2 hours in the milk. Then have ready boiling hot fat (375° F.). Seize the shrimp by the top tuft, dip in the rice (or other) flour, then roll in the beaten egg, then in the flour again. Drop, a few at a time, in the deep fat. Cook 3 to 4 minutes, turning once. Drain on absorbent paper. Season with salt and pepper. Serve very hot. Mix the Soy Sauce with the horseradish, and warm slightly. The shrimp are to be dipped into this sauce, while holding them by the top tuft.

(The Japanese soy sauce is called Shoyu Sauce, but either this or any bottled soy sauce will do.)

LOBSTER BRULOT, CONSCIENCE POINT

1 medium-sized Lobster, boiled	1 egg yolk, slightly beaten
	¼ cup cream
3 tablespoons butter melted	Salt, pepper, paprika
½ clove garlic, halved	Melba toast
¼ cup brandy	

Pick the meat from the lobster and cut into pieces. Melt the butter in a saucepan with the garlic. Cook 2 minutes. Remove garlic, and add lobster meat. Sauté 3 minutes. Remove from fire. Then pour on the brandy and light it, and let burn for 1 to 2 minutes. Blend the egg yolk into the cream and pour over lobster. Add seasonings to taste. Cook in a chafing dish or casserole for only 1 to 2 minutes, stirring constantly. Serve immediately on Melba toast.

SHRIMPS AND FRIED RICE, ORIENTALE

1½ lbs fresh Shrimp
1 large onion, chopped
1 stalk celery, chopped
½ cup mushrooms, halved
2 tablespoons peanut or
   olive oil

4 cups cooked Rice
3 tablespoons bottled soy
   sauce
1 teaspoon salt
4 eggs, beaten

Cook the shrimps in salted boiling water for 10 minutes. Let cool and shell, removing black vein. Fry the onion, the shrimps, the celery, the mushrooms in the oil for 5 minutes. Then add the rice, soy sauce, salt and ¼ cup of the liquid in which the shrimp has been boiled. Let cook for 5 minutes, stirring to mix well. Stir in the eggs, and cook over moderate heat for 5 minutes more.

BAKED SHRIMPS AND OYSTERS, ABDULLAH

1½ pint Oysters
1 lb fresh Shrimp
2 cups cracker crumbs
1¼ cups melted butter
Pepper, cayenne

1 teaspoon salt
1 teaspoon celery salt
Paprika
1 cup light cream

Drain the liquor off the oysters and add water if necessary to make one cup liquid. Boil the shrimp and shell, removing black vein. Mix the cracker crumbs with the melted butter, and the cayenne, pepper, salt, celery salt. Butter a baking dish and put in a layer of the buttered crumbs, then a layer of oysters mixed with the shrimp. Then add a second layer of buttered crumbs and another layer of oysters and shrimp. Top with remaining crumbs. Dot with butter, sprinkle with paprika. Pour over this the oyster liquor and cream. Bake in a moderate oven (350° F.) for 30 minutes.

FISH WITH SHRIMP SAUCE, ATLANTIC BEACH

2 lbs Fish fillets
½ pint Chablis (white
  wine)
1 tablespoon minced onion
Pinch of thyme
Juice of ½ lemon

Shrimp Sauce
2 hard-cooked eggs, sliced
1 tablespoon parsley,
  chopped
3 lemon slices

Clean and wash the fillets, dry them thoroly. Lay in a buttered saucepan, add the wine, onion, thyme, lemon juice. Simmer gently for 20 minutes. Make the Shrimp Sauce as follows: add 1 egg yolk and ½ cup of minced shrimp to 1 cup drawn butter sauce. Arrange the fillets on a hot platter, pour on the shrimp sauce. Arrange the sliced boiled eggs around the edge, garnish dish with the parsley and lemon slices.

SHRIMP AND LOBSTER PATTIES, SOUTHAMPTON

1 lb cooked Lobster meat
2 lbs cooked picked Shrimp
1 tablespoon minced pars-
  ley
1 sprig thyme, minced

½ clove garlic, minced
1 cup rolled cornflakes
2 eggs
3 teaspoons melted butter
½ cup flour

Grind lobster and shrimp meat together, through medium knife of food chopper. Mix well, add all the other ingredients (except flour). Shape mixture into little patties, and roll each lightly in flour. Fry in hot oil or butter. Serve, if desired, tartare sauce. Garnish with lettuce leaves, watercress and lemon slices.

SHRIMP IN PANTIES, PATCHOGUE

1 lb extra large Shrimp
2 cups olive oil

Salt, pepper
1 lemon, sliced

The larger the shrimp the better. After washing thoroly, and drying them with linen towel, drop them, a few at a time, into a deep frying pan filled with the very hot olive oil (375° F.). Turn them frequently until done (4-5 minutes), then lay on hot dish covered with absorbent paper while the others are being cooked. The diners shell the shrimp themselves at the table—they are served hot, sprinkled with salt and pepper, and with lemon.

BATTER SHRIMP, OCEAN BEACH

3 tablespoons olive oil
½ teaspoon salt
Dash of pepper
2 tablespoons lemon juice
1 lb raw Shrimp, shelled

1 cup sifted flour
1 egg, beaten
¾ cup warm water
Small skewers or toothpicks
½ teaspoon minced parsley

Beat together 1½ tablespoons of the olive oil with ¼ teaspoon salt, pepper and the lemon juice. Pour this mixture over the shelled shrimp, and let stand to marinate for 30 minutes. Make the batter as follows: mix the sifted flour and remaining ¼ teaspoon salt, combine beaten egg, 1½ tablespoons of olive oil and water, add gradually to flour, beat until smooth. Skewer four or five shrimp on toothpicks, and dip them into the batter, making sure they are entirely covered. Then fry in deep fat heated to 375° F. Drain on absorbent paper; sprinkle with parsley.

OYSTER-SHRIMP PILAU, LONG ISLAND

1 cup Oysters
1 cup oyster liquor
5 slices bacon
1 onion, chopped
3 cups canned tomatoes

1 cup rice, uncooked
1 cup cooked Shrimp
Salt, pepper, few grains cayenne

Simmer oysters in the oyster liquor for 5 minutes. Drain. Cut the bacon into inch squares, fry until crisp. Then take from the pan, and in the fat fry the onion. Put in the tomatoes and 1 cup oyster liquor; let cook 3 minutes. Turn into the upper part of double boiler, add the rice, and cook for 45 minutes. Add the shrimp, and the bacon, and the oysters and the seasonings. Butter a shallow baking dish, fill it with the mixture and bake in a moderate oven for 15 minutes.

(The "pilau" is a dish which came from the Orient to the southern American shores via clipper ships, and the pilau has therefore been known for several centuries in Charleston and southern seaports. But it was also known (for the same reason) to very old Long Islanders.)

CORN-SHRIMP-CLAM PIE, SUFFOLK

2 cups Corn, grated from the cob (or whole-kernel canned Corn)
3 eggs, beaten
2 tablespoons butter, melted
½ cup milk
Salt, pepper, few grains cayenne
1 cup raw Shrimp, shelled
1 cup soft shell Clams, steamed and cut in half
Clam broth

Mix together the corn, the eggs, the butter, milk, seasonings, the shrimp and the clams. Reduce the clam broth to ½ cup over a hot fire and add. Butter a casserole or baking dish, put this mixture in and bake for 30 minutes in a moderate oven (300° F.).

SHRIMP SOUP, SHIP'S GALLEY

1 lb raw Shrimp, shelled
3 cups fish broth
1 pint cream or evaporated milk
Salt, pepper, few grains of cayenne
1 tablespoon chopped parsley
½ cup broken saltine crackers
2 tablespoons butter

Boil the shrimp in the fish broth, having placed in the broth a little cheese cloth bag containing some crushed shrimp shells. As soon as broth comes to a boil add the cream or evaporated milk which has been brought to a boil. Season with salt, pepper, cayenne and the chopped parsley, and then add the broken crackers and the butter. Let it cook until the butter is melted, then remove the bag of shrimp shells. Serve soup in soup plates, on each of which has been laid a toasted pilot cracker.

FISH AND SHRIMP, ISLIP

2½ lbs Flounder, Bass or Cod or Haddock
3 cups water
2 slices onion
½ carrot, sliced
4 tablespoons butter, melted
4 tablespoons flour
1 pint Grade A milk
White pepper, nutmeg
Allspice, cloves
1½ cups sifted dry bread crumbs
1 lb raw Shrimp, shelled
2 tablespoons grated cheese

Fillet the fish. Prepare a fish stock by simmering the fish head, tail, bones and trimmings in 3 cups water with onion and carrot slices. Poach fillets in stock for 10 minutes, lift out. Reduce broth to 2 cups over a hot fire. Strain through fine sieve. Melt 3 tablespoons butter, blend in flour, add gradually the milk and fish stock. Season, and add ½ cup dry bread crumbs. Add shrimp. Arrange fish fillets in a buttered baking dish, in layers, with the shrimp sauce between. Mix remaining ½ cup bread crumbs with the remaining tablespoon melted butter, and sprinkle over top of casserole. Cover top with grated cheese. Bake in a moderate oven for 25 minutes.

SHRIMP CROQUETTES, EAST QUOQUE

1 lb fresh Shrimp
4 tablespoons butter
1 tablespoon onion, chopped
4 tablespoons sifted flour
2 cups milk
6 egg yolks, slightly beaten
1 tablespoon parsley, chopped
½ cup bread crumbs
Crisco, or Spry

Shell the shrimps, cook in boiling salted water for 15 minutes; drain. Melt the butter, fry the onion in it until yellow but not brown. Blend in the flour, but do not brown, then add the milk, stirring until smooth. Bring to a boil and cook 5 minutes or until mixture thickens. Remove pan from fire. Add gradually half the liquid to the egg yolks, beating constantly. Add remaining liquid and cook over hot water for 3 minutes until thickened, stirring constantly. Add the parsley and the cooked shrimp. Mix, and then pour out on a floured baking board and let cool; divide into little heaps of the same size. With floured hands shape these heaps into rolls, after which dip the rolls into the breadcrumbs and fry them in deep fat until brown.

CURRIED LOBSTER IN CUCUMBERS

2 large cucumbers
1 can ($\frac{1}{2}$ lb) Lobster
1 cup white sauce
Salt
Paprika

$\frac{1}{2}$ teaspoon curry powder
1 hard-cooked egg
1 tablespoon minced parsley

Peel cucumbers and cut in half lengthwise. Scoop out seeds and cook in rapidly boiling salted water 15 minutes, or until tender. Drain carefully. Shred lobster meat and add to white sauce, seasoned to taste. Cook over hot water 5 minutes or until lobster is thoroly heated. Fill cucumber shells with creamed mixture and garnish with chopped egg and parsley.

LOBSTER SOUFFLE ANGOSTURA

2 tablespoons butter
3 tablespoons flour
$\frac{1}{4}$ teaspoon salt
Dash of tabasco
2 teaspoons minced parsley
1 cup milk

1 cup fresh or canned Lobster, chopped
3 eggs, separated
1 teaspoon Angostura
1 teaspoon lemon juice

Melt butter and blend in flour. Add salt, tabasco and parsley. Gradually add milk and cook over low heat 5 minutes or until thick and smooth, stirring constantly. Remove from heat, add lobster. Add to beaten egg yolks. Beat egg whites stiff and fold in. Turn into greased casserole, place in a pan of warm water and bake in a moderately slow oven (325° F.) about 1 hour.

LOBSTER CREOLE, CHESTER MORRIS

1½ cups Lobster meat
1 clove garlic
2 tablespoons butter
3 green onions, minced
1 green pepper, chopped fine
2 tablespoons flour

½ teaspoon salt
¼ teaspoon pepper; few grains cayenne
1 cup solid-pack tomatoes
1 cup cream
Toast or pastry shells

Wash the lobster meat in cold water, cut in medium pieces. Rub a deep saucepan with the cut clove of garlic. Melt the butter in the pan, and fry the onions and green pepper in it for 5 minutes, stirring constantly. Then blend in the flour, salt, pepper, cayenne and cook for several minutes. Gradually add the tomatoes and the cream; then add the lobster and heat through. Serve on hot buttered toast squares, or pastry shells.

FRIED SHRIMP IN SOY BATTER

1 cup flour
1 teaspoon baking powder
¼ teaspoon salt
1 cup milk
1 tablespoon melted butter
1 egg white

½ teaspoon soy sauce (or worcestershire sauce)
3 cups raw Shrimp, shelled
6 sprigs parsley
1 lemon, sliced

Sift together the flour, baking powder and salt, blend in the milk and melted butter and beat well. Fold in the egg white, beaten stiff, and the soy sauce. Into this batter dip the shrimp and lay in a deep fat frying basket. Cook in deep fat at 375° F., until brown, about 4 minutes, turning once. Drain, serve on hot platter with parsley and lemon.

TIMBALE OF LOBSTER, IOLANTHE

2 onions, chopped	1½ cups cream
3 tablespoons butter	6 small mushrooms
2 boiled Lobsters, picked and sliced	2 sweetbreads
	1 teaspoon lemon juice
1 glass sherry	Cooked noodles

Fry the onion in one tablespoon butter then add the lobster meat, sliced. Heat for 10 minutes, blend in the sherry, the cream and the mushrooms. Cook for 15 minutes. Meanwhile parboil sweetbreads and fry in remaining butter. Take out the lobster and mushrooms and set aside on a hot dish. To the lobster cream sauce add the lemon juice, season, and pour over the lobster. Cut up the sweetbreads, spread them on a hot platter. Top them with the lobster, mushrooms and the sauce. Serve with buttered noodles.

TOASTED LOBSTER, STIRRUP CUP

1 2-lb Lobster	Salt, pepper
1 clove garlic	1 strip salt pork
2 tablespoons drawn butter	2 tablespoons melted butter

Plunge the live lobster in boiling salted water and boil for 15 minutes. Then split, rub with garlic, baste with drawn butter and salt and pepper and toast gently 15 minutes on a plank before a wood fire (in a fireplace, or on the shore). Then cover the cut surface with the strip of salt pork and bake in the oven until completely done. Serve with melted butter.

SEAWATER LOBSTER, CAPTREE

1 Lobster	Fresh Seawater

Fill a kettle two-thirds full of genuine fresh, clean seawater—but be quite sure it *is* clean seawater, secured not too near the shore and not in any spot where any pollution or dirt exists. Then bring this seawater to an active boil. Put in the lobster, tail downward, entirely immersing it. Boil actively for 15 to 20 minutes. If more than one lobster is put in kettle, always be sure the water is boiling again before putting another lobster in.

CURRY OF LOBSTER

4 Lobsters
5 tablespoons sweet butter
2 tablespoons curry powder
2 teaspoons shallots, minced
½ cup Chablis (white wine)
4 peeled tomatoes, crushed and seeded
1 teaspoon minced parsley

¼ teaspoon salt
Pinch cayenne pepper
3 cups hot boiled rice
½ cup cooked raisins or currants
3 tablespoons sliced, skinned, slightly scorched almonds
1 tablespoon lemon juice

Boil lobsters for 5 minutes. Drain. Take out the meat and cut into cubes. Melt butter in saucepan, put in lobster, fry for 5 minutes, then add the curry, shallots, wine. Cook for 5 minutes, add tomatoes, parsley, salt, pepper. Cover, cook 15 minutes to blend well. Serve from hot chafing dish, with hot rice on the side, to which the raisins, almonds and lemon juice have been added.

KINGFISH WITH SHRIMPS, HUEY LONG

2 lbs Kingfish fillets
Salt and pepper
½ cup milk
2 tablespoons flour
3 tablespoons butter

½ lb cooked Shrimp
6 sprigs parsley
12 asparagus tips
Potato balls
1 lemon, decoratively cut

Wash the fillets and dry thoroly. Rub with salt and pepper. Dip in the milk, roll in flour and fry in the butter until browned. Lay on hot platter, place the shrimps on

top. Garnish with parsley sprigs, asparagus tips, potato
balls and the cut lemon.

SHRIMP AND GREEN CORN SOUFFLE

6 large ears of Corn (or 1
   large can of whole-grain
   Corn)
3 eggs, separated

2 teaspoons sugar
1 tablespoon butter, **melted**
$\frac{1}{2}$ teaspoon salt
$1\frac{1}{2}$ lbs Shrimp, cooked

Cut the corn from the cob, stir into the beaten egg yolks,
add the sugar, melted butter, salt and shrimps; then fold in
the stiffly beaten egg whites. Turn into a buttered baking
dish, cover and set in a pan of hot water. Bake in a slow
oven (300° F.) for 1 hour, until firm. For the last 15 minutes remove cover and let brown.

LOBSTER-STUFFED MUSHROOMS, NASSAU

6 large Mushroom caps
1 tablespoon butter
3 tablespoons olive oil (or
   butter)
4 tablespoons flour
1 teaspoon salt
$\frac{1}{2}$ teaspoon black pepper

2 cups fish stock, or clam
   broth
1 Lobster coral, pounded
1 cup cooked Lobster meat,
   chopped
Toast slices

Broil the mushroom caps on a buttered wire broiler under
a moderate flame, exposing the top side first. After 5 minutes turn the mushrooms and put a bit of butter in each
cap, and broil 4 minutes more. In a saucepan make a Cardinal Sauce as follows: blend the olive oil or butter with the
flour; when it bubbles add the salt, pepper and fish
stock. Cook until it boils, then let simmer slowly for 5
minutes. Add the coral and the lobster meat. Fill the
mushroom caps with the mixture, arrange on toast slices,
on a platter around the lobster shell, and surround with the
rest of the sauce.

LOBSTER ROYAL, SCHNEIDER

1½ tablespoons chopped onion
1½ tablespoons butter
1½ tablespoons flour
Salt, pepper, dash of mace
¾ cup light cream
2 tablespoons soft bread crumbs

1½ cups Lobster meat, diced
1½ teaspoons lemon juice
1 tablespoon parsley, minced
2 egg yolks, beaten
2 tablespoons fine bread crumbs

Cook the onion in the butter for 3 minutes. Then add the flour, salt, pepper, mace and cream. Stir until it thickens. Then blend in the soft bread crumbs and the lobster meat; cook for a few moments, then add the lemon juice, parsley and egg yolks. Clean the lobster shell and fill with meat mixture, cover with the fine bread crumbs and brown in a quick oven.

LOBSTER THERMIDOR, MANHATTAN

1 good-sized Lobster
4 tablespoons butter
6 mushrooms, diced
1 green pepper, diced
1 pimento, diced
½ teaspoon paprika
¼ cup sherry
3 tablespoons medium cream sauce

Salt, pepper
1 egg yolk
3 tablespoons cracker crumbs
2 tablespoons melted butter
Paprika
2 partly crisped slices of bacon

Plunge lobster in furiously boiling salted water for 20 minutes; cool in cold water. Take off claws and legs, split lengthwise from head to tail on the under side, taking care not to cut through the shell, as you want the shell for filling. Take out and discard the sac in the head, also membrane running through the tail. Take meat from tail and claws and dice, leaving the butter fat inside the shell. Sauté in butter the mushrooms and green pepper, add pimento, lobster meat, paprika and sherry wine. Add cream sauce, salt and pepper, to taste, and egg yolk. Place mixture in lobster shell, mound up, sprinkle with crumbs and melted butter, slightly dust with paprika. Cut bacon in thin slivers, place on top diagonally. Brown slightly under broiler, place in oven until thoroly heated.

SHRIMPS, SUI MING HAR

1 lb large-sized Shrimp
1 tablespoon crushed powdered almond
6 strips bacon

1 egg, beaten
4 tablespoons worcestershire sauce
1 tablespoon catsup

Wash and shell the shrimp, cut open along the back with a sharp knife (but do not cut in half). Flatten the cut shrimp with a knife, and sprinkle on them the crushed powdered almond. Cut the bacon in small strips the size of the shrimp, dip them in the beaten egg, and lay one piece on top of each shrimp; arrange shrimp on a broiling rack. Broil under a good flame for 6 to 8 minutes. Place on a hot platter and pour over them the worcestershire sauce and catsup brought to a boil together.

LOBSTER DIAVALO, RENATO

1 Lobster
3 tablespoons olive oil
1 tablespoon parsley, minced

1 clove garlic, crushed
½ cup Italian peeled tomatoes
Oregano (Italian thyme)

Plunge the live lobster in salted furiously boiling water for 15 minutes; drain. Pick out meat, cook for 3 to 4 minutes in the olive oil. Add then the parsley, garlic, tomatoes and oregano; let simmer for 6 or 8 minutes. Serve piping hot.

XI

The Scallop Is a Lovely Shellfish!

THE sea is full of both fearful and beautiful things—but none lovelier than the fluted shellfish, the scallop. We even use the scallop shell for serving other foods. The scallop is also, I believe, a misrepresented fish. The scallop is of two kinds, the large deep-sea scallop and the lesser size bay or cape kind, found in the general North Atlantic waters, inclusive of some waters off Long Island. Long Island Bay Scallops are a preferred item. Most of us think a scallop looks like what we see for sale, but what we see is only the abductor muscle which holds this mollusk's shells together. There are gourmets who like the *body* part of the scallop. At Tom Moore's restaurant in Bermuda, and at certain European places, it is served as a delicacy.

But the muscle of the scallop is itself surely good eating —even raw (which is not usually known). Here are various scallop recipes:

SCALLOPS AND OYSTER-CRABS, SEAFORD

36 small Scallops	Salt, pepper
1 lb Oyster-Crabs	Hollandaise sauce (No. 16)

Roll both scallops and oyster-crabs in flour, shake off the excess flour. Fry in a frying pan with half an inch or more of very hot fat, for only two to three minutes. Then sprinkle with salt and pepper, and serve very hot, heaped on a plate together. Serve with Hollandaise sauce.

SCALLOP FRY, PLUM ISLAND

8 pieces bacon
36 Bay Scallops
½ cup bread crumbs,
    finely sifted

2 eggs, slightly beaten with
    2 tablespoons water
Salt, pepper
4 sprigs parsley
1 lemon, cut in pieces

Fry the bacon; drain on absorbent paper, and cut into 1-inch squares. Cut a slit in the scallops and insert one or two pieces of the bacon in each. Roll the scallops in the bread crumbs then dip into the eggs, then again in crumbs. Fry the scallops in the hot bacon fat. Season and serve with parsley and lemon slices.

SCALLOPS AND MUSSELS, EN BROCHETTE

32 small Bay Scallops
24 good-sized Mussels (or
    small hard shell clams)
6 pieces of bacon
½ cup olive oil

1 cup rolled seasoned
    bread crumbs
4 slices hot toast
4 sprigs parsley
Maitre d'hotel sauce
    (No. 6)

Cook the scallops in their own liquor until they begin to shrink. Then dry again thoroly. Steam open the mussels, shell and dry them thoroly also. Cut the bacon into inch squares. Take 8 6-inch skewers and thread on each one alternately four scallops, three mussels, three squares of bacon. Dip the skewerfuls in olive oil, drain off and coat with the seasoned breadcrumbs. Place the skewers on the broiler rack and broil for 4 or 5 minutes on each side. Have four hot plates ready, laid with four slices of toast. Place 2 skewers on each; garnish with a sprig of parsley. Pour over each serving some of the maitre d'hotel butter and serve promptly.

SCALLOP STEW, SHOREHAM

1 pint milk	24 small Scallops
½ teaspoon salt	2 tablespoons freshly rolled
Dash of cayenne	pilot cracker crumbs
2 tablespoons butter	Slices of buttered toast

Heat the milk just to the boil, then add the salt and pepper and the butter. Put in the scallops and simmer slowly (do not boil) for 12 minutes. Thicken with the cracker crumbs, and pour over the pieces of toast laid in soup plates.

WHOLE FRESH SCALLOPS, BERMUDA

18 fresh Scallops, in their shells	2 tablespoons butter
2 tablespoons chopped mushrooms	1 cup Chablis (white wine)
2 tablespoons chopped shallots	½ cup fish stock
1 tablespoon fresh herbs	1 cup Hollandaise sauce (No. 16)

The fresh, whole scallops (of which we usually eat only the muscle) are to be opened; then *entire* scallop (body part and muscle) removed carefully. Throw away the black part and cut off the beards. Blanch these beards and then chop. Saute mushrooms, shallots and herbs in butter, and add to chopped beards. Simmer the familiar scallop muscle in the wine until they are tender; lift out. Then reduce the liquid by simmering; remove from fire, add the fish stock and very carefully the Hollandaise Sauce. To half of this sauce add the beard mixture; spread on the cleaned shells. On top of this lay the scallop muscles; spread with remaining sauce, and glaze under the broiler.

RAW SCALLOPS, CUTCHOQUE

36 Scallops	Lemon slices
Marinade	Salt
Cocktail sauce	

For 10 minutes let the washed scallops lie in a marinade consisting of 2 tablespoons of olive oil, ½ tablespoon tarragon vinegar, 1 tablespoon Chablis (or any dry white wine), 1 small sliced onion, 1 clove of garlic, 1 sprig parsley and ½ bay leaf. Then serve with oyster crackers and oyster cocktail sauce, or salt and lemon slices.

SCALLOPS AND MUSHROOMS, GLEN HEAD

2 tablespoons butter	¼ cup liquor drained from
4 tablespoons chopped	Scallops
onion	Salt, pepper, few grains
2 tablespoons flour	cayenne
1 cup cream	1 lb Bay Scallops
	1 cup mushrooms, sliced

Melt butter, add onion and fry 3 minutes. Blend in flour; gradually add cream and scallop liquor, stirring until smooth. Season. Add scallops and mushrooms. Turn mixture into buttered baking dish and bake 30 minutes in a moderate oven.

SCALLOP SOUP, MERRICK ROAD

1 quart Bay Scallops	6 peppercorns, bruised
4 cups milk	1 onion, chopped fine
Salt and pepper	2 tablespoons butter
Pinch of nutmeg	1 tablespoon flour
Pinch of ground clove	3 egg yolks, slightly beaten
½ bay leaf	

Clean the scallops, and chop fine one half of them, leaving the others whole. Scald the milk, add the chopped scallops, the seasonings, and the onion; cook gently for 20 minutes. Meanwhile bring the whole scallops to boil in just enough water to cover, boil 2 minutes, then drain. Blend together one tablespoon of the butter and the flour. Add carefully to the milk, stirring constantly until smooth. Bring just to a boil, take off the fire. Add the egg yolks one at a time, stirring constantly until mixture thickens. Beat in remaining tablespoon of butter. Add parboiled whole scallops. Serve on soup plates on each of which a toasted pilot cracker has been laid.

DEVILLED SCALLOPS, SEA BISCUIT

1 quart Bay or deep-sea Scallops
½ cup butter
½ teaspoon English mustard
2 tablespoons flour

¾ teaspoon salt
Pinch of cayenne
1 cup Grade A milk, hot
¼ cup bread crumbs
1 tablespoon melted butter

Chop the scallops into quite small pieces and heat slightly in their own liquor; drain. Beat the butter to a creamy consistency, blend into it the mustard, flour, salt and cayenne; add to the scallops. Pour the hot milk in gradually, stirring constantly until smooth. Arrange this mixture on scallop shells or in a shallow baking dish. Sprinkle over it the bread crumbs which have been mixed with the melted butter. Bake 20 minutes in moderate oven.

SCALLOPS, THERMIDOR

1 quart Scallops
½ cup flour
4 tablespoons butter
½ cup chili sauce
1 tablespoon parsley, minced

½ teaspoon dry English mustard
1 teaspoon sugar
½ teaspoon salt
⅛ teaspoon cayenne
1 teaspoon scraped onion
Boiled rice

Clean the scallops and dry thoroughly. Roll them in the flour, shaking off any excess flour. Melt the butter, but do not brown it, and fry the scallops in it by tossing them in the pan for 5 minutes over a hot flame. Then add the chili sauce, parsley, the mustard which has been blended with the sugar, salt, and cayenne, and the scraped onion. Cook together for 5 minutes, and serve on a hot plate inside a circle of boiled rice.

BAKED SCALLOPS, BOSSERT

2 tablespoons butter
3 shallots, chopped
1 cup Bay Scallops, diced
¼ cup Chablis (white wine)
3 mushrooms, diced
2 tablespoons chopped chives

Salt, pepper
½ cup cream
4 washed large hard shell clam shells
4 tablespoons Hollandaise sauce (No. 16)

Melt the butter in a saucepan, add the shallots, and cook until tender; add the scallops, stir, then add the wine, and simmer until nearly tender. Then add the mushrooms and chopped chives. Add the salt and pepper, and stir for 3 minutes, then add the cream, and let simmer slowly until scallops are thoroughly tender. Butter the clam shells, lay them on pan, and fill them with the mixture, cover with the Hollandaise Sauce, and put in hot oven to brown, not more than 6 minutes. Serve immediately.

SCALLOPS, FILIPPINI

1 pint Bay Scallops, chopped
4 tablespoons butter
2 onions, chopped
2 tablespoons flour
1 cup scallop liquor (or fish stock)
Pinch of salt, pepper, few grains cayenne

1 clove of garlic, crushed
½ cup fresh buttered bread crumbs
1 tablespoon chopped parsley
4 egg yolks, slightly beaten
Parsley sprigs

Cook the scallops for 10 minutes in two tablespoons of the butter, and then drain. Brown the onion in another saucepan with remaining butter, then blend in the flour; add the scallop liquor, or stock, stirring until smooth. Add the salt, pepper, cayenne, and cook for 5 minutes. Add the chopped scallops, garlic, bread crumbs, parsley. Remove from fire, carefully stir in egg yolks, beating constantly.

Let cool to nearly lukewarm. Then fill clean scallop shells with the mixture and sprinkle with buttered breadcrumbs. Brown in the oven for 5 minutes. Serve garnished with parsley sprigs.

SCALLOPS AU DIABLE

1 lb Bay Scallops	$\frac{1}{2}$ cup chili sauce
$\frac{1}{4}$ cup butter	1 teaspoon lemon juice
$\frac{1}{2}$ cup flour	Few drops onion juice
$\frac{1}{2}$ teaspoon dry mustard	1 tablespoon parsley, finely
Pinch of cayenne	minced
$\frac{1}{8}$ teaspoon salt	Boiled rice

Wash the scallops and dry thoroly. Melt the butter. Roll the scallops in the flour, shake off surplus flour and cook in the butter. Then blend in the dry mustard, cayenne, salt, chili sauce, lemon and onion juice, parsley. Cook for 5 minutes, and serve on a mound of rice.

SHRIMP AND SCALLOP LOAF, NORTHPORT

8 stale bread slices	1 tablespoon melted butter
2 cups milk	4 tomatoes, chopped fine
Salt, pepper, few grains of cayenne	$\frac{1}{2}$ cup celery, chopped
Nutmeg	Sprig thyme
80 raw Shrimps, shelled	1 bay leaf
20 Bay Scallops, halved	1 cup oyster liquor or clam broth
1 teaspoon parsley, minced	

Grate the crusts of the bread slices and set aside. Break the rest into bits, and moisten with the milk and season with salt, pepper, cayenne and nutmeg. Mix with 50 of the shrimp and all the scallops, and parsley. Bake 30 minutes in a moderate oven. Sprinkle with the grated crust and butter and serve this loaf in slices with a shrimp sauce, made as follows: boil the remaining 30 shrimp, mix with melted butter, the tomatoes, the celery, thyme and bay leaf. Let cook for 3 or 4 minutes, add 1 cup oyster liquor or clam broth. Heat thoroly and serve over the shrimp and scallop slices.

OYSTERS AND SCALLOPS, JAMBALAYA

1 lb Bay Scallops, chopped	1 cup canned tomatoes
24 Oysters	1 teaspoon salt, few grains
3 tablespoons butter	cayenne
1 onion, minced	$\frac{1}{2}$ chili pepper, minced
1 clove garlic, minced	2 cups rice, washed

Wash the scallops, put in water to cover; bring to a boil and drain thoroughly, reserving the liquor. Cook oysters in their own liquor for 4 or 5 minutes; drain thoroly, reserving liquor. Then fry the scallops and the oysters in the butter for just 2 minutes, add the onion and garlic and cook 5 minutes longer. Then add the tomatoes, seasoning, chili pepper and rice and mix well. Add the liquor drained from oysters and scallops, adding water if necessary to make 3 cups. Let simmer, covered, for 40 minutes, or until rice is tender. Serve from a soup tureen.

XII

A Grand Fish Miscellany

There are over 250 varieties of food fishes, and there are an average of 25 different ways of cooking a fish. Some fish can only be cooked in half a dozen ways, but others in literally hundreds of ways. So we may say that there is a possible total of about 6250 different fish dishes! This, we may calculate, is enough for *a different fish meal for every meal of the day for almost 20 years!*

Still one hears people say, "I get tired of fish too easily," as did one person interviewed in a recent survey on eating fish.

How very natural, fish cookery being what it is in most instances! Who wouldn't get tired of only a few *kinds* of fish, and only two or three *methods* of cookery! In this chapter is illustrated the remarkable scope of fish cookery, which certainly matches the varieties which meat has to offer, and (in the author's opinion) exceeds the range of meat in flavor and change of taste.

Not even the most ardent lover of fish dishes will fail to find here recipes he has never heard of before. Here are enough recipes to provide a new fish cookery sensation several times a week for almost a year. Sameness in the food served, or in the cookery method, is just as bad when the food is meat or potatoes as when it is fish. I shall never forget the sensation of adventure in dining I experienced when traveling abroad on the French Line for the first time. Potatoes were served at every one of the 27 meals I ate on board, but *not once* was the method of cooking them the same! I had not before known there were so many ways to prepare the simple potato. The French chef could, equally as readily, have taken just one fish (sole or flounder) and served it at every meal every day on a trip around the world, and still never exhausted the different ways of treating it!

This chapter is a general group of recipes of many kinds, for all kinds of fish which are taken out of the eastern sea.

FISH SPINACH NEST, À LA AIDA

2 lbs spinach, cooked and drained
2 lbs Fish fillets, poached
1 cup cooked or canned shrimp
½ pint medium-sized oysters

6 mushrooms, broiled
Salt, pepper
1 pint Sauce Supreme (No. 31)
½ cup grated cheese

Lay the spinach on the bottom of a buttered baking dish, and put the fillets on top of the spinach. Arrange the shrimps in a row around the edge, then, inside of this a row of oysters, then the mushrooms in the center. Cover with the sauce, sprinkle with cheese, and brown under the broiler.

ROE SURPRISE, FREEPORT

½ lb fish Roe
1 egg
3 eggs, hard-cooked and sliced
1 cup cooked fish
1 tablespoon lemon juice
1 cup mashed potatoes

½ cup melted butter
1 teaspoon minced parsley
1 teaspoon minced celery
1 teaspoon minced green peppers
2 teaspoons minced onion
Salt, pepper

Parboil the roe, skin and dry. Mix it with the raw egg, and the yolks of the hard-boiled eggs, and the cooked flaked fish; season with lemon juice. Butter a deep baking dish and put in a layer of potatoes, then alternate layers of the fish mixture, and the sliced egg whites and the potato, and moisten with butter. Sprinkle each layer with the parsley, celery, pepper, onion, seasonings. Cover and bake in a hot oven (400° F.) for 20 minutes. Then uncover and brown for about 5 minutes more.

FISH SCRAPPLE, MINEOLA

2 cups cornmeal	6 cups boiling water
1 cup cold water	3 teaspoons salt
1 teaspoon onion, minced	1 cup cooked Fish

Mix well the cornmeal, onion and cold water, then add it to the boiling, salted water. Cook in a double boiler for 1½ hours. Then add the fish and continue cooking for 30 minutes more. Line a baking pan with oiled paper. Pack the mixture in this pan and let cool; covering to prevent crust forming. When ready to use, slice into half-inch slices and fry brown on both sides.

GRILLED PICKLED MACKEREL, CRANE NECK

2 or 3 Mackerel	1 cup water
2 tablespoons tarragon vine-gar	½ cup flour
1 teaspoon chopped onion (or shallot)	1 tablespoon lemon juice
Thyme, parsley, few bruised peppercorns	Orange (or Cranberry) Sauce (No. 19)

Clean, wash, bone and split the mackerel. Let them stand for one hour in a pickling mixture composed of the vinegar, onions and seasonings, and 1 cup water. Then lift out, sprinkle with flour and broil until tender. Sprinkle with lemon juice, and serve with an Orange or Cranberry Sauce.

STRIPED BASS, SHEEPSHEAD BAY

3 lbs Striped Bass fillet	2 cups crab meat
Salt, pepper	Mornay Sauce (No. 7)
1 teaspoon shallots, chopped	4 strips pimento
2 tablespoons butter	5 capers

Rub fillet with salt and pepper. Cook shallots in butter until tender and arrange on the bottom of a buttered baking dish, with the crab meat. Then lay the fillets over this and cover with Mornay Sauce. Lay strips of pimento crisscross over the fish, and place washed capers on the open spaces. Bake in a hot oven for 25-30 minutes.

STRIPED BASS AU GRATIN, PIPING ROCK

3 lbs Striped Bass fillets	1 tablespoon butter
$\frac{1}{2}$ cup seasoned flour	$\frac{1}{4}$ cup bread crumbs
1 teaspoon chopped parsley	$\frac{1}{4}$ cup grated American
1 teaspoon chopped onion	cheese
$\frac{1}{2}$ cup fish stock	1 tablespoon melted butter

Roll fillets in flour. Lay them in a buttered baking dish which has been sprinkled with the parsley and onion mixed. Add the fish stock (made from the trimmings of the fish, including the head). Dot with butter and cover with the bread crumbs and cheese. Sprinkle with the melted butter, cover the dish with buttered paper and bake in a hot oven for 15 minutes. Remove the paper and bake for 5 minutes more. Serve from baking dish.

BROILED MACKEREL, HAUPPAGE

1 Mackerel	Anchovy butter
Salt and pepper	Lemon quarters
1 tablespoon butter	

Split the mackerel for broiling, place in a broiling pan, sprinkle with salt and pepper and dot with a little butter. Broil for 20 minutes until browned, basting occasionally.

Remove to a hot platter, spread the anchovy butter over it, and garnish with lemon.

BROILED SPICED MACKEREL, SHINNECOCK

3½ lbs Mackerel
10 crushed peppercorns
 1 yellow onion, chopped
1½ tablespoons salt

 1 sprig dill
1½ cups wine vinegar
 2 tablespoons butter

Fillet the mackerel and remove the bones. Lay half the fillets in a deep baking dish, sprinkle over them half the peppercorns, onion, salt and dill; lay the other half of the fillets on top, add the other half of the seasonings; pour on the vinegar. Cover the baking dish and let stand over night. The next day lift out the fillets, and wipe off. Broil. Reduce the seasoned vinegar over a hot fire. Pour the drippings from the broiling pan into the vinegar, add butter and use as a sauce over the fillets. Serve with spinach and mashed potatoes.

ANCHOVY-COD, HAMPTON BAY

3½ or 4 lbs small Cod (or haddock), filleted
Juice of 1 lemon
 1 tablespoon salt
 6 or 8 anchovies
 1 egg, beaten with 1 table-spoon cold water

 ½ cup sifted breadcrumbs
1½ tablespoons flour
 2 tablespoons butter
 ½ cup fish stock
 ½ cup light cream

Cut fillets in half if too large. Then sprinkle with lemon juice and let stand one hour. Then rub with salt, and on each fillet piece lay one or two cleaned boneless fillets of anchovies, and roll the fillet and anchovies together into rolls with small skewers or toothpicks. Dip them in the beaten egg, and then roll in the bread crumbs which have been mixed with the flour. Brown some butter in a baking pan, lay in the fish rolls, baste with butter and bake in a hot oven (450° F.) for 25 minutes. When browned, baste frequently with both the pan juice and with the cream mixed with fish stock. Serve on warm platter; and heat the pan gravy, season, thicken if desired, and serve over the fish rolls.

FISH HASH, OYSTER BAY

2 cups cold Fish, flaked	Salt, pepper
2 cups cold boiled potatoes, chopped	Pinch of cayenne
	1 (2-inch) cube salt pork
1 tablespoon minced onion	

Mix the fish and potato, onion and seasonings. Fry the fat out of the salt pork, take out pork, put the potato-fish mixture in the pan with the fat. Fry until brown, and fold like an omelet.

WEAKFISH FRIES, SPEONK

8 or 10 Weakfish	Fritter batter
Salt and pepper	Parsley, deep-fried

Trim fillets from the weakfish carefully; remove the skin, rub with salt and pepper and let stand several hours. Meanwhile prepare a fritter batter as follows: sift one cup flour with $\frac{1}{2}$ teaspoon salt, then add to it a beaten egg with $\frac{3}{4}$ cup of water; and beat until smooth. Wipe the fish fillets thoroly, and roll in the batter, twisting each fillet like a spiral. Drop in hot fat at 375° F., and turn it with a perforated spoon. Fry to golden brown, cooking only a few fillets at a time. Drain on double sheets of absorbent paper on a hot platter. Wash and dry well some large sprays of parsley, and immerse in the frying fat with a wire basket, for just a few *seconds*. The parsley must hold its green color.

BAKED SEA BASS, COPIAGUE

1 3½- or 4-lb Bluefish
Salt
1 can sardines
3 tablespoons butter
1 cup Chablis (white wine)

1 slice onion
1 teaspoon minced parsley
½ cup bread crumbs
2 egg yolks, slightly beaten

Clean and wash the fish, leaving the head on. Rub with salt and let stand for one hour. Then wipe thoroly, and cut 3 or 4 gashes diagonally across each side. Into these gashes fill a paste made by blending crushed sardines and the butter. Then put the fish in a buttered pyrex baking dish, spread more of the sardine mixture across the top. Add to the pan the wine, onion and parsley. Sprinkle on the bread crumbs and bake in fairly hot oven (400° F.) for 35 minutes or more until tender. Baste occasionally with the wine. Lift out the fish and put on hot platter. Pour the pan gravy into the egg yolks, stirring constantly. Return to low heat and beat constantly just until mixture thickens. Remove from heat immediately and pour over the fish.

STRIPED BASS, FLORENTINE

1 Striped Bass (or Halibut or other fish), filleted
4 tablespoons butter
1½ lbs spinach

Salt, pepper
Sauce Mornay (No. 7)
¼ cup grated cheese

Cook fillets in butter until tender. Wash the spinach thoroly, remove stems. Cook 5 minutes with no additional water. Drain thoroly. Saute spinach in butter, season with salt and pepper. Spread spinach in the bottom of a buttered baking dish, lay the fillets on top. Cover with Sauce Mornay. Sprinkle with grated cheese and brown in hot oven.

BONITO SOUFFLÉ JERICHO

3 eggs, separated
2½ cups flaked cooked Bo-
   nito
½ cup soft bread crumbs
1 tablespoon melted shortening

1 teaspoon salt
⅛ teaspoon pepper
1 tablespoon minced pars-
   ley
Caper Sauce

Beat the egg yolks until thick and lemon-colored. Flake the fish, add it with the remaining ingredients to the egg yolks. Beat the egg whites until stiff and fold into fish mixture. Transfer to a greased baking pan and bake in a slow oven (300° F.) about 1 hour. Serve with Caper Sauce.

KINGFISH, STONY BROOK

3 or 4 Kingfish
Salt, pepper

½ cup Chablis (white wine)
Creole Sauce (No. 34)

Clean and dry the Kingfish, rub with salt and pepper. Place in buttered baking dish, add the wine and bake for 20 minutes or until tender. Cover with Creole Sauce and serve.

BOILED WEAKFISH, LONG BEACH

1 celery root, chopped
1 onion, chopped
1 sprig parsley
3 good-sized Weakfish
Water
1 teaspoon vinegar
2 eggs, hard-cooked

1 cup sweet cream
2 tablespoons flour
2 tablespoons cold milk
1 dozen blanched almonds
1 tablespoon chopped parsley

Place celery root, onion and parsley in a kettle. Wrap the fish in cheesecloth or parchment and lay it on the vegetables. Pour in enough boiling water to cover and add vinegar (the vinegar keeps the fish firm). Simmer just below the boiling point until tender, allowing 6-8 minutes to the lb. In the meantime hard-cook two eggs. Drain fish and lay on a hot platter and prepare the following sauce: Heat sweet cream in a saucepan. Blend flour with cold milk; add to cream, stirring until smooth. Boil about one minute, stirring constantly; pour over the fish. Stick almonds into the fish, points up. Shell the hard-cooked eggs, chop the whites and yolks separately; garnish the fish, first with a row of chopped yolks, then of whites, until all are used; lay chopped parsley all around the platter.

CRANBERRY-STUFFED MACKEREL, DUCK POND POINT

2 Mackerel
½ lb Cranberries
4 tablespoons bread crumbs
4 tablespoons butter

1 teaspoon anchovy paste
Salt, few grains pepper
Cayenne

Clean and wash the mackerel, bone and split in two. Chop the cranberries, and add the bread crumbs, butter, anchovy paste and seasonings. Stuff each mackerel with this mixture, wrap the fish in greased paper, and bake in a buttered baking dish for 30 minutes. Remove the paper carefully and serve.

(This dish is an adaptation of an English dish, in which green gooseberries are used instead of the cranberries. Gooseberries are not often in the market in the U. S.; use them if obtainable. An additional variation that is rather delightful is Diced Grapefruit in place of cranberries.)

SEA FOOD RISOTTO, ITALIENNE

Seafood miscellany: 1 boiled lobster, ½ lb raw shrimp, 15 mussels, 15 clams, 2½ lbs fish of any kind
2 teaspoons salt

½ onion, chopped
½ clove garlic
1 tablespoon olive oil
2 cups brown rice

Pick meat from lobster, leaving pieces as whole as possible. Shuck raw shrimp. Steam mussels and clams and remove from shells; reserve broth. Fillet fish. Put into a pot, with cold water to cover, the lobster claws and shells, shrimp shells, mussel shells and the heads, tails, bones, skin of fish. Add salt; simmer 45 minutes to make fish stock. Fry the chopped onion and garlic in the olive oil, then add the rice, and cook for 5 minutes, stirring quite frequently. Then add a pint of the strained fish stock and the reserved mussel and clam liquor. Stir well, and continue to add more fish stock as needed, until the rice is cooked and tender; about 45 minutes. Wipe dry the fish fillets, the shrimp, lobster pieces, mussels, etc., then roll each in flour and fry brown in hot olive oil. Serve on top of a platter of the rice.

WEAKFISH WITH EGG SAUCE, PECONIC

3 large Weakfish	1 lemon, quartered
Juice of 1 lemon	Potato Balls
Salt, pepper	Egg Sauce (No. 13)
4 sprigs parsley	

Clean, wash and dry each fish thoroly, then rub with the lemon juice. Wrap in cheese cloth or cooking parchment. Drop into a kettle of actively boiling water. Cover, reduce heat, and let simmer for 15 minutes. Then take out, remove wrappings, and arrange on a hot platter, season with parsley, lemon quarters and potato balls. Serve with it Egg Sauce.

WEAKFISH, FISHERMAN'S SPECIAL

12 small Weakfish	2 tablespoons parsley, chopped
Salt and pepper	Juice of 1 lemon
2 tablespoons anchovy butter	

Clean the fish, slash the back from head to tail, dry thoroly, rub with pepper and salt, and lay in a hot buttered baking dish. Lay on top of each fish a small piece of anchovy butter, sprinkle with 1 tablespoon of the parsley, and then put in the oven, cover with buttered paper. Bake for 25 minutes in a hot oven (400° F.), basting frequently. Take out and squeeze the lemon juice over the fish, and sprinkle the other tablespoon of parsley. Serve with string beans and French fried potatoes.

GRILLED WEAKFISH, GARDINER'S BAY

6 Weakfish
2 tablespoons tarragon vinegar
2 tablespoons olive or peanut oil
¼ teaspoon freshly ground black pepper

½ teaspoon salt
Sour gherkins
2 sprigs parsley
1 lemon, quartered
Drawn butter sauce (No. 9)

Clean and wash the fish, dry thoroly. Rub with vinegar, then roll in the oil into which have been mixed the pepper and salt. Then place on a well greased broiler rack and broil slowly, turning frequently and basting with the oil. Serve on hot platter, garnished with the gherkins, parsley and lemon, and some Drawn Butter Sauce.

STRIPED BASS, MONTAUK LIGHTHOUSE

2 onions, sliced
2 green peppers, finely sliced
½ cup olive oil
4 cloves garlic, halved
2 cups claret
1 dozen sliced fresh mushrooms
6 peeled, sliced tomatoes

½ can sliced pimentos
5 lbs Striped Bass fillets
Salt, pepper, paprika
8 slices bread
2 tablespoons additional olive oil
1 tablespoon chopped parsley

Fry the onions and the peppers in the olive oil. Then add 3 cloves of the garlic and let stand in the oil for a few moments. Add the claret, the mushrooms, the tomatoes, the pimentos, and bring to a boil. Then put in the bass fillets, season with salt, pepper, paprika; cover and let simmer for 30 minutes. Fry eight slices of bread in 2 additional tablespoons of hot oil; remove from pan and rub the bread slices with remaining clove of garlic. Lay bread in a deep platter and put the fish on it; pouring over it the sauce, and garnish with the parsley.

SPANISH MACKEREL, MONTEBELLO

6 Mackerel fillets
Salt, pepper, few grains cayenne

Sauce Béarnaise Tomatée
Potato Balls

Wash and dry the mackerel fillets thoroly, rub with salt and cayenne. Lay them in a buttered baking dish, cover with buttered paper. Bake in a moderate oven until tender. Arrange on a platter with potato balls, dress fish with Béarnaise Sauce Tomatée made as follows: Put in a saucepan 6 finely chopped shallots, a good pinch of white pepper, $\frac{1}{4}$ cup tarragon vinegar. Reduce over a hot fire to 3 tablespoons. Put the saucepan over hot water, stir in 5 beaten egg yolks. Add $1\frac{1}{2}$ cups of sweet butter, cut into pieces, stirring constantly, until the sauce becomes thick. Remove from heat immediately. Add teaspoon of meat extract, some chopped fresh tarragon leaves, a little cayenne pepper and 4 tablespoons thick purée of tomato.

STRIPED BASS, MONTAUK POINT

1 large Striped Bass
Cold water
1 tablespoon salt
2 lemons, sliced
1 small piece ginger root
1 onion, sliced

1 bouquet garni
Potato balls
Soy sauce
Lemon slices
Parsley
Indian Soy Sauce

Put the washed and cleaned bass into a kettle, head and tail left on. Cover with cold water, add the salt, the lemons, the ginger root, the onion, the garni. Bring to a boil, and cook just below the boiling point for 20 minutes. Lift out carefully, serve on a platter. Garnish with potato balls and parsley, and lemon halves.

The Indian Soy Sauce (served separately) is made by cooking two tablespoons of butter with two chopped shallots until tender; then adding 3 tablespoons of flour, 1 cup scalded milk, $\frac{1}{4}$ cup of bottled Soy Sauce; also $\frac{1}{2}$ teaspoon salt and a few grains of cayenne. Cook for 2 minutes, then add 1 cup of thick cream and the juice of 1 lemon.

MACKEREL, SOUTHAMPTON

3 Mackerel	3 sprigs fennel
Chablis Courtbouillon	3 sprigs parsley
12 bruised peppercorns	1 lemon quartered

Clean and dress the mackerel, removing heads and tails. Dry thoroly and cut into $3\frac{1}{2}$- or 4-inch pieces. Cook in Chablis Courtbouillon made as follows: place in the cooking kettle with the fish, 1 quart cold water, 2 tablespoons salt, 2 sliced carrots, 2 onions, sliced, 5 thyme leaves, small bouquet garni, and add 1 bottle Chablis. Allow 6 to 10 minutes to the pound. Just before fish is tender, add the bruised peppercorns then the sprigs of fennel. Lift to hot platter, garnish with parsley and lemon quarters; serve with boiled potatoes.

FISH MESS, NORTH SHORE

½ cup olive oil
2 onions, chopped fine
2 leeks (white parts), chopped fine
1 full bottle Chablis (white wine)
1½ teaspoon salt
½ teaspoon pepper
1 pinch saffron
1 bouquet garni
4 tomatoes, peeled, crushed
2 cloves garlic
1 tablespoon chopped parsley
2 flounders
3 weakfish
2 eels
2 small snappers
2 small bluefish
12 mussels
12 oysters
12 hard shell clams
2 tablespoons butter

In a large saucepan mix ¼ cup olive oil, the onion and leeks. Cook, just until tender and golden but not brown. Add the wine, then a teaspoon of salt and add the pepper, the saffron, the garni, the tomatoes, the garlic and parsley. Bring to a boil, then let simmer for 20 minutes.

Cut the fish meanwhile into two-inch pieces. Steam open the mussels, oysters and clams, and shell; but place 6 clam shells and 6 mussel shells in the fish mixture. Cook the fish separately in a deep frying pan with remaining ¼ cup olive oil, for 5 minutes, shaking the pan occasionally. Turn the fish into the other pot containing the onions and wine and cook for 10 minutes. Take off the fire, add butter and remaining salt, stirring meanwhile; let stand for a few minutes. Then lift out the fish on a big hot platter, together with half a cup of the liquid. Serve the rest of the liquid (including the clam and mussel shells) from a soup tureen, ladling it onto soup plates with pilot crackers on the bottom; give one or two shells to each portion. Serve fresh cucumber pickles with this meal.

The variety used in this recipe may be altered according to supply available; there should be about 1 pound of fish for each person, and there should be about the same amount of each kind of fish.

SEA PLATE, SOUTHERN PARKWAY

1½ lbs Striped Bass fillets
¼ cup Chablis (white wine)
¾ cup fish broth
1 scallion, minced
Salt, pepper

4 tablespoons butter
12 clams or oysters
3 mushrooms, chopped
1 tablespoon flour
½ cup lobster meat, diced

Butter a baking dish and arrange the fish fillets on the bottom. Pour in the wine, then the fish broth (made by boiling the head, tail and trimmings of the fish). Sprinkle with the scallion, salt and pepper. Dot with 2 tablespoons of the butter. Cover tight and bake until tender. Bring the oysters and clams to a boil in their own liquor. Drain. Brown the mushrooms in remaining butter, blend in the flour, thin with ½ cup of the clam or oyster liquor; season and boil 5 minutes. Add the lobster meat and bring again to a boil. Pour this sauce over the fish in the baking dish and serve.

FLOUNDER-LOBSTER JELLY, FOREST HILLS

1 lb fillet of Flounder
3 small Lobsters
3 tablespoons gelatin

1 tablespoon vinegar
3 hard-cooked eggs
Salt, pepper

Wipe fish and cook in simmering water to generously cover until done, about 10 minutes. Cool in stock. Plunge lobsters in boiling salted water and cook 20 minutes. Plunge into cold water. Remove and split down center front. Cut off heads, saving for garnish. Remove meat in as large pieces as possible. Place cold fillets, carefully drained, on a cold platter and arrange lobster meat around them attractively. If the lobster has coral, dice it and sprinkle over fish. Heat 2 cups of the water in which flounder was cooked and soften 1 tablespoon gelatin in 2 tablespoons cold water and dissolve in hot fish stock. Add 1 teaspoon vinegar, salt and pepper to taste and the chopped white of 1 hard cooked egg. Pour over fish on platter and chill until firm.

Soften remaining gelatin in $\frac{1}{2}$ cup cold water and dissolve in remaining fish stock, heated to boiling with enough boiling water added to make 1 quart. Add remaining vinegar and seasoning to taste. Chill until slightly thickened and then stir in the chopped whites of the two remaining hard cooked eggs. Pour into a pan and chill until firm. Cut in squares and place on rim of platter around fish. Garnish with lobster heads. Approximate yield: 6 portions.

FISH MIT SAUERKRAUT, YAPHANK

2 lbs striped bass, cod, halibut or any white, firm-fleshed fish	3 tablespoons butter
	2 tablespoons flour
	2 tablespoons chopped ham
2 carrots, sliced	$\frac{1}{2}$ cup sour cream
2 onions, sliced	$\frac{1}{4}$ cup grated Parmesan
Salt, pepper	cheese
$2\frac{1}{4}$ lbs sauerkraut	

Clean and wash the fish, removing skin and bone. Place the heads, tails, skin, bones, etc., in a kettle with the carrots and one onion; season with salt and pepper, and add water to cover. Simmer just below boiling point for 30 minutes. Boil the sauerkraut, drain thoroly. Melt the butter, stir in the flour until slightly browned, then add the remaining onion, the ham, 1 cup of the broth made from the fish trimmings, and the sour cream. Mix well and let simmer. Then butter a baking dish, place a layer of sauerkraut in it, a layer of the fish, then some of the sour cream sauce, then more sauerkraut, then more fish and sauce. Sprinkle with the cheese, put in a moderate oven for 30 to 40 minutes, until fish is tender.

LEMON FISH, OCEANSIDE

1½ lbs striped bass, cod, hali-
    but or any white, firm-
    fleshed fish
3 tablespoons cooking fat
5 onions, finely sliced
Salt, pepper
½ cup sour cream

Juice of 1 lemon
1 teaspoon grated lemon
    peel
1 teaspoon parsley, minced
3 tablespoons capers,
    chopped

Clean and wash the fish, cut into 2- or 2½-inch lengths; take out bones. Melt fat in a frying pan, and cook the onions in it until lightly browned. Add the fish, season with salt and pepper. Stir in the sour cream, then the lemon juice, the lemon peel, the parsley, the capers. Simmer 20 minutes and serve hot.

FISH GOULASH, LYNBROOK

1½ lbs striped bass, cod, hali-
    but, or other white, firm-
    fleshed fish
3 cups cold water
7 onions, sliced
5 tablespoons butter or
    other fat

Salt, pepper, few grains of
    cayenne
1½ tablespoons paprika
Boiled rice, noodles or
    macaroni

Clean the fish, cut into 2- or 3-inch lengths and remove bones. Prepare fish stock by boiling for 25 minutes the heads, tails and trimmings of the fish in 3 cups cold water with a few slices of the onion. Melt fat in a frying pan and fry the remaining onions until brown. Add the fish, sprinkle with salt, pepper, cayenne, paprika and enough of prepared fish stock to cover. Let simmer 25 minutes without stirring. Add more stock if necessary for serving. Serve boiled rice with it, or noodles or macaroni.

MACKEREL, HORSERADISH, BELMONT TRACK

1 Mackerel	2 tablespoons grated horse-
6 boiled potatoes	radish
1 tablespoon butter	1 tablespoon tarragon vine-
1 tablespoon flour (scant)	gar
½ pint sour cream	Salt, pepper

Wash and clean mackerel, leaving head and tail on. Wrap in cheesecloth, lower into boiling water and simmer just below boiling point, allowing 6 to 8 minutes to the pound. Serve with boiled potatoes, and horseradish sauce (No. 12) or as follows: Melt the butter, blend in with the flour, then stir in the sour cream, the horseradish, the vinegar, salt, pepper. Stir well and let simmer for 5 minutes.

FISH À LA KING

½ cup green pepper, minced	1 cup milk or part stock
½ cup celery, minced	Salt and pepper
1 tablespoon pimento, minced	2 cups cooked or smoked fish, flaked, or shellfish
2 tablespoons butter	Toast
2 tablespoons flour	

Simmer green pepper, celery and pimento in butter until tender. Add flour, then stir in milk, gradually. Season and add fish. Heat thoroly and serve on toast.

BAKED SOUR CREAM FISH, MECOX BAY

1 3-lb haddock or cod	¼ cup Parmesan cheese, grated
Salt, pepper	
¼ lb bacon strips	1 pint sour cream
2 tablespoons butter	2 tablespoons flour

Clean and wash the fish, dry thoroly. Remove skin. Rub flesh with salt and pepper. Cut the bacon into long thin strips, and thread them through the surface of the fish with a larding needle. Place in a baking dish, dot with the butter, sprinkle with the grated cheese, and pour in one cup of the sour cream. Bake for 20 minutes in a moderate oven, basting frequently. Add the second cup of sour cream and cook about 10 minutes more. Thicken the pan gravy with the flour and cook 5 minutes. Serve with parsley boiled potatoes.

MADRAS FISH, GOWANUS BAY

1 lb haddock fillets
2 tablespoons butter
1 onion, minced
2 tablespoons flour
1 teaspoon ground ginger

1 diced red pepper (or $\frac{1}{8}$ teaspoon cayenne pepper)
Pinch turmeric
2 cups milk
Juice of 1 lemon
Boiled rice

Fry the fillets in the butter, then keep warm. Add the onion to the butter, blend in the flour, ginger, cayenne and turmeric. Cook for 2 or 3 minutes. Then add the milk. Let simmer for 5 minutes. Put in the fish and let simmer for 12 to 15 minutes more. Add the lemon juice, mix well; and serve with boiled rice.

BLACKFISH, NAPEAGUE BAY

1 Blackfish
1 cup milk
Salt and white pepper
1 cup flour

Tartare Sauce (No. 1)
4 sprigs parsley
1 lemon, quartered

Fillet the fish and then cut the fillets into long strips about $\frac{1}{2}$-inch wide. Wash and dry thoroly. Dip them in the milk, to which have been added salt and pepper, then roll them in flour. Using the wire basket of a deep-fat fryer, dip the fish strips into boiling hot fat (375° F.) for about 3 minutes. Then drain on absorbent paper. Place on hot platter and cover with a napkin, and when ready serve with Tartare Sauce and parsley and lemon quarters.

BAKED BLACKFISH, ORIENT HARBOR

1 Blackfish	3 slices onion
Salt, pepper	1 sprig parsley
4 tablespoons butter	1 pint milk
1 bay leaf	2 tablespoons flour
1 crushed clove	

Clean fish, cut off head and tail; wash and dry, and rub with salt and pepper. Butter a baking dish, lay in fish and dot with half of the butter; add the bay leaf, clove, onion slices and parsley. Pour in the cold milk, and bake in hot oven 10 minutes to the pound. Place fish on a hot platter, keep hot. Melt remaining butter in saucepan, blend in flour; add milk from baking dish, stirring constantly. Cook 5 minutes, adjust seasonings. Serve separately with fish.

BROILED BLUEFISH, MUSSEL SAUCE, MORICHES

1 3-lb bluefish	4 sprigs parsley
½ cup melted butter	Mussel Sauce (No. 8)
1 lemon quartered	

Clean the fish, split open from the back and remove the large bone, wash and dry. Roll in melted butter, and then broil, turning often and basting with melted butter. Serve with Mussel (or Oyster) Sauce, and French fried potatoes.

SNAPPERS AU GRATIN, SEATUCK COVE

6 or 8 young Bluefish ("Snappers")	1 can mushrooms
1 teaspoon shallots, chopped	3 tablespoons Chablis (white wine)
1 teaspoon parsley, minced	½ cup bread crumbs
1 teaspoon flour	2 teaspoons melted butter
1¼ cups water	

Clean and fillet the fish and place them in a buttered baking dish. Make a fish stock from the fish trimmings, heads and all, and add the shallots, parsley and flour, and the water, bring to a boil, then let simmer for 10 minutes. Then strain it and pour over the fish. Put the mushrooms over the fish and the white wine and bread crumbs, and melted butter. Cover the dish with buttered paper and bake at 350° F. for 20 minutes. Remove the paper then and cook until brown. Sprinkle a little lemon juice and minced parsley over it and serve with potatoes.

BAKED SNAPPER, PLUM ISLAND

6 or 8 young Bluefish ("snappers")	2 cups Creole Sauce (No. 34)
	Salt, pepper
	½ cup bread crumbs

Clean and dry the fish, lay in buttered baking dish, add the Creole Sauce, and bake for 20 minutes at 350° F., with buttered paper over the dish. Then remove the paper, sprinkle seasonings and bread crumbs over it, and cook for 15 minutes more. Serve from the casserole.

BAKED FRESH TUNA STEAK, FRANCIS LOW

6 slices fresh Tuna	4 tablespoons butter
Salt, pepper	4 teaspoons tomato puree
Nutmeg, grated	Juice of 1 lemon
1½ cups fish stock or clam broth	3 sprigs parsley

Salt and pepper the tuna slices and sprinkle with a little nutmeg. Lay in a buttered baking dish, and then add the fish stock or clam broth. Cover with buttered paper and bake in moderate oven (350° F.) for 30 minutes, frequently basting. Take paper off and cook 5 minutes longer. Take fish out and put on hot platter; meanwhile transfer the liquor to a saucepan and reduce over a hot fire; then add slowly the butter, the tomato. Adjust the seasoning, add the lemon juice, and pour this sauce over the fish. Garnish with the parsley.

(Francis Low is the man who holds the U. S. record for tuna fishing, having caught a 705-pounder off Rockaway Beach).

SEA-STUFFED EGGS, ROSLYN

1 cup cooked lobster	½ teaspoon pepper
1 cup cooked crabmeat	½ teaspoon paprika
½ cup cooked chopped shrimp	½ teaspoon mustard
½ cup oysters, chopped	1 teaspoon worcestershire sauce
1 egg, beaten	12 hard-cooked eggs, hot
2 tablespoons cream	Toast
1 teaspoon salt	Lobster Sauce (No. 15)

Mix the lobster, crabmeat, shrimp, oysters, together with the beaten egg and cream, and seasonings. Cut the boiled eggs in half, take out the yolks and refill with the seafood mixture. Place in a pan under a broiler for a few minutes. Serve on thin toast slices in a small deep dish, with Lobster Sauce.

GRILLED YOUNG MACKEREL, ORIENT POINT

3 tablespoons olive oil	4 young small Mackerel, filleted
1 tablespoon onion juice	
Juice of ½ lemon	1 teaspoon minced parsley
½ teaspoon Maggi Sauce	

Prepare a marinade by mixing the olive oil, onion juice, lemon juice, Maggi sauce. Split the mackerel the entire length; remove backbones. Wash and dry the fillets and lay in a shallow dish; pour the marinating liquid over them; let stand for 3 hours, turning occasionally.

Lift out fillets, and broil. To serve, sprinkle with parsley and pour over them the heated marinating liquor.

FISH, YAPHANK

1 large fish (about 6 lbs)
½ lemon
Salt, pepper, paprika
1 clove garlic, mashed
1 onion, minced

1 tablespoon worcestershire sauce
1 teaspoon Maggi Sauce
1 tablespoon A-1 Sauce

Grease a deep baking pan with plenty of butter. Rub the fish well with lemon, salt and pepper, and place in a baking dish. Place the other ingredients over the fish. Bake in moderate oven, allowing 12 minutes for each pound of fish. Baste frequently.

FISH-BANANA FRY, WADING RIVER

5 lbs Long Island flounder, filleted
1 cup milk
½ cup flour
5 tablespoons butter or peanut oil

3 bananas
1 lemon
½ teaspoon minced parsley
Paprika, salt, pepper

Cut fillets into long strips. Dip these strips in milk, roll in seasoned flour; fry in the butter or oil. When tender remove from pan and keep hot. Cut the bananas into thin strips (halves or thirds) and fry in the same butter or oil. When done, take out the bananas, squeeze juice of ½ lemon into the fat and let cook for a minute. Pour this sizzling fat over the fish and banana strips. Garnish with the minced parsley, thin slices of lemon (or lime), and paprika.

COLD SPICED MACKEREL, PINELAWN

1 lb Mackerel
Cold water
1 teaspoon salt
6 whole allspice

3 bay leaves
1 onion, sliced
Watercress

Clean and wash the mackerel, and fillet it. Place in a saucepan with cold water to cover, adding the salt, allspice, bay leaves, onion. Let simmer for 10 minutes or until tender. Turn with its liquor into a covered dish; chill in refrigerator. Serve ice cold, garnished with watercress. Horseradish or Mustard Sauce go well with it (Nos. 12 or 17).

FRESH TUNA FISH STEAK, PORTUGUESE

6 Tuna fish steak slices	Salt, pepper
$\frac{1}{2}$ onion, chopped	2 cups fish stock or clam
1 cup stewed tomatoes	broth
1 tablespoon butter	$\frac{1}{2}$ cup Chablis (white wine)

Lay the steaks in a frying pan together with the onion, tomatoes, butter, salt, pepper. Fry lightly, add half the fish stock or clam bouillon; cover the pan and let simmer for 25 minutes. Then add the wine, more fish stock, and let simmer for 25 minutes more. Serve with the sauce in a separate dish.

SEA BASS, OYSTER SAUCE, ROCK POINT

2 lbs Sea Bass or similar fish	$1\frac{1}{2}$ tablespoons flour
	2 tablespoons bread crumbs
$1\frac{1}{2}$ tablespoons lemon juice	Salt, pepper, few grains of
1 cup Chablis (white wine)	cayenne, few grains of nutmeg
1 cup water (approx.)	12 oysters
2 tablespoons butter	1 lemon sliced

Clean and wash the fish, dry thoroly. Rub with 1 tablespoon lemon juice, and let stand for one hour. Then simmer until tender, about 25 minutes, in the white wine and water enough just to cover. Melt the butter, add flour, crumbs and seasonings. Add $\frac{3}{4}$ cup liquor in which fish was cooked and any liquor drained from oysters, and remaining lemon juice. Cook the oysters in this sauce for 3 or 4 minutes. Pour sauce over the fish, garnish with lemon slices.

FRIED OYSTER-CRABS AND WHITEBAIT, MEADOWBROOK

1 pint Oyster-Crabs	½ cup cracker dust
1 lb Northern Whitebait	Salt
½ cup flour	Pepper
1 cup cold milk	

Wash the oyster-crabs and whitebait, dry carefully. Then toss them gently together in a paper bag containing the flour, then in cold milk, then in cracker dust. Fry in fat for no more than two minutes; if very small, only *one* minute. Serve heaped together on a plate, garnished with parsley, sprinkling a little salt and a very small amount of pepper on them. Serve very hot. This dish should be prepared immediately before eating.

BLUEFISH, BUSTANOBY

1 3-lb Bluefish	Pinch salt, pepper
3 tablespoons mushroom liquor	3 tablespoons tomato sauce
½ glass Chablis (white wine)	1 tablespoon cooked smoked beef tongue, finely minced

Clean the bluefish, score each side with a slanting cut, wipe dry. Place in a buttered baking dish. Add the mushroom liquor, the wine, and season. Cover the dish with buttered paper; cook 30 minutes in moderately hot oven (375° F.) Lay the fish on a hot plate and keep hot. Pour the sauce from baking dish into a saucepan, add the tomato sauce and the tongue, and boil for 2 minutes. Pour sauce over the fish and serve.

PAN-FRIED BUTTERFISH, KINGS PARK

6 Butterfish	½ cup flour
1 teaspoon salt	Olive oil
1 cup milk	

Clean and wash the fish and dry thoroly. Dissolve salt in milk. Dip the fish in the milk. Roll lightly in the flour and fry in olive oil.

YOUNG MACKEREL WITH LEEKS, OZONE PARK

6 fillets young Mackerel	Salt, pepper
4 leeks	½ teaspoon onion juice
2 tablespoons butter	½ cup American cheese,
½ cup fish stock	grated
2 tablespoons flour	

Clean and wash the fillets, dry thoroly. Cut the leeks (white parts only) into short, thin strips; blanch in boiling water, drain. Fry the leeks in the butter until they start to brown. Add enough fish stock to cover (which can be made from the heads, tails, bones of the mackerel), and let simmer for 3 minutes. Lay the mackerel fillets in a buttered baking dish. Lift the leeks out of their juices and lay them on top of the fillets. Blend the flour into the juices left in pan, heat until it thickens, stirring constantly, then add salt, pepper, onion juice. Pour this over the fillets, sprinkle the cheese over the dish, and bake for about 30 minutes in a moderate oven, basting frequently.

COCONUT FISH, HAWAIIAN STYLE

6 fillets of flounder, striped bass, or bluefish or any fish	2 tablespoons butter
	½ fresh coconut
2 eggs, beaten	1½ cups boiling water
½ cup bread crumbs	2 bell peppers, chopped
½ teaspoon turmeric	Boiled rice

Fillet the fish, wash and dry each one thoroly. Dip in the eggs, which have been beaten with a little cold water. Mix bread crumbs with turmeric and roll fish in crumbs. Fry in the butter. Remove meat from coconut and shred. Pour boiling water over it; let stand ½ hour and then squeeze out. Add 1 cup of water to this "coconut milk" and cook the peppers in it until tender. Then add the fish and let simmer uncovered, until tender, about 25 minutes. Sauce should have thickened at end of this time; if not, remove fish and cook sauce 10 minutes over hot fire. Arrange boiled rice in a ring on a round hot platter, and lay the fish inside the ring. Pour the sauce over it. Serve with India Chutney or other hot relish.

SEA BASS, STUFFED WITH CHESTNUTS

1 good-sized Sea Bass	Sprig thyme
Salt, pepper	1 tablespoon grated lemon
½ lb chestnuts	rind
1 tablespoon bread crumbs	Juice of 1 lemon
1 teaspoon parsley, finely minced	1 egg yolk, slightly beaten
	1 tablespoon olive oil

Clean and wash the bass, take out center bone. Dry thoroly and rub with pepper and salt. Puncture chestnut shells with a knife and cook in boiling salted water for 15 to 20 minutes, or until tender. Shell. Press meats through a sieve. Mix this purée with bread crumbs, the parsley, the thyme, lemon rind, lemon juice, egg yolk, salt, pepper. Stuff the fish with this mixture. Sew up the fish, brush with olive oil, and bake in a moderately hot oven (375° F.) for 25 minutes.

LIVER-STUFFED HADDOCK, LEMON SAUCE, GULL ISLAND

1 Haddock
½ lb liver
1 cup bread crumbs
6 slices bacon, cooked and minced
1 tablespoon parsley, minced
Thyme, dash marjoram
1 lemon, grated rind and juice

1 tablespoon butter
1 egg, beaten
Lemon Sauce:
  1 tablespoon butter
  1 tablespoon flour
  ½ cup milk
  ½ cup liquid in which liver was cooked

Clean and wash fish and dry thoroly. Take out center bone. Simmer the liver until tender, mince very fine. Add the bread crumbs, bacon, ½ tablespoon of the parsley, seasonings, one half of the grated lemon rind, and one half of the lemon juice, the butter, and the egg which has been beaten with a little cold water. Stuff the fish with this mixture. Put in buttered baking dish, bake 40 minutes to 1 hour, depending on size, in fairly hot (375° F.) oven, basting frequently. Serve with Lemon Sauce, made as follows: melt butter, blend in flour; adding the other half of the grated lemon rind and the other half of the juice, and remaining parsley, the milk and liquid in which the liver was cooked. Season to taste and let come to a boil. Pour over the fish.

BAKED BLUEFISH, CUCUMBER STUFFING, LINDBERGH

1 2½-lb Bluefish
Salt, pepper
1 tablespoon melted butter
Cucumber Stuffing:
  1 onion
  ½ cup mushrooms

2 slices bacon
2 cups cucumbers, finely chopped
1 tablespoon melted butter
1 cup soft bread crumbs
2 eggs, beaten lightly

Clean and wash the fish, dry thoroly. Sprinkle with salt

and pepper inside and out. Stuff with the Cucumber Stuffing, and sew together the edges with thread or tie securely with a string. Lay in greased baking dish, brush with melted butter, and bake in a moderately hot oven (375° F.) for about 25 minutes.

For the Cucumber Stuffing, chop together the onion, mushrooms, bacon, then add and mix well the other ingredients.

BAKED STRIPED BASS À LA SPENCER

1 Striped Bass (3 to 4 lbs)
Salt
Stuffing
Sauce Allemande (or Cucumber-Tomato, No. 35)

1 slice salt pork, $\frac{1}{2}$ inch thick or 6 strips bacon
3 tablespoons cooking oil

Clean and scale fish, removing head and tail or not as desired. Rub with salt inside and out. (Striped bass is a dry-meated fish, therefore cannot be cooked in its own fat). Lard with salt pork or arrange strips of bacon over the fish after it is stuffed and tie with string to hold it in place. Place on cooking paper in baking pan and brush with oil. Bake 10 to 15 minutes in a hot oven (550° F.), then as it begins to brown, reduce heat to moderate (350° F.), allowing 30-45 minutes for a 3-4 pound fish. Serve with Sauce Allemande or Cucumber-Tomato Sauce.

MAYONNAISE OF MACKEREL, COW NECK

$1\frac{1}{2}$ tablespoons gelatin
$\frac{1}{2}$ cup cold water
2 lbs Mackerel
$\frac{1}{2}$ cup vinegar
12 cloves
2 tablespoons chopped parsley

1 teaspoon peppercorns
1 teaspoon salt
$\frac{1}{2}$ bay leaf
Parsley sprigs
3 hard-cooked eggs, sliced
$\frac{1}{2}$ cup mayonnaise

Soften gelatin in $\frac{1}{2}$ cup of the cold water. Wash and dry mackerel. Place in baking tin. Add remaining water, vinegar and seasonings. Cover and bake in moderately hot oven (375° F.) 30 minutes. Lift carefully to serving platter. Remove skin, strain liquor fish was baked in, and add to gelatin, stirring until gelatin is dissolved. Pour over fish. Chill until firm. Garnish with sprigs of parsley. Between each sprig place slices of hard-cooked egg, topped with mayonnaise.

BAKED SHAD ROE, KEW GARDENS

1 Shad Roe	1 egg yolk
2 tablespoons chopped mushrooms	1 tablespoon chives, finely chopped
2 tablespoons shallots, chopped	$\frac{1}{2}$ clove garlic
1 teaspoon lemon juice	1 tablespoon tarragon vinegar
$\frac{1}{2}$ cup cream	1 tablespoon butter

Prepare the roe by parboiling and skinning. Then lay it in a buttered baking dish with the mushrooms, shallots, lemon juice, cream. Bake in a moderate oven for 10 minutes. Then lay the roe on a hot platter. Add the egg yolk, chives, garlic, tarragon and butter to the sauce left in baking dish; bring to a boil, and cook over low heat until thickened, stirring constantly. Strain the sauce over the roe.

MUSTARD SHAD ROE, MANHATTAN

1 Shad Roe (from a 4-lb Shad)	$\frac{1}{2}$ teaspoon dry English mustard
2 tablespoons butter	3 tablespoons heavy cream
Mustard Sauce:	$\frac{1}{2}$ teaspoon lemon juice
1 teaspoon butter	Salt, pepper

Parboil and skin the roe. Then broil it in a broiling pan with the butter over it, browning on each side about 5 minutes. Make the Mustard Sauce by blending the butter and mustard together, then the cream; simmer for 10 minutes, then add the lemon juice, salt, pepper. Serve over roe.

MIXED GRILL, SHAD AND ROE

1 Shad Roe	4 tomatoes, sliced
1 lb Shad fillets	4 strips bacon
1 tablespoon butter	4 baked potatoes

Parboil and skin the roe. Cut it into strips. Also cut the shad fillets into strips of approximately the same size. Dot with butter. Broil with the tomatoes. Serve piping hot with the grilled bacon, and baked potato.

FISH KEDGEREE, LIONHEAD ROCK

2 tablespoons butter	2 hard-cooked eggs
2 cups cooked fish, flaked	Salt and pepper
1 cup cooked rice	

Melt the butter in a frying pan, add the flaked fish, stir gently, then add the rice and the chopped egg whites. Season, then heat well. Serve on hot platter, and sprinkle the egg yolks, forced through a seive, over the top of the dish.

HALIBUT WITH CUCUMBERS, GREAT RIVER

1 lb Halibut fillet	$\frac{3}{4}$ teaspoon salt
Vinegar courtbouillon	2 tablespoons flour
2 cucumbers	Pepper
3 tablespoons butter	1 egg yolk

Poach the halibut fillets in vinegar courtbouillon to cover. Peel and seed the cucumber, cut into thin strips $1\frac{1}{2}$ inches long, barely cover with boiling water; add 1 tablespoon of the butter and the salt and let simmer until tender. Drain. Lay the cucumber in a serving dish and place the fillets over them. Blend remaining butter, flour, and 1 cup court-bouillon together into a sauce; season; stir in the egg yolk carefully, stirring over low flame until just thickened. Pour this sauce over fillets and serve.

FISH ASPIC, SANDS POINT

½ teaspoon celery seed
¼ cup vinegar
3 cups hot water
¼ teaspoon salt

2 eggs, beaten
2 tablespoons gelatin
½ cup cold water
2 cups cooked fish, flaked

Add the celery seed, vinegar, hot water and salt to the eggs and cook in a double boiler, stirring constantly, until thickened. Soften the gelatin in cold water for 5 minutes, then add to the egg mixture, stirring until dissolved. Then, add the fish, flaked. Pour into individual oiled baking cups or molds, and let chill. When firm, turn out on large platter laid with lettuce leaves, and serve with mayonnaise.

SEA BASS, ONDERDONCK

1 large Sea Bass
3 cloves garlic
1 teaspoon olive oil
1 tablespoon butter
6 large tomatoes, sliced

6 large onions, sliced
2 green peppers, sliced
Salt, pepper
½ teaspoon worcestershire
  sauce

Clean and wash the bass, rub it with salt and pepper. With a sharp knife open the fish in three places and in each opening stuff one clove of garlic. Rub the olive oil over the bottom of a baking pan, add the butter, and heat it. Then lay in the fish and cover with the sliced veegtables, salt and pepper. Cook until the vegetables are done (about 1 hour), and baste frequently, adding the Worcestershire sauce when half done.

FISH PUDDING, GREAT COVE

1 lb haddock or cod
2 cups water
1 bay leaf
2 peppercorns
1 small onion, sliced
1 small carrot, sliced
¼ cup butter

¼ cup flour
½ teaspoon dry mustard
1 teaspoon salt
⅛ teaspoon pepper
1 cup milk
1 cup fish stock
½ cup buttered crumbs

Place fish in water with bay leaf, peppercorns, onion and carrot. Cook 10 minutes. Drain, reserving liquor. Separate fish into large flakes. Make white sauce of butter, flour, mustard, salt, pepper and milk, stirring in fish liquor last. Blend in fish, place in greased casserole, top with crumbs and bake 30 minutes in a moderate oven (350° F.)

FISH AND SAUSAGE ROLLS, COVE NECK

6 fillets of fish	½ teaspoon scraped onion
6 link sausages	1 cup fine dry bread crumbs
1 egg, beaten	2 tablespoons melted butter
1 tablespoon lemon juice	2 tablespoons soup stock

Wipe fillets with damp cloth. Force sausage meat from casing and spread over fish in a thin layer. Roll fish up, fasten with a toothpick, dip in combined egg, lemon juice and onion, then roll in crumbs. Place in greased baking pan and add melted butter and stock. Cover and bake in hot oven (400° F.) 35 minutes.

SEA BASS, DUGLERE

2 or 3 Sea Bass (1 lb each)	¼ cup Chablis (white wine)
4 tablespoons butter	Juice of ½ lemon
1 small onion, chopped	¼ cup water
4 tomatoes, peeled, chopped	Salt, pepper
1 tablespoon parsley	

Clean, wash and split fish as for broiling. Melt half the butter in a saucepan, add the onion, tomato, parsley and cook 3 minutes. Lay the fillets over the vegetables, pour on the wine, the lemon juice and ¼ cup water. Cover the dish, cook for 20 to 30 minutes, until the fish is tender. Arrange fish on a hot platter, and reduce the sauce until it thickens, then add remaining butter, and salt and pepper to taste. Pour sauce over fish and serve.

BAKED SHAD WITH RAISINS, HALL'S

1 Shad
1 tomato, sliced
2 tablespoons butter

1 tablespoon parsley, chopped
1 cup seedless raisins
½ cup Chablis (white wine)

Split the shad, and lay in a long buttered baking dish. Arrange the tomato slices on top and dot with butter. Sprinkle with the parsley, and the raisins. Add the wine, and bake in a moderate over for 30 to 45 minutes, basting frequently.

BROILED SHAD ROE, MONTAUK MANOR

1 Shad Roe
Salt and pepper
1 clove garlic
3 tablespoons olive oil

½ cup Maitre d'hotel butter
2 vinegar pickles, finely chopped
1 teaspoon French mustard

Parboil roe for 15 minutes in 3 cups water to which ½ tablespoon vinegar is added. Drain. Remove membrane. Rub roe with salt and pepper, and a bit of garlic; roll in olive oil and broil on a greased grill. Lay on a hot platter, cover with a sauce made by mixing the Maitre d'hotel butter with the pickles and the mustard. Serve with French fried potatoes.

BAKED SQUID, CEDARSHORE

1 Squid
1 cup milk
1 tablespoon salt

½ cup bread crumbs
1 tablespoon butter

The squid is prepared by splitting the belly and removing the quill or backbone. Wash, and dip the squid in the milk mixed with the salt. Then roll in bread crumbs, until well covered. Lay in a buttered baking dish and dot with little pieces of butter. Bake in a hot oven (450° F.) for

10 minutes only. Serve with Spanish or Curry Sauce (Nos. 18 or 37).

(Squid is also excellent when rolled in flour and fried in deep fat, or when baked in a casserole with a Creole or rich Italian tomato sauce.)

HADDOCK, SWEET AND SOUR, CRAB MEADOW

2 lbs Haddock	2 tablespoons sugar
1 cup water	1½ doz. raisins
½ cup vinegar	2 egg yolks
1 lemon, sliced	½ doz. almonds, blanched
1 onion, sliced	and quartered
½ doz. cloves	

Clean fish; slice crosswise in 2-in. strips. Put in saucepan the water, vinegar, lemon, onion, cloves and the sugar. Bring to a boil, add fish and cook gently for half hour. When almost done add raisins. Remove fish to platter, arranging lemon and raisins between fish slices. Strain the liquor in which fish was cooked. Beat egg yolks slightly, blend in gradually the fish liquor; return to stove, and cook over low heat, stirring constantly, until just thickened. Remove from heat immediately. Pour sauce over fish and add the almonds. The fish alone may also be served cold.

FISH AND BEET HASH, HICKSVILLE

¾ cup cooked fish, flaked	¼ teaspoon paprika
¾ cup cooked cold potatoes, diced	1 teaspoon worcestershire sauce
2 cooked beets, diced	2 tablespoons thick cream, or 4 tablespoons rich milk
1 tablespoon minced onion	
1 tablespoon minced parsley	1 tablespoon bacon fat
½ teaspoon salt	

Mix together the fish, potatoes, beets and seasonings;

blend in the cream or milk. Fry in the fat, keep stirring until hot, then shape into a large cake and fry until brown, then fold over like an omelet.

FISH DIABLE, MEADOWBROOK

1 lb cooked cod, halibut or canned salmon
1 tablespoon olive oil
1 tablespoon minced onion
1 teaspoon vinegar
1 teaspoon salt
1 teaspoon kitchen seasoning sauce

$\frac{1}{4}$ cup tomato catsup
1 tablespoon butter
3 chopped capers
$\frac{1}{4}$ cup hot water
$\frac{1}{2}$ cup cooked peas
Rye bread toast

Marinate the fish in a mixture of the olive oil, onion, vinegar, salt and sauce for ten minutes. Drain. Remove to chafing dish and add catsup, butter, capers, hot water and peas. Cook for ten minutes. Serve hot with rye bread toast.

CUCUMBER-FISH ASPIC, FREEPORT

2 packages aspic gelatin
1 pint tomato juice
2 hard-cooked eggs, sliced
2 large fresh cucumbers, thinly sliced

$1\frac{1}{2}$ lbs boiled cod, halibut or salmon, flaked
Lettuce
French dressing

Prepare aspic according to directions, adding tomato juice instead of water. Pour a little in bottom of a fish mould. When it is hardened slightly, arrange alternate layers of sliced hard-cooked eggs, and one of the thinly sliced cucumbers, and the fish, pouring the aspic between each layer and on top. Place in refrigerator to set. Unmold and serve surrounded with shredded lettuce leaves and remaining cucumber which has been pared, chopped, drained and mixed with French dressing.

BAKED STUFFED PERCH, MANHATTAN

2 tomatoes	1 egg, well beaten
2 onions, chopped	$\frac{1}{2}$ cup bread crumbs
$\frac{1}{3}$ cup celery, chopped	$\frac{1}{8}$ teaspoon salt
2 tablespoons butter	Pinch of pepper
Sprig of parsley, chopped	4 Perch

Skin tomatoes, cut up in small pieces, add onions, and celery; cook together in butter for about 10 minutes. Add parsley, cook a few minutes more. Remove from stove, add egg and bread crumbs, salt and pepper. Clean perch, without opening belly; wash and rub with salt. Fill with prepared vegetable stuffing. Place in well-buttered baking dish and bake in hot oven, basting often until fish is nicely browned.

(Perch is not found in Long Island waters but sold for New York and Long Island consumption.)

BAKED ALBACORE, AMITYVILLE

2 or 3 lbs Albacore	2 tablespoons flour
$\frac{1}{2}$ teaspoon salt	6 stuffed olives, sliced thin
Juice of 2 lemons	2 tablespoons butter

Clean the fish, brush with salted butter, rub with salt, inside and out, and sprinkle with the juice of two lemons. Let stand for one hour. Then dredge with flour, place upon a greased rack in a baking pan. Arrange the stuffed olive slices on top of the fish. Dot with butter. Bake in a very hot oven (500° F); and when it is browned, reduce the heat and baste with boiling water. Serve hot, garnished with lemon quarters.

BLOWFISH, SCHWIDETSKY

4 Blowfish	Maitre d'Hotel Butter Sauce (No. 6)

Clean and wash the fish, remove the small fillets carefully.

Then brush them with melted butter and broil. Serve with Maitre d'Hotel Butter Sauce.

WEAKFISH FLORENTINE

4 or 5 Weakfish
Salt and pepper
2 tablespoons flour
2 cups cooked spinach

2 cups cooked rice
Meunière Sauce (No. 20)
Cucumbers with sour cream

Clean and bone the fish and dry thoroly. Rub with pepper and salt, roll in flour, then stuff each fish with a mixture of the spinach and the rice and Meunière Sauce, and bake in a quick oven. Serve with a side dish of cucumbers with sour cream dressing.

ALMOND SNAPPER, CHARPENTIER

6 Snapper (young bluefish)
  or weakfish
4 tablespoons butter
2 tablespoons almonds,
  sliced

1 teaspoon lemon juice
1 lemon, quartered
6 sprigs parsley
Sliced cucumber

Clean the fish, wash and dry. Fry on both sides in two tablespoons butter. Lay the fish on a hot platter. Add the 2 tablespoons butter to the pan, and the sliced almonds, and cook until almonds are lightly browned. Add the lemon juice. Then with a spoon pour this sauce over the fish. Garnish with lemon, parsley and cucumber slices.

ROE-STUFFED SHAD, ANJOU

6 ounces Shad Roe
1 cup soft bread crumbs
1 cup milk
1 tablespoon parsley, finely
  minced
1 tablespoon chives, chopped
1 teaspoon mixed fresh
  herbs

Pinch of basil
1 Shad
6 young cabbage leaves
3 leeks (white part only),
  minced
Few sprigs sorrel
Salt, pepper
1½ cups cream, scalded

Make a "forcemeat" of the roe as follows: parboil and skin the roe; soak bread crumbs in milk and squeeze out and combine with roe, parsley, chives, mixed herbs, basil. Then clean and trim the shad, wash and dry. Stuff it with the forcemeat, and tie or sew it shut. Cut the cabbage into thin long strips; parboil and plunge into cold water. Butter a baking dish, lay the cabbage leaves in it, and the leeks and sorrel. Lay the shad on top, season with salt and pepper, add the cream and bake in a moderately hot oven (375° F.) basting frequently.

SKATE WITH BLACK BUTTER SAUCE

1½ lbs Skate flippers	1 tablespoon parsley,
1 tablespoon salt	chopped
2 tablespoons vinegar	1 cup Black Butter Sauce
7 tablespoons capers	(No. 32)
	1 tablespoon vinegar

Scrub skate flippers (the only edible part of this fish) thoroly to remove stickiness. Cook them until tender in water to cover and the salt and 2 tablespoons vinegar. Then drain, and skin the pieces by scraping; cut off the bone extremity, and wipe dry; lay on hot platter. Season them, sprinkle with capers and parsley. Pour over them the Black Butter Sauce, which with the vinegar has been heated for a moment. Serve hot with steamed potatoes.

(This is a famous recipe in Europe under the name *Raie à Beurre Noir*)

PORGY FISH FRY, WYANDANCH

6 Porgies	nut oil (or other frying
2 cups corn meal	fat)
Bacon fat mixed with pea-	3 lemons, quartered
	6 sprigs parsley

Get fresh good-sized porgies, clean them by chopping away the heads, tails and gills. Gash each one twice on each side with a knife. Wash and clean, then dry thoroly.

Roll in the corn meal and fry in a good-sized pan with $\frac{1}{2}$ inch of the peanut oil, to which has been added 3 tablespoons of bacon fat. When tender, lay upon a hot platter on which has been spread three thicknesses of absorbent paper. Let drain thoroly. Garnish with lemon quarters and parsley.

(Porgy, of which there are quantities in Long Island waters, is an excellent fish when fresh and when not greasily cooked. It is also excellent brushed with oil, rolled in bread crumbs and broiled.)

FISH STEAK DINNER, LONG ISLAND

1 large Striped Bass	2 teaspoons salt
1 halibut or cod	$\frac{1}{2}$ teaspoon onion juice
1 blue fish	$\frac{1}{2}$ teaspoon minced parsley
1 cup olive oil	3 lemons, quartered
1 teaspoon pepper	1 cup Creole Sauce (No. 34)

Clean the fish, wash and cut into thick steaks. Marinate for one hour in the oil which has been seasoned with the salt and pepper, onion juice and parsley. Lift the steaks from the marinating oil to the broiling rack and broil until tender. Lift out on a hot platter, on which has already been poured the hot Creole Sauce, and serve with lemon slices and French fried potatoes. Each person served is to get a piece of each kind of fish. Any other firm-fleshed fish may be used in this recipe.

FISH IN WINE ASPIC, OLD WESTBURY

1 package aspic gelatin	$1\frac{1}{2}$ lbs boiled fish
1 cup Chablis (white wine)	2 cups fresh fruit salad
	1 bunch watercress
3 cups seedless grapes	

Dissolve aspic according to directions on package, substituting the wine for part of the water. Pour a thin layer of this mixture in the bottom of a ring mold. When it is slightly hardened, arrange part of the grapes on top of aspic, alternate with little mounds of fish. Pour the rest of the aspic carefully on top of this, and chill in refrigerator until firm. Unmould and fill center with fruit salad mixed with rest of grapes and watercress.

SKATE, À LA FRISCO

2 Skate flippers
½ cup cold water
⅛ teaspoon salt
½ cup milk
Pepper

2 tablespoons tarragon vinegar
1 tablespoon capers
1 tablespoon chopped parsley
¼ lb butter

Blanch flippers in boiling water to cover for 3 minutes; drain and scrape skin off. Place in ½ cup water, salt and milk and bring just to the boil. Take off the stove, and let stand for 10 minutes; drain. Lay fish on a hot platter, sprinkle with salt and pepper and the vinegar, capers and parsley. Brown the butter until it turns almost black, and pour this over the fish.

WEAKFISH, FORT POND

6 Weakfish
Salt and pepper
1 cup flour
2 eggs, beaten
½ cup bread crumbs, finely rolled

Clarified butter
Maitre d'hotel butter (No. 6)
1 lemon, quartered
4 sprigs parsley

Open the fish along the backbone and remove the bone. Clean and wash, and dry them thoroly; rub with salt and pepper. Then roll in flour, dip in the beaten egg, and then in the bread crumbs. Fry in clarified butter over a slow fire. Spread over a hot platter and pour the Maitre d'hotel butter over the fish, and garnish with lemon quarters and fresh parsley sprigs.

STEWED FISH AND VEGETABLES, BAITING HOLLOW

2 lbs fish	3 young carrots, diced
1 teaspoon salt	3 potatoes, diced
1 tablespoon tarragon vinegar (or lemon juice)	½ pint Chablis (white wine)
3 medium-sized onions, sliced	3 medium-sized tomatoes
	1 tablespoon flour
	Juice of ½ lemon
3 tablespoons olive oil	1 tablespoon mixed herbs

Fillet the fish, sprinkle with ½ teaspoon salt and the tablespoon lemon juice or vinegar; let stand for one hour in a deep kettle. Fry the onions in the olive oil until lightly browned, then add the carrots and potatoes. Cook 5 minutes, then add the wine and remaining salt. Lay the fillets on top of the vegetables, then add the tomatoes. Simmer for 15 or 20 minutes. Strain out upon a hot platter, with the vegetables in the middle and the fillets attractively arranged around the edge. Blend the flour with juice of ½ lemon, add to liquid left in the saucepan; stir constantly until smooth. Add the mixed herbs and simmer for 5 minutes. Pour over both the vegetables and fish.

SKATE WITH SAUCE VINAIGRETTE

3 lbs Skate flippers	½ lemon, sliced
1 onion, sliced	Salt, pepper
1 bayleaf	Vinaigrette Sauce (No. 36)
4 cloves	

Wash and clean the skate flippers (the only thing edible on a skate), and boil until tender in water to which has been added the seasonings listed. Skin the flippers and lay on hot platter, pour over it the Sauce Vinaigrette and serve hot.

WHALE STEAK, NORTHPORT

3 or 4 lbs Whale Steak   2 onions
3 cloves garlic   1 bay leaf
Salt, pepper   1 pint boiling water
½ cup oil   2 tablespoons flour

Wash the steaks, dry, and rub with a cut clove of garlic. Stick the other cloves of garlic, cut, into the meat. Sprinkle with salt and pepper. Sear the steak in the oil, boiling hot. Then add the onions, bay leaf, and boiling water and cover tightly. Simmer about 2 hours, until tender. Lay on hot platter, thicken the sauce with the flour and pour over.

(Whalemeat has been coming into the New York market occasionally in recent years. Long Island was for several centuries a whaling center.)

HERRING SALAD, DAHLSTROM'S

1 salted Herring   3 tablespoons vinegar
2 cooking apples   2 tablespoons sugar
4 medium-sized potatoes   ¼ teaspoon white pepper
5 beets   ¾ cup heavy cream
1½ tablespoons chopped   1 hard-cooked egg
  onion

Cut the herring into fillets, and soak overnight in plenty of water. Dry with cloth, bone, skin and cut into tiny cubes. The beets and potatoes cut in larger cubes, peel the apples and cut them into smallest possible cubes. The onion should be peeled and chopped very fine. All these ingredients should be kept separate and covered, and should only be mixed together just before they are to be served. Then mix in bowl, careful not to break the cubes. At the same time season and taste carefully. Lastly, stir in the heavy cream which has been beaten to the consistency of thick sauce; care must be taken not to beat it stiff or it will curdle slightly when mixed with the salad. Pile on platter and garnish with yellow and white strips of chopped hard-cooked egg. To be served cold, no dressing is needed.

(Not everybody knows that a good deal of herring is taken from Long Island waters. The Swedish chefs are the most expert cooks of herring, and there are half a dozen first-class Swedish restaurants on Long Island. Herring salad is a famous delicacy in all Scandinavian countries.)

FISH CURRY, MEADOWBROOK

6 fillets of flounder (or had-dock, or any white-fleshed fish)
1 fresh coconut, shredded
3 cups milk
½ onion
4 tablespoons butter
1 tablespoon curry powder
1 teaspoon ground ginger
Boiled rice

5 tablespoons flour
Chutney sauce
3 hard-cooked eggs, sliced
8 small gherkins
4 tablespoons shredded kip-pered herring
Spiced grapes or guavas (or any fruit jelly pressed through ricer)

Grate the coconut meat and let stand for 1 hour in the 3 cups of milk. Brown the onion in 2 tablespoons of the butter, then blend in the curry powder and ginger. Add then the shredded coconut and the 3 cups of milk in which it was mixed, and if there was any "milk" in the coconut itself, use it, adding cow's milk to make 1 cup. Add the fish fillets and simmer slowly, covered, until tender.

Arrange the rice in rings on hot individual plates, place a fish fillet inside each ring. Blend the flour and remaining butter to a paste and add to liquid left in pan; simmer for 5 minutes. Spoon this sauce on each fish fillet on each plate. Put some of the Chutney sauce, hard-cooked egg slices, gherkins, kippered herring, spiced grapes or guavas or riced fruit jelly around the edges of each plate.

SHAD WITH SORREL, SHEEPSHEAD BAY

1 Shad, medium size
1 tablespoon olive oil
½ lemon, sliced
¼ bunch parsley roots, chopped
½ onion, sliced
⅓ cup Chablis (white wine)

3 tablespoons mushroom liquor
Bouquet garni
2 bunches sorrel
¼ teaspoon salt
⅛ teaspoon pepper
1 tablespoon white sauce

Pare and scale the fish, then steep for as long as possible in a marinade made of the olive oil, lemon, parsley roots, onion. Drain, reserving marinade. Then put the fish in a deep buttered pan with the white wine, mushroom liquor, bouquet, sorrel, salt and pepper. Cook for nearly 1½ hours over a slow fire. Lay the fish on a hot platter. Add the white sauce to strained marinade, thicken and pour over the fish. Serve its own juice in separate sauce boat.

SEA BASS WITH CLAM JUICE SAUCE

2 2-lb Sea Bass
Salt and pepper
2 tablespoons flour
1 tablespoon bacon fat, (or butter)
1 tablespoon grated Parmesan cheese
4 sprigs parsley

4 tablespoons butter
4 tablespoons flour
2 cups clam broth or liquor
¼ cup Italian tomato purée (or ½ cup condensed tomato soup)
½ cup capers

Clean and wash the fish, dry thoroly. Gash the fish twice across the back, rub with salt and pepper, roll in flour lightly, and fry in a hot frying pan with the bacon fat. Do not cook fish longer than it takes for easy separation of flesh from the bone. Put on a hot platter. Dust the fish with the cheese, and garnish with parsley sprigs. Make Clam Juice Sauce as follows: blend the butter with the flour, and gradually add the clam liquor or broth. Stir until it boils. Season with salt, add the tomato and the capers. Serve from a sauce boat.

BAKED SEA BASS WITH TOMATOES, QUEENS

4 lb Sea Bass	1 cup cold water
1 onion, chopped	2 tablespoons butter
1 teaspoon minced parsley	*Sauce:*
2 cups strained tomato pulp	1 tablespoon butter
$\frac{1}{2}$ green pepper, minced	3 tablespoons flour
$\frac{3}{4}$ teaspoon salt	6 baked tomatoes

Wash and clean the fish, dry thoroly. Cut a deep gash, lengthwise, on each side of the fish. Lay on a buttered baking pan, add the onion, parsley, tomato pulp, green pepper, salt, and water. Dot the fish with the butter and bake in a moderate oven (375° F.) for 45 minutes, basting 4 or 5 times. Take out the fish and lay on hot platter. Melt the butter and blend in the flour, cook until it bubbles; then add $1\frac{1}{2}$ cups of the liquid from the baking pan, stir and let come to a boil. Then pour over fish. Arrange baked tomatoes around platter.

BLUEFISH SHORTCAKE, STONY BROOK

2 cups cold cooked Bluefish (or other fish)	3 tablespoons flour
	$\frac{1}{2}$ teaspoon salt
2 cups flour	$\frac{1}{8}$ teaspoon pepper
$\frac{1}{2}$ teaspoon salt	1 cup fish stock (or oyster or clam liquor)
4 teaspoons baking powder	
$\frac{1}{4}$ cup butter	Paprika
$\frac{2}{3}$ cup light cream	Pickled cucumbers
2 tablespoons butter	

Flake the fish, remove the skin or bone. Sift the flour with the salt, and baking powder. Cut in the butter; add cream and mix to a soft dough. Roll on floured board into a round about half an inch thick and bake for 15 or 20 minutes in a hot oven (450° F.). Make a white sauce by blending the butter and flour, and seasonings; add the fish stock and cook 5 minutes. When thick add the fish and cook until hot through. Split open the biscuit; lay bottom half on platter. Spread with butter, sprinkle with paprika, and pour on one half of the fish mixture. Lay on the upper part of biscuit and pour remaining fish mixture over it. Serve very hot, with the cucumbers.

FRESH COD OR HADDOCK FRY, SAYVILLE

1 fresh Cod or Haddock	Salt, pepper
1 lb salt pork	4 sprigs parsley
3 tablespoons flour	

Fillet the fish and cut the fillets into 3-inch pieces; dry thoroly. Cut the salt pork into very thin slices, roll in the flour, and let fry out slowly until brown, turning frequently. Then take the pork out of the pan, roll the fish in the flour and fry slowly in the pork fat, first on one side, then on the other. Lay on a hot platter, put the pork around the fish, and serve with parsley sprigs.

STUFFED STRIPED BASS, RAISIN SAUCE

4 or 5 Striped Bass	2 tablespoons flour
2 cups stale bread crumbs	1 teaspoon salt
Hot water	$\frac{1}{4}$ teaspoon pepper
2 tablespoons butter	1 tablespoon brown sugar
1 tablespoon minced onion	$1\frac{1}{2}$ cups water
1 tablespoon chopped pars-	$\frac{1}{4}$ cup chopped raisins
ley	$\frac{1}{4}$ cup blanched almonds,
1 tablespoon capers	ground
1 teaspoon salt	2 tablespoons grated horse-
$\frac{1}{2}$ teaspoon black pepper	radish
1 egg, beaten	$\frac{1}{4}$ cup sifted bread crumbs
Raisin Sauce:	Juice of 1 lemon
2 tablespoons butter	

Clean and wash the bass, dry. Moisten bread crumbs with hot water, press dry; season with the butter, onion, parsley, capers, salt, pepper, and mix in egg. Stuff the fish with this mixture and sew up. Bake in a hot oven for 40 minutes, or until tender. Arrange the fish on the platter and pour over it the Raisin Sauce, made as follows: melt the butter, blend in the flour, salt, pepper, sugar, water. Stir until it boils, then add the raisins, almonds, horseradish. Heat through and before serving add the bread crumbs and lemon juice.

SHAD ROE CASSEROLE, HALL'S

2 Shad Roe	1 egg, well beaten
2 tablespoons butter	1 tablespoon lemon juice
2 tablespoons flour	$\frac{1}{4}$ cup buttered bread
$\frac{1}{4}$ teaspoon salt	crumbs
Pinch of cayenne	6 slices bacon
1 cup thin cream	

Parboil two shad roes 10 to 15 minutes and remove membranes. Gently mash the roes with a fork, without breaking the roe-eggs. Melt the butter, blend in the flour, salt and cayenne. Then add the cream, bring just to a boil, stirring constantly. Remove from fire. Add the beaten egg and lemon juice, stirring until thickened; then add the roe. Put the mixture in a buttered casserole, and cover with the bread crumbs. Bake in a hot oven until crumbs are brown. Serve hot with crisped bacon.

HADDOCK, GLASGOW STYLE

1 3-lb Haddock	2 tablespoons tomato catsup
$\frac{3}{4}$ cup butter	1 tablespoon vinegar
2 onions, chopped	8 boiled potatoes
2 tablespoons worcestershire sauce	1 lemon, sliced

Clean the haddock, removing head and tail, cut into 6 pieces. In a large saucepan melt the butter, brown the onions, and add the worcestershire, catsup and vinegar. Stir and lay in the fish pieces (not on top of each other). Cover and cook for 10 minutes; then turn the pieces and cook 10 minutes more. Arrange on a hot platter with the potatoes around the edge. Pour on the sauce and lay a lemon slice on each fish piece.

SWORDFISH STEAK, THERMIDOR

4 Swordfish Steaks
2 tablespoons softened butter
2 tablespoons flour
2 cups milk (or fish stock or clam broth)
1 teaspoon salt

2 teaspoons onion juice
$\frac{1}{2}$ green pepper, chopped fine
1 tablespoon minced parsley
$\frac{1}{2}$ teaspoon tabasco sauce (or $\frac{1}{4}$ teaspoon cayenne)

Wash the steaks and dry thoroly. Broil them under a hot flame until *half* done. Then have ready a sauce in a hot pan, made as follows: blend the butter with the flour, then add the milk or fish stock, the salt, onion juice, green pepper, parsley and tabasco or cayenne. Lay the fish steaks in this mixture in the hot pan and cook, turning once or twice. When tender arrange the steaks on a platter and pour the sauce over them.

(This recipe can be used for tuna fish or any fish steaks.)

SEA BASS, BROOKVILLE

6 slices Sea Bass
1 tablespoon butter
3 onions, chopped fine
2 peppers, sliced
1 pimento, sliced
1 clove garlic, halved
1 bay leaf
1 teaspoon salt
1 teaspoon paprika
Pinch mace
1 teaspoon chopped tarragon

$\frac{1}{4}$ cup pitted olives, sliced
$\frac{1}{2}$ cup okra, sliced
1 tablespoon chopped cooked ham or bacon scraps
1 cup mussel liquor
2 mussel shells
12 mussels, steamed open, shelled and halved
2 tablespoons parsley, minced

Wash and dry the fish thoroly. In a saucepan put the butter, onions, peppers, pimento, garlic, bay leaf. Fry for 10 minutes, stirring, until light brown. Then add salt, paprika, mace, tarragon, olives, okra, ham. Heat through, put in the fish, mussel liquor and shells; let simmer gently for 10 minutes. Add mussels and simmer 10 minutes more. Remove mussel shells and serve sprinkled with parsley.

LEMON HADDOCK, LLOYD'S NECK

1 3-lb Haddock	1 tablespoon butter
1 lemon (or lime), sliced	1 glass Chablis (white
4 tomatoes, sliced	wine)

Clean and wash the fish, and dry thoroly. Gash one side with 5 or 6 incisions, and insert in each a very thin slice of lemon (or lime). Arrange the fish in a buttered baking dish, surrounded with the tomatoes. Season with pepper and salt, dot with butter, and add the wine. Bake in a moderate oven (375° F.) for 25 or 30 minutes. Serve from the baking dish.

FISH FRICASSEE, CRAB HOLLOW

1½ lbs haddock fillets	1 tablespoon worcestershire
4 tablespoons butter	sauce
1 onion, chopped	6 whole cloves
2 cloves garlic, chopped	Salt, pepper
2 tablespoons flour	1 cup Chablis (white wine)
1 medium (No. 2) can to-	
matoes	

Wash the fillet and dry thoroly. Cut the fillets into two-inch square pieces and fry in 2 tablespoons of the butter. In another pan brown the onion and the garlic in remaining butter, then blend in the flour, the tomatoes, worcestershire, cloves, salt, pepper. Let simmer for 30 minutes, then add the wine. Heat and pour over the fish. Serve hot.

FISH WITH MUSHROOMS AND LOBSTER SAUCE

1 stalk celery, chopped fine	1½ teaspoons salt
1 carrot	3 lbs fish (any white
1 onion	fleshed fish), cleaned
3 tablespoons butter	1 lb spinach, cooked,
½ cup cider vinegar	chopped and seasoned
4 cups water	12 or 15 broiled mushrooms
4 cloves	*Lobster Sauce:*
¼ small pepper, seeded	3 tablespoons butter
½ bay leaf	3 tablespoons flour
2 sprigs parsley	½ cup lobster meat, cubed

Cook the celery, carrot and onion in the butter, without browning. Add the vinegar, the water, cloves, the pepper, bay leaf, parsley, salt. Bring to a boil and skim, then let cool. Then put the cleaned fish into a deep-fat frying basket, place into the liquid as prepared above and bring to a boil quickly; then let simmer about 25 minutes or more, according to fish's thickness. Serve on a platter surrounded by the spinach. Pour over this the lobster sauce, made as follows: melt the butter until it bubbles, blending in the flour, cooking until it becomes light brown. Add 1 cup of the liquid in which the fish has boiled, stirring constantly; bring to a boil and cook 5 minutes. Then add the lobster meat. Dress the platter with the mushrooms.

FISHERMAN'S DELIGHT, LE POISSONNIER

6 mushrooms, sliced	½ teaspoon shallots
1 tablespoon butter	¼ cup sherry (as old as pos-
½ cup Bay scallops	sible)
1 cup oysters	1 to 2 cups cream
24 shrimp	1 egg yolk
1 teaspoon chives, chopped	

Fry the mushrooms in the butter for 3 or 4 minutes, then add the scallops, oysters, shrimp, chives, shallots, sherry and cook for 7 or 8 minutes. Then add cream enough to cover, bring just to the boil. Blend in egg yolk carefully, stirring constantly so that it does not curdle. Serve immediately.

CURRIED SEA FOOD PLATTER

1 small onion, minced
4 tablespoons butter
$\frac{1}{4}$ teaspoon whole cloves
1 teaspoon black pepper
1 bouquet garni
2 tablespoons sweet pepper, minced
2 tablespoons celery, minced
1 leek, sliced thin
4 teaspoons curry powder mixed with 1 tablespoon flour and 1 teaspoon salt

$1\frac{1}{2}$ lbs cooked lobster, oysters, clams, mussels, shrimps, whitefish, scallops or what have you
1 pint clam broth, oyster liquor or fish stock (or plain water)
1 egg, beaten with 2 tablespoons thick cream
Boiled rice and fresh pickled cucumbers

Brown the onion in the butter, and then add the following tied in a bit of cheese cloth: cloves, black pepper, bouquet garni. Add to the pan also the sweet pepper, celery, leek. Cover the pan and cook over low heat until vegetables are tender. Take out spice bag, put in the curry mixture and blend smooth. Then add the sea food, together with the broth or fish stock. Cook for 7 or 8 minutes, then take from fire. Add half the stock to the egg and cream mixture, stirring constantly; add this to ingredients in saucepan, stirring until smooth. Serve inside a ring of rice, with a border of cucumber pickle.

HALIBUT STEAK, CUCUMBER SAUCE

3 Halibut steaks (cut 1 inch thick)
1 tablespoon parsley, minced
2 medium onions, chopped
1 teaspoon salt
¼ teaspoon pepper
1 egg yolk, beaten lightly
Juice of one lemon

3 tablespoons butter
Cucumber Sauce:
2 large cucumbers, grated
1 small onion, grated
1 teaspoon tarragon vinegar
1 teaspoon salt
3 tablespoons thick cream

Wash the steaks and cut them in half. Butter a roasting pan, sprinkle with half of the parsley and onion, pepper and salt. Brush the steaks with the beaten egg yolk and lay them in the pan. Sprinkle on them the other half of the parsley, onion, salt and pepper. Bake in a moderately hot oven (375° F.) for 30 minutes. For the Cucumber Sauce have the cucumbers thoroly chilled; then grate them into a dish, add the onion, vinegar, salt, then slowly blend in the cream. Serve in a sauce boat with the fish.

PICKLE-STUFFED FISH, SPENCER TRACY

1 Halibut or Mackerel
1 cup bread crumbs
⅓ teaspoon salt
⅛ teaspoon pepper
¼ cup melted butter

1 egg, beaten
1 teaspoon minced onion
1 teaspoon minced parsley
1 teaspoon chopped pickles

Clean and prepare the fish, and then dry thoroly. Mix other ingredients, and stuff the fish, but not to the bursting point. Hold together with toothpicks or skewers. Bake in an uncovered baking dish in a moderately hot oven (375° F.) 10 minutes for each pound.

FISH AND APPLES

2 lbs fillets or steaks about $\frac{1}{2}$ in. thick

3 tablespoons butter or cooking fat

$2\frac{1}{4}$ lbs apples (about 9 of medium size)

2 tablespoons water

$\frac{1}{2}$ teaspoon salt

1 teaspoon sugar

Basting oil made by mixing:

$\frac{1}{4}$ teaspoon black pepper with

4 tablespoons melted butter

Cover fish with a salt solution made in the proportion of 2 tablespoons salt to 1 cup cold water and allow to stand for 3 minutes and drain.

Heat slowly 3 tablespoons fat in a deep frying pan. Wash, quarter, and core apples and slice to $\frac{1}{4}$ in. thick. Place the apples into the hot fat, adding the water, salt, and sugar. Cover tightly and cook slowly with one turning, until apples are almost tender. Lay the fish, flesh side down, on the apples, cover and allow to steam 3 to 5 minutes. Remove cover, turn fish, baste it with the butter mixture, and place for 5 to 10 minutes under the broiler until well browned. Remove the fish to a hot platter and surround with the apples.

FISH AND CABBAGE

3 lbs cabbage

2 lbs fillets or steaks

Cooking oil

Basting oil made by mixing:

4 tablespoons melted butter

$\frac{1}{4}$ teaspoon black pepper

4 tablespoons garlic vinegar, or onion vinegar

Quarter the cabbage and soak in salted water long enough to cleanse thoroly. Cut the cabbage into coarse shreds and boil in plenty of salted water in an uncovered kettle. For each quart of water allow 1 teaspoon salt.

While the cabbage is cooking, place the fish for 3 minutes in a salt solution made in the proportion of 2 tablespoons salt to 1 cup cold water. Drain the fish and brush oil on all sides. When the cabbage is almost tender, place fish (flesh side down) in a well-oiled basket or steamer and suspend over the cabbage for 5 minutes with the kettle covered. Remove fish and as soon as the cabbage is tender, spread it out on an oiled plank or heat-proof platter. Lay the fish (flesh side up) on the cabbage and baste with the melted butter mixture. Broil the fish for 5 or 10 minutes until well browned.

FISH IN PARCHMENT PAPER

2 lbs absolutely boneless fillets or steaks
$\frac{1}{4}$ teaspoon pepper
2 tablespoons melted butter
or cooking oil
2 tablespoons grated onion
2 tablespoons grated carrot

1 tablespoon lemon juice
1 tablespoon parsley,
chopped fine
Cooking oil
2 sheets parchment paper
about 2 feet square

Prepare a salt solution in the proportion of 2 tablespoons salt to 1 cup cold water. Fish that is $\frac{1}{2}$ in. thick should be kept in the salt solution for about 5 minutes, but this time may be varied from 5 to 10 minutes, depending upon thickness of flesh and variety of fish.

Fill a kettle two-thirds full of water and start heating. Oil or wet both sides of parchment paper and lay flat. Cut fish to serving size pieces and divide between the two papers, arranging the pieces one layer deep on each paper. Mix the pepper with the butter and put one teaspoon each of butter, onion, and carrot over each serving of fish. Sprinkle with lemon juice and chopped parsley. Bring edges of paper together and tie. Immerse in boiling water. After water boils, continue cooking until tender. This will take from 8 to 15 minutes, depending upon thickness of flesh and variety of fish. Remove to a hot platter, and pour juices over the fish or thicken them for a gravy.

A tightly covered steamer lined with oiled or wet parchment paper may be used in this method of cooking. The fish must be laid in a single layer. Steaming will require more time to cook than will boiling.

(The "En Papillotes" method of fish cookery in parchment paper has much to be said for it, as it retains all flavor faithfully. In New Orleans a famous dish is *Pompano en Papillote*.)

BROILED BLUEFISH, PIERRE CAMIN
(MONTAUK MANOR)

1 large Bluefish
Salt and pepper
2 tablespoons cooking oil
2 tablespoons butter, melted
2 tomatoes, broiled
Sauce Mexicaine:
   6 red pimentos, chopped fine

4 teaspoons tarragon vinegar
6 shallots, chopped fine
4 egg yolks, slightly beaten
$\frac{3}{4}$ cup butter, melted (approx.)
$\frac{1}{2}$ teaspoon tarragon leaves
$\frac{1}{2}$ teaspoon chopped parsley

Bone and fillet the fish. Season fillets with salt and pepper, dip in combined oil and butter. Broil under broiler. To serve, arrange on platter with half-broiled tomatoes. Serve with Sauce Mexicaine.

Make the sauce as follows: Combine pimentos, vinegar and shallots and cook together until almost dry. Beat this mixture into the egg yolks. Cook mixture in double boiler over hot water, stirring constantly until mixture begins to thicken. Add melted butter little by little until mixture is as stiff as mayonnaise. Add tarragon leaves, parsley and seasonings. Serve at once.

XIII

Fun With Outdoor Seafood Cookery

LONG ISLAND—like California, Texas, Eastern Shore Maryland and Florida—has fostered, and for the same reasons, a great deal of *outdoor cookery,* which is one of America's newest pastimes and amateur arts. "Dining al fresco" was once a delight which only Italy and Southern France knew well, but in those few places in America where nature has made it especially favorable, both with food and climate, a great many people in recent years have tasted of the immense fun and zest of appetite which come with preparing and eating food in the open. And once having tasted it, such folk have become enamored of it.

Long Island is especially such an outdoor dining place, because it has a range of even temperature (average monthly day temperature 60.9° F) which only Texas, California and Florida can boast of, and a 5-year record of 77.6% of sunshine per month; a record only Florida and California can equal. Long Island also has an amazing total of nearly 1000 miles of waterfront—130 miles of it on the broad Atlantic Ocean, the rest on every kind of sound, bay, inlet, lake, strait, etc. Deep water, shallow water, rough water, smooth water, narrow water, broad water, salt water, fresh water, sandy shore, rocky shore, low shore, high bluff shore—it is all there on Long Island, ready to use for outdoor fun. The owners of sail and motor boats are legion; Long Island is a yachtsman's paradise. There is still plenty of shore front open to the public for picnicking and bathing, fire-making, cookery and dining. There are hundreds of such places easily accessible by means of 1500 miles of boulevards, parkways and surfaced highways, where one can duplicate a "scene on a desert island"; that is, have shore meal and picnic on the sands, using driftwood for a fire, and not be near another human being. Since the automobile era many thousands have learned this delight.

This was *nature's* contribution, but *man* (largely in the person of Robert Moses, famous State Park Commissioner) has now added incredibly greater outdoor enjoyments to Long Island, through the public park facilities. Nowhere else in the United States are there public facilities in such quantity (12,000 acres in 17 state parks), and up to such a level of convenience and scope; and few with such facilities for outdoor cookery fun.

There are at least 12 public parks of large size on Long Island, and in each of them are attractive picnic tables (of a quality and convenience superior to any I have ever met with), and in most of them there are also *cookery fireplaces* with grids, free to picnickers. Some of these parks (Fire Island on the ocean shore, Hither Hills, Wildwood, etc.) have also facilities for all-season tent campers, at low rates. Jones Beach is of course the pride of Long Islanders, probably the most beautiful, extensive and highly developed public park in the world, with two miles of ocean-front, and bath-house and parking accommodations for 16,000. Along the Ocean Parkway nearby are many more miles of shore open to those who would picnic and dine on the ocean sands.

You bring your food and pots and make your own dinner at these shore or park places—or you fish or dig for your food. There are vast beds of mussels, plenty of clams at certain favored shore points, and plenty of fish in the waters. Digging, or water-treading, for clams is even a form of exercise—culinary calisthenics, if you please! So are foraging for driftwood, building clam bake ovens, etc.

There is an immense coterie of fishermen—men and women—who go out on Long Island waters to fish, and often stay to eat their catch. They do everything from fishing off a dock, to wrestling with a 300-lb broadbill swordfish from the rear end of a cruiser, miles from the Long Island shore. The Long Island railway runs "Fishermen's Special" trains (45,000 fishermen carried on 200 trains a year) from New York, starting as early as 3 a.m. Special fishermen's boats, charging two dollars for the day per person, including bait, go out into waters, their decks crowded.

At Montauk there is a large fleet of open boats for bottom fishing, while on the sands are to be seen at almost all times men and women in high fishing boots doing "surf-casting" for the wary striped bass. Long Island is visited in May and June by a fish phenomenon—the run of weakfish—a vast mass of them, and you can't miss. From Canoe Place, South Jamesport, Shelter Island, New Suffolk, Greenport to Sag Harbor, chartered boats as well as "open" boats for fishermen go out in large number to drag in all the weakfish one could want. Fishing in any of the waters of Long Island is usually productive, for Long Island is a natural "fisherman's idea of paradise." His catch being so demonstrably fresh, he often cooks it himself, with gusto, or has someone do it for him, or takes it home for his own and his friends' enjoyment.

With all this background of food, sun, sand, water, driftwood, open space, public facility, it is no wonder that, like the Californians, the Floridians and the Texans, the Long Islander has been rapidly increasing his lore about outdoor food cookery. In recent years more and more outdoor cooking fireplaces have been built on Long Island home plots. Designs for such outdoor fireplaces have developed amazingly. So has inventive genius in the making of simple portable outdoor cooking grids, using charcoal or briquettes. Even the 5-and-10-cent stores have offered simple little grids for the purpose. All America seems to be entering upon an era of outdoor cookery, largely because the automobile and good roads have made it so readily possible, and modern ideas of greater health and gourmet food enjoyment have rendered it so much more desirable.

But we greatly need to know more about the arts of

outdoor cookery. So often the sheer enthusiast succeeds only in spoiling good food by his crude, uninformed methods. There is such a very great difference between food burned in acrid picnic smoke, and food intelligently prepared!

Herewith are some suggestions, developed on Long Island, for good outdoor seafood cookery.

CORN HUSK FISH, HAWAIIAN STYLE

3 snappers or weakfish or young mackerel or striped bass (or one larger fish)	Green corn husks Salt

Clean the fish and wipe thoroly dry. Have ready some green corn husks, from which the ear of corn has been removed so as to leave the whole husk empty. Sprinkle the husks with salt, both inside and out, and place the fish inside, and wrap as closely as possible, one fish to a husk. Lay these in a roasting pan and add 3 cups of water. Bake in a very hot oven (500° F) for 15 to 20 minutes, basting constantly. Serve with the husks on.

(This recipe can be used outdoors, using two frying pans topping each other for the oven, or merely placing the corn husk fish in the hot embers of a shore fire.)

FISH BARBECUE, LONG ISLAND

6 mackerel, bluefish or striped bass	2 teaspoons chili powder
Barbecue Sauce:	1 tablespoon worcestershire sauce
1 cup butter	$\frac{1}{2}$ teaspoon tabasco sauce
$\frac{1}{2}$ cup vinegar	1 tablespoon black pepper
1 teaspoon dry mustard	2 tablespoons paprika
2 tablespoons sugar	$\frac{1}{2}$ clove garlic
3 cups water	$\frac{1}{2}$ onion, minced
2 teaspoons salt	$\frac{1}{2}$ teaspoon red pepper

Mix the sauce ingredients, and boil together for 10 minutes. This is the authentic "cowboy" barbecue sauce, hot enough to burn your fingers! (By the way, double these portions for the sauce, and you can use it for a *meat* barbecue anytime.)

Build an outdoor fire, and let it die down to red hot embers. Then have the fish ready, in fillets, and the barbecue sauce nearby in a large pan. Have everybody gather round the fire with 3- or 4-foot greenwood sticks, or long wire forks, or iron skewer rods. On each stick or rod spear a fish fillet securely, piercing it in two places to make sure it can't fall off. Dip the fish fillets in the sauce and then gently broil over the open coals. Dip the fish in the barbecue sauce every 2 minutes or so—but be careful not to lose the fish off the stick! Eat with potato chips and bottled fresh cucumber pickle.

(A milder and less expensive Quick Barbecue Sauce is mixed by simmering together for 15 or 20 minutes, 1 pint vinegar, $\frac{1}{2}$ can tomatoes, 2 teaspoons red pepper, 1 teaspoon black pepper, 1 teaspoon salt, 2 tablespoons butter.)

BALSAM FISH-BAKE, BELMONT LAKE PARK

3 or 4 fish—any fish   Salt
Green Balsam twigs   Pepper

Clean and wash the fish, and dry them thoroly. Make a hot fire, let die down to a good pile of embers. Rake half of these away. Then quickly pile a layer of small green balsam twigs on the hot coals, and lay the fish right on top of these twigs, without any wrappings. Place another layer of balsam swigs on top of the fish, and then replace the other half of the red hot embers on top of the balsam swigs, and let steam for about 30 minutes.

SHORE CLAM BAKE, SHINNECOCK

200 soft shell Clams   Corn on the cob, sweet po-
  $\frac{1}{2}$ lb melted butter   tatoes if desired
Salt, pepper

Gather a lot of stones and lay close together. Gather driftwood and lay it on these stones and build a really good hot fire. Meanwhile, nearby dig an 18-inch or 2-foot hole in the ground, and after the fire has died down and the stones are piping hot, get a stick and roll them into the hole, enough to cover the bottom well. Have ready some seaweed, and pile on a layer 4 or 6 inches deep. (If seaweed is not available, gather plenty of green leaves.) Lay the clams over the seaweed. Then on top of the clams place all the rest of the seaweed or leaves. Let steam for 30 minutes. Corn on the cob, or potatoes can be added to the clams.

(If you are not able to manage a shore fire from driftwood, or hole-in-the-ground clam bake, and can bring a briquette broiler or other form of portable cooker, then you may have a fair semblance of a shore clambake by bringing along a large pot, and in this pot put your seaweed, clams, corn, etc.)

SHORE FISH-BAKE, FORT SALONGA

4 dozen soft shell clams
3 or 4 fish—any kind
Sheets of oiled or buttered paper
(add if desired mussels, oysters, scallops, corn on the cob, potatoes, or what have you)
$\frac{1}{2}$ cup melted butter
Salt, pepper

Gather medium-sized stones and pave a 2-foot circle with them, ringing this circle with some larger stones. Build on this a very hot fire of driftwood. When it is reduced to red-hot embers, rake away and cover the stones with seaweed or wet leaves. Spread the clams and other shellfish on this. Clean fish, leaving heads and tails on, rub with salt and wrap in oiled paper or vegetable parchment. Lay the fish on top of the shellfish. Pile on the fish the ears of corn, potatoes, etc. Cover with a layer of seaweed or wet leaves, and then top everything with an old piece of dampened canvas or old cloth or blanket. Let steam for 30 to 40 minutes. Then draw off seaweed coverings and serve some of each kind of fish to each person. Pass melted butter, salt and pepper as the only accompaniments.

SHORE FISH FRY, OAK ISLAND BEACH

6 weakfish, snapper, butter- $\frac{1}{2}$ cup cornmeal
   fish, flounder or other   Salt
   small fish   Pepper
6 slices bacon   Olive oil

Clean the fish, wash and dry each one thoroly. Put a strip of bacon inside of each fish, rub with salt and pepper. Roll in cornmeal, place in a frying pan in hot olive oil. Have *another* frying pan of equal size ready and cover the first one with it. Have a hot driftwood fire going, with plenty of red hot embers. Then put the double frying pan in the embers, piling more embers on top, and let it bake and fry for 25 minutes.

FISH-BAKE, FIRE ISLAND

3 or 4 fish (any kind, any   oiled paper, or vegetable
   size)   parchment
Grape leaves, seaweed, or   Salt, pepper

Make a bang-up hot shore fire and when the embers die down have the fish ready cleaned (but with heads and tails left on). Rub the fish with salt and pepper, wrap around each one some wet grape leaves (or other large green leaves); bury each fish individually in the hot embers. Or if you have seaweed, use it instead of the leaves. If there is no seaweed or leaves, use oiled or buttered brown paper, or vegetable parchment for wrapping fish. Do not use *waxed* paper. If the fish is large, wrap *first* in oiled or buttered paper, then in leaves or seaweed. If there is no seaweed or leaves, wet a newspaper thoroly and wrap it around instead. If you can get some sweetfern, tie some of it on the first oiled paper, then 2 or 3 sheets more of brown paper, and bury in the embers. Let steam for about 25-30 minutes.

SHORE-SKEWERED FISH, WILDWOOD

6 weakfish, snappers, young
  mackerel or other small
  fish

6 or 8 slices bacon
Salt
Pepper

Clean the fish, but do not cut off heads or tails. **Dry** each one thoroly. Rub with a piece of bacon, sprinkle with salt and pepper. Cut a 3- or 4-foot straight piece of green wood stick about $\frac{3}{4}$-inch thick; sharpen at one end. Then thread on the fish and bacon alternately, placing a piece of bacon between every fish or every two fish. Hold this over a fire of shore driftwood which has burned down to red-hot coals, turning frequently to let the juices roll over the fish. Serve promptly.

SHORE PLANKED FISH, SUNKEN MEADOW

1 striped bass, bluefish,
  mackerel or other good-
  sized fish
3 slices bacon
Salt, pepper

Large chip of oak or scraped
  strip of driftwood board
  or plank (of unpainted
  hardwood)

Clean and wash the fish, split it. Wipe dry with paper towel. With an axe cut a large thick chip from a piece of green oak; the chip should be at least 2 inches thick and about 2 feet long, and wider than the split fish. Or look among the driftwood or elsewhere for an old hardwood board or plank, and chip off the surface, free of any impurities, wash well. Prop this chip immediately before a good-sized fire of driftwood, so that the heat of the fire reaches it. Pin the fish on the plank, skin side down, with an oak splinter. Keep the fire hot. Baste continually by spearing bacon on a long stick and holding it just above the fish. When tender, salt and pepper it, grease with the bacon drippings or some butter. Serve on the plank, with potato chips.

SHORE-STEAMED FISH, HECKSHER PARK

2 or 3 fish (any fish)	Salt
$\frac{1}{4}$ butter or oil	Pepper
Some thin manila or butch-er's paper, and newspapers	Few grains cayenne

Clean the fish, leaving on heads and tails; dry thoroly. Grease the manila paper with butter or the oil. Sprinkle salt, pepper, cayenne on fish and roll each fish separately in a piece of the buttered paper. Then wrap the bundle of wrapped fish in a larger piece of the buttered paper, and again wrap this bundle in a newspaper which has been laid in water for 5 minutes. Meantime build a good-sized hot fire, and when it gets to the red-hot coal stage, push the coals aside and dig a hole in the sand or ground directly under the coals, and put in the wrapped bundle of fish. Rake the hot coals back on top of it, and let steam for 25 or 45 minutes, according to number and size of fish and heat of fire. Then unwrap and serve.

SHORE CLAM BAKE, MATTITUCK

48 soft shell or cherrystone Clams	Sweet corn on the cob Sweet potatoes
Salt, pepper	$\frac{1}{2}$ cup melted butter

Select a good spot, bring plenty of driftwood of fair thickness; break or cut it to no longer than 18-inch size, and gather plenty of seaweed. Gather also a pile of stones of 3-inch to 6-inch diameter. Lay down a flat, round circle, 20 inches to 2 feet in diameter, of these stones, for the bed of the fire. Build up an edging of stones about 6 inches high around this circle, except for a four-inch space in front. Then start a fire in this circular oven and keep it going in lively fashion, letting the wood finally die down to a pile of red-hot embers

Now move quickly: Rake out the half-burned, smoking pieces. Throw on top of the stones a layer of about 6 inches of wet seaweed. Place the clams on top of this, also a corn cob or two for each person, and a sweet potato. Top this with a 10- or 12-inch layer of seaweed. Let stand for 40 minutes, and then serve promptly. Always allow a full hour, or an hour and a half, from the time the fire is started to the time for sitting down to eat.

RAW TUNA APPETIZER, À LA JAPANESE

6 tuna fish steak slices cut about $\frac{1}{2}$ inch thick, 2 inch squares	$\frac{1}{2}$ cup Shoya Sauce 1 tablespoon freshly grated horseradish

Clean tuna fish slices, wash, rub some salt in, let stand 5 minutes; then wash in another water. Mix the grated horseradish in the Shoya Sauce (obtainable at Japanese stores). To eat, spear the tuna fish steak slice on a fork, dip well in the sauce and eat! (Yes, it's good! the Japs grow strong, even fierce, on raw fish!)

XIV
Seafood Pies

THERE is too little known, in this homeland of pies, about *seafood pies*. Even the Oyster Pie is eaten by only a handful compared to those who eat oysters in other ways. The Clam Pie is even less known, yet Princess Kropotkin has maintained that the clam pie is the most gallant and distinctively native dish America has produced.

England, with her centuries of meat pie traditions, and eating three times as much fish per capita as America, knows seafood pies much better, of course. She lifted Eel Pie to a high place, and knows many other fish pies. But England's pies, it must be confessed, have too little benefit of good cookery and combination, therefore they sin along the lines of both flavor and digestibility. Even the famous Cheshire Cheese "pudding" (Steak-oyster-kidney-lark pie) with so much tradition behind it, is acknowledged by most frank Englishmen as lacking in taste appeal.

In America we are in a renaissance of cookery, and because the fruit pie is quite particularly a national favorite with us, we are "pie-minded" enough to avoid sneering, as the French do, at nearly all pies. We are trying—and succeeding—in making pies both more palatable and more digestible. Our vegetable shortenings, our greater care with combinations, and our awakened gourmet sense are combining to produce delectable—and digestible—pies of the heavier kind, in wide variety, for the first time in all pie history.

The Clam Pie is, in my opinion, the king of all seafood pies. A pie is an ideal way of drawing out full clam flavor.

It is superior to oyster pie, in my judgment, because of the fact that cooked oysters cloy the taste, after a certain point, in a manner that clams do not. It also seems to me that clam flavor imparts itself more definitely to other ingredients, and that the broth is more acceptable. Thus we drink clam broth with relish, but never oyster broth. The mussel has not been much used for pie, but I venture to say it also makes a good one. Combination seafood pies are also excellent.

Seafood pies are met with remarkably seldom in recipe books, and when they are, often they are called pie only by courtesy. That is to say, they are not pastry pies at all, but baking dish combinations of potatoes, fish and milk. Even the standard cook books do not have an oyster, clam, or fish pie in their entire assembly of recipes. I am aware that some people assert that fish and pastry are bad gastronomic combinations, yet these very people will consider seafood good in pastry patty shells. I do not see the difference in principle, and I suspect there is none; only some memories of indigestible seafood pies, which, like meat pies, have many friends among the poets, but few among the dietitians! Some such timid cooks offer oyster and seafood pies which for crust are topped with mashed potatoes or buttered bread crumbs browned in the oven! That is a particularly low trick—good in itself, but a sad substitute for a real pie!

At considerable difficulty, some trepidation, but much hope, I present here at least a small gathering of seafood pies. The Clam Pie is a result of the loving care and experimentation of myself and family. Those who have not warmed to clam pie have doubtless eaten the common, slap-dash, ordinary clam pies which are met with in New England, and alas! even at restaurants on Long Island which should know better. It is to me a great wonder that clam pie has weathered the years weighted down by low standards of cookery. It must be basically a good pie or it never would have come through! As for Eel Pie,

England long ago perfected it. The Twickenham Eel Pie is especially famous. There is an Island on the Thames named Eel Pie Island; history seems to afford little record why. Doubtless someone, ages ago, caught the eel fresh there and served it there to the gourmets of the day.

I look for a rebirth of the fish pie; and this, the first collection of such recipes, may help.

CLAM PIE, APPLECROFT

48 soft shell Clams
2 cups hot boiled potatoes, sliced ¼-inch thick
2 onions, chopped finely
2 cups celery, diced finely
5 tablespoons butter

2 tablespoons flour
Salt, pepper
¼ cup cream
2 tablespoons parsley, minced
Biscuit or pastry dough

Steam well-scrubbed clams to open; remove meats, and save liquor separately. Butter a 2-quart baking dish, and set inverted glass mixing cup in center. Line bottom and sides of casserole with potatoes slices. Fry onions and celery in 3 tablespoons of the butter until golden brown. Add clam liquor and simmer until tender. Make a 'roux" of flour rubbed with remaining butter and add to clam liquor, stirring until smooth, making a thin gravy. Season. Combine cooked clam meats, gravy, and the cream; turn into casserole, pouring carefully so as not to disturb potatoes. Sprinkle with minced parsley. Have ready either biscuit crust or richer flaky pastry crust to fit top of casserole. Fit, trim, and prick with air holes. Make a "rose" of narrow strips of paste and set on top of pie. Bake in hot oven (450° F.) for about 15 minutes, or until browned.

(The inverted glass cup supports the crust and acts as a vacuum to hold juices in. The trick of making this pie so tasty is the cooking of onions and celery in the clam liquor.)

OYSTER PIE, SEWANAHAKA

6 tablespoons butter
1 cup sliced mushrooms
7 tablespoons flour
1¼ teaspoons salt
¼ teaspoon nutmeg

¼ teaspoon celery salt
3½ cups milk
1 pint Oysters
Pepper
Crumbly pastry

Melt the butter, add mushrooms and cook two minutes. Stir in flour and seasonings and when well blended add milk. Stir over low fire until smooth and thick. Add drained oysters and pour into individual baking dishes or into a large casserole. Cover with pastry, make two or three slits in top and bake in a hot oven, 450° F., about 10 minutes or until brown.

OYSTER-EGG PIE, POLO GROUNDS

1 recipe plain pastry
1 pint Oysters
4 hard-cooked eggs, sliced
4 tablespoons butter
Salt and pepper

1 cup celery and onions, diced and mixed
1 teaspoon parsley, minced
½ cup milk

Line a deep baking dish with a thin pastry crust made with milk instead of water. Drain liquor from oysters and save. Arrange a layer of the oysters on the bottom crust, then a layer of egg slices, then dots of butter and salt and pepper. Then arrange one more layer of oysters and of eggs. On top of all place the celery and onions and sprinkle the parsley. Then pour in ½ cup milk and the oyster liquor. Top with a pastry cover, vented well. Bake in moderate oven for 35 minutes.

OYSTER PIE, BLUE POINT

2 tablespoons butter
1 clove garlic, minced
8 shallots or chives, minced
3 tablespoons flour
Oyster liquor with enough water added to make 2 cups
1 cup milk
3 tablespoons white wine (such as Chablis)

6 tablespoons cream
1 can mushrooms
40-50 Oysters (Bluepoints or other small ones)
1 tablespoon chopped parsley
Salt, pepper
1 recipe biscuit dough

Melt the butter; fry the garlic and shallots in it until lightly browned. Add the flour and blend well. Stir in gradually the liquor drained from the oysters and the milk, wine and cream. Add the mushrooms, oysters, parsley and salt and pepper. Simmer for 10 minutes. Line a large deep baking dish or casserole with half the biscuit dough rolled thin; fill with oyster mixture. Cover with remaining dough; pierce holes in top with a fork, making an extra large "X" hole in center. Bake a light brown for 15 minutes in a quick oven until lightly browned. Serve very hot.

INDIVIDUAL SHRIMP AND OYSTER PIES

2½ cups milk
1 cup cracker crumbs
¼ teaspoon celery salt
¼ teaspoon paprika
Salt, pepper
¼ cup grated American cheese

1 cup uncooked shrimp, shelled and chopped
36 Robbins Island or other large Oysters
¾ cup chopped cooked celery
½ recipe pastry crust

Scald the milk in a double boiler; add the crumbs and seasonings and cook, stirring frequently, until it thickens. Take off the stove, stir in the cheese. Combine the shrimps, oysters and celery. Grease six individual casseroles. Pour in each one a layer of the cheese sauce mixture, then a layer of the oyster-shrimp mixture, cover with pastry crust. Bake in hot oven (400° F) for 15 or 20 minutes, or until crust is brown.

SOFT SHELL CLAM AND CHICKEN PIE, BETHPAGE

1 recipe plain pastry
1 pound tin of Chicken or meat from 2½ pounds roast Chicken
1 can (1 pound) steamed soft shell Clams

3 tablespoons butter
3 tablespoons flour
¾ cup juice from clams
¾ cup milk
½ teaspoon salt
Dash of pepper

Line 8-inch pie tin with half of pastry. Cut meat into slivers. Drain clams and place in alternate layers with chicken in pastry shell. Melt butter, blend in flour and add combined clam juice and milk. Cook over low flame, 5 minutes, until thick and smooth, stirring constantly. Season to taste. Turn over clams and chicken. Top with remaining crust, slash well and bake in hot oven (450° F.) 20-25 minutes.

INDIVIDUAL OYSTER PIES, CONEY ISLAND

6 tablespoons butter
1 cup mushrooms, sliced
7 tablespoons flour
1¼ teaspoons salt
¼ teaspoon nutmeg
¼ teaspoon celery salt

Pepper, a few grains of cayenne
3 cups Grade A milk
1 pint Oysters
Pastry

Melt the butter, fry the mushrooms in it for 2 minutes. Blend in the flour and the seasonings; then add the milk. Let simmer and stir meanwhile until thick and smooth. Add the oysters with ½ cup of their liquor. Place this mixture into individual baking dishes and cover with a pastry crust, making 2 or 3 slits in the top. Bake in a hot oven (450° F) for about 10 minutes or until brown.

SHRIMP AND FISH PIE, FARMINGDALE

1½ lbs fillets of any white-
  fleshed fish
1 onion, finely chopped
½ cup dry bread crumbs
½ teaspoon salt
⅛ teaspoon pepper
¾ cup sour cream

1½ lbs cooked Shrimp
1 cup cooked peas
Pastry crust
1 egg yolk
2 tablespoons butter
2 tablespoons flour

Wash fish and dry thoroly. Wrap fish in clean cloth and drop for 5 minutes in boiling salted water. Lift out, reserving liquor, and take off cloth, and mince the fillets with a fork. Mix the onion, bread crumbs, seasoning and ½ cup of the sour cream. Then blend in the fish, shrimps and peas; fill this mixture into 6 individual ramekin cups or casseroles, and cover with pastry crust; cut a small hole in center of crust. Brush crust with slightly beaten egg yolk, bake in a hot oven (450° F) for 15 minutes. Melt the butter in a saucepan, blend in the flour. Add gradually one cup of the water in which fish was cooked and the remaining ¼ cup sour cream. Cook over low heat, stirring constantly for 5 minutes. When the pies are done, place a funnel in the hole in the crust, and pour sauce into each one. Serve piping hot.

OYSTER AND CHICKEN PIE

1 fricassee Chicken
1 pint Oysters
2 hard-cooked eggs, sliced
1 tablespoon butter
¼ cup celery, chopped

¼ teaspoon salt
Pinch cayenne pepper
1½ tablespoons flour
1 cup milk
Puff pastry

Cut chicken in small pieces and parboil for 40 minutes. Drain. Arrange in deep baking dish. Pour the oysters with their liquor over it. Add the sliced eggs, butter, celery, salt and cayenne. Add flour mixed with milk. Cover dish with puff paste crust. Bake 35 minutes in moderate oven.

OYSTER, BEEFSTEAK AND KIDNEY PIE, KINGSTOWN

1½ lbs round steak, 1 inch thick
2 tablespoons flour
2 teaspoons mixed herbs
1 teaspoon salt
½ teaspoon freshly ground black pepper
1⅓ cups boiling water
½ lb Kidneys, sliced
1 tablespoon butter
1 pint Oysters
Pastry dough

Cut the steak into strips 2½ inches wide. Roll these pieces in a mixture of the flour, the herbs, salt and pepper. Add boiling water, cover and simmer about 1 hour or until tender. Cook kidneys in butter for 10 minutes, turning frequently. Roll an oyster into each strip of meat and pin with a toothpick. In a deep baking dish lay these pieces. mixed with the kidneys; add the liquor strained from oysters and enough stock (in which meat was cooked) to almost cover. Cover with a flaky pastry crust, bake for 20 minutes in a hot oven (450° F).

RUMP STEAK, OYSTER AND CLAM PIE, HUNTINGTON

1 lb rump Steak
Salt and pepper
2 tablespoons flour
12 Oysters
12 hard shell Clams, shelled
1 tablespoon butter
Pastry dough
1 egg yolk, slightly beaten
1 strip of lemon peel, finely chopped
1 tablespoon walnut catsup
½ blade mace

Cut the steak into thin, narrow strips 2½ inches long and 1 inch wide. Mix salt, pepper and the flour on a plate and roll the steak in it. Simmer until nearly tender in water just to cover. Then roll up inside each meat strip one oyster and one clam, and pin with a toothpick. Fill a deep baking dish with these rolls, pour in ½ cup of liquor drained from clam and oyster and one cup of gravy or stock in which meat was cooked. Dot with butter and cover with vented pastry dough brushed over with beaten egg yolk. Bake 25 minutes in moderately hot oven (425° F). Pour with a funnel through vent in crust, a mixture of the rest of the oyster and clam liquor, the lemon peel, the walnut catsup, the mace, which have been brought to a boil together.

FISH PIE, GREENPOINT

1 loaf unsliced day-old bread
4 tablespoons butter, melted
4 tablespoons flour
2 cups milk
Salt, pepper, few grains cayenne

1½ teaspoons anchovy sauce or 3 crushed anchovies
1½ lbs cold cooked fish (cod, salmon, halibut, etc. flaked)
4 sprigs parsley

The loaf of bread best suited to this recipe is a square sandwich loaf and at least a day old; cut off the entire top of it, in one lengthwise slice half an inch thick; scoop out all the soft inside, leaving walls about ½ inch thick. Blend together the butter and flour, add the milk, salt and cayenne. Simmer 5 minutes, add anchovy sauce and flaked fish. Put this mixture into the hollowed-out bread. Place back the "lid" of bread which had been sliced off, and bake it for 20 minutes in a moderate oven. Serve this "pie" as it is, garnished with parsley.

LAYER FISH PIE, BAYSHORE

1½ lb fillets of flounder (or hake, haddock, cod or pollock)
1 onion, thinly sliced
2 tablespoons fat

1½ cups potatoes, sliced
1 tablespoon butter
1 teaspoon salt
½ teaspoon black pepper
2 or 3 cups hot milk

Clean and wash the fillets, and dry thoroly. Cook the onion in the fat in a large frying pan. Parboil the potatoes for 8 minutes in boiling water, drain and add; cook for

5 minutes more, tossing occasionally. Butter a casserole, lay in the fish, then a layer of potatoes, then one of fish. Add the onion, dot with butter, and sprinkle with the salt and pepper. Pour on the hot milk, enough to cover the top layer. Bake in moderate oven (375° F) for 1 hour.

HALIBUT-AND-HERRING PIE

½ lb stale bread
1 or 2 cups milk, hot
2 tablespoons butter
Salt, pepper
4 or 5 capers, chopped
2 boneless Herrings (smoked or kippered form), chopped finely

1½ lbs Halibut, in thin steaks
1 cup fish stock
3 or 4 thin strips bacon
Pastry dough

Break up the stale bread into pieces, and pour over it enough milk to moisten. Add the butter, salt, pepper and capers and beat until smooth. Then mix in the boneless herring, beating all together, to the consistency of a thick batter. Cut the halibut steaks into strips, and lay half of these in the bottom of a buttered baking dish. Sprinkle with salt and pepper, then cover with the prepared mixture. Add another layer of halibut, another of the mixture, then pour the fish stock over it, and lay on the bacon pieces. Top with a light pastry crust with a hole in it, and bake in a moderately slow oven (325° F.) for 1½ hours.

VEAL, HAM AND OYSTER PIE, RIVERHEAD

1½ lbs fillet of Veal
2 tablespoons bacon fat
24 Oysters
½ lb cooked Ham, sliced
2 hard-cooked eggs, sliced
½ cup oyster liquor

Potato Crust:
1 lb white potatoes
½ cup flour
1 teaspoon salt
¼ teaspoon pepper
2 tablespoons butter
1 or 2 tablespoons milk

Cut the veal into inch-wide strips and sear and brown in bacon fat in a very hot pan. Then cut the strips into inch squares. Lay in a baking dish, together with oysters and ham. Arrange the egg slices on top. In the pan in which the veal was cooked heat the oyster liquor, and pour over the baking dish. Top this pie with a mashed potato crust, made as follows: boil the potatoes, put through a ricer, dredge with the flour, which has been sifted with the salt and pepper. Add to this the butter and a bit of milk to give a soft dough consistency. Pat into a pie-crust-like "round," on a floured baking board, and place over the baking dish. Bake 45 minutes in a moderate oven (350° F.).

ST. DAVID'S FISH PIE

6 leeks	fleshed fish, flaked
4 tablespoons butter	$\frac{1}{2}$ cup thick white sauce
Salt and pepper	$\frac{1}{4}$ lb cheese
1 lb cooked any white-	$1\frac{1}{2}$ cups bread crumbs

Cut the leeks in 2-inch pieces, and cook in 3 tablespoons butter until slightly browned. Butter a baking dish, lay the leeks in the bottom, season, then add the flaked fish, then the white sauce, then the grated cheese, then the bread crumbs. Dot with remaining butter and brown in a moderate oven.

DOGFISH PIE

2 Dogfish	Salt, pepper
1 tablespoon chopped pars-ley	Pie crust

Skin the dogfish and cut into 2 inch pieces. Put in a saucepan, just cover with cold water and let come to a boil. Then simmer gently until tender. Lay in a deep baking dish, season to taste, add the parsley, and cover with the liquid it was stewed in. Cover with vented pie crust and bake until brown. (This pie, when thoroly chilled in a refrigerator, "jells" and is liked by many people.

OYSTER PIE, SALT-AIRE

2 tablespoons butter
3 tablespoons flour
1 cup milk
1 pint Oysters
Salt and pepper

2 cups whipped potatoes
1 egg-white, slightly beaten
1 teaspoon parsley, chopped
Paprika

In a double boiler blend the butter and flour, add the milk gradually, stirring constantly; cook 5 minutes. Add the oysters with their liquor, the salt and pepper. Cook until the edges of the oysters begin to curl. Pour this mixture into a buttered baking dish, and place the whipped potatoes on top. Brush with the egg-white, sprinkle with paprika and bake in a moderately hot oven (375° F) for 20 minutes. Serve with sprinkled parsley.

SEA PIE, MONTAUK

3 lbs fish
72 oysters
4 tablespoons butter
2 teaspoons flour
1 stalk celery, chopped
1 teaspoon parsley, minced

1 clove garlic, minced
2 lbs cooked crabmeat
Salt and pepper
$\frac{1}{2}$ cup cream
Pie crust

Boil fish in its skin; cool. Remove skin and bones. Separate fish meat into small pieces. Run the oysters through a meat grinder. Melt half the butter, mix with the flour, and the oyster pulp, together with the celery, the parsley, the garlic, and also the water in which the fish was cooked. To this mixture add the crabmeat and the fish and let simmer for 3 minutes. Then add the salt, pepper and 2 tablespoons of butter. After simmering for 10 minutes more, add the cream, blending it in thoroly. The mixture is then ready to put into a deep baking dish, pan or earthen casserole, covered with a rich pie crust, baked in a hot oven (450° F) until crust is brown. Serve in baking dish.

XV

Forty Good Sauces for Seafood

FAR too many American cooks are badly educated about fish, for the very simple reason that they do not realize how often seafood is only *as good as its sauce*. There is a careless idea, even among many American seafood lovers, that, after all, the only way to eat fish is the "natural" way, the "simple" way—and that French cooks bother too much with sauces. Thus in America we *fry* fish overmuch, and then wonder why it has a tendency to be monotonous; why some fish when fried are not appetizing (not to say indigestible).

We are usually very careful to provide a gravy or sauce for *meat,* and as a rule abhor just plain boiled meat without any accompaniment. We "gild the lily" by serving onions with steak, which needs sauce less than any other meat. We are even guilty of dumping a lot of catsup on it, or other bottled sauce, or mustard. This is the sign of too little attention to sauces—we instinctively reach for something to make it less monotonous. Like steak, seafood is surely wonderful in taste, all by itself, prepared in certain competent ways. But precisely as with meat, fish often needs to be varied in taste with sauces so that we may like to eat fish more frequently. After all, if we must eat meat (or fish) every day, we need to learn how to intrigue our palates; how to ring changes on taste. It is the sauce which accomplishes this. One may admit that French cooks carry the sauce idea very far indeed, and probably pay too little attention to food in its more natural state. But this is merely an indication of how far the

French have perfected the art of cookery. It advertises their wider range of technique.

Many people have never eaten with fish even some of the well-known sauces (as for example Sauce Mornay). They will find fish very much more delightful and more frequently desired if, with intelligent discrimination, they learn to prepare and eat fish with *appropriate* sauces. There are hundreds of such sauces. I shall give only a selected number here, for convenience:

1. *Sauce Tartare* (for fried fish especially).—Add 1 tablespoon each chopped capers, green olives, pickles and parsley to 1 cup mayonnaise.

2. *Cucumber Sauce* (fluffy; for any fish).—Whip $\frac{1}{2}$ cup heavy cream, sweet or sour, until stiff. Fold in 1 cucumber chopped and drained, and season with $\frac{1}{2}$ tablespoon salt and 1 tablespoon vinegar.

3. *Cucumber Sauce* (mustard; for fatty fish especially). —Combine 1 teaspoon salt, $\frac{1}{4}$ teaspoon dry mustard, 3 tablespoons vinegar, 1 teaspoon minced onion, 1 cup evaporated milk, 2 teaspoons minced parsley, with $\frac{1}{2}$ cup finely diced cucumber.

4. *Anchovy-Sherry Sauce* (for panned oysters).—Dissolve 2 teaspoons anchovy paste in 1 cup of melted butter. Gradually add $\frac{1}{3}$ cup dry Sherry. Heat to boiling point and simmer 5 minutes, or until sauce thickens slightly, stirring vigorously.

5. *White Wine Sauce* (for boiled and broiled fish).—3 tablespoons butter, 3 tablespoons flour, $\frac{3}{4}$ cup water, $\frac{1}{4}$ cup white wine, 1 cup milk, salt, 1 tablespoon Sherry. Melt butter, blend in flour, and add liquids slowly while stirring constantly. Season. Add grains cayenne.

6. *Maitre d'Hotel Butter Sauce* (for broiled fish especially).—Blend 2 teaspoons finely minced parsley with 5 tablespoons of soft butter, add salt and pepper and 1 tablespoon strained lemon juice.

7. *Sauce Mornay* (for au gratin dishes especially).— Blend $\frac{1}{2}$ cup white wine and fish stock mixed, with 1 cup seasoned cream sauce, and boil over a hot fire while stir-

ring to reduce by one-third. Then blend in 1 tablespoon of grated Parmesan cheese and one of grated Swiss cheese, stirring frequently. Then add a tablespoon of butter and take off fire.

8. *Oyster Sauce* (for broiled or boiled fish especially).— For 3 minutes stew 12 oysters in their own liquor with 1 tablespoon of Chablis (white wine). Then separate oysters from liquor and cut into pieces. Blend 2 tablespoons of flour with 2 tablespoons butter; then add slowly the oyster liquor mixed with scalded milk to make 1 cup. Season with salt, pepper, few grains of nutmeg, few grains cayenne pepper, add 1 teaspoon of strained lemon juice; then mix with the oysters, and bring to a boil. Sprinkle over it some parsley and add 1 tablespoon of butter.

9. *Drawn Butter Sauce* (for broiled or boiled fish).— Blend 3 tablespoons of flour with 3 tablespoons of melted butter, add $\frac{1}{4}$ teaspoon of salt, pepper to taste, then stir in slowly $1\frac{1}{2}$ cups of hot water, and boil for 5 minutes. Then add 3 tablespoons of butter, in small pieces, while stirring, alternating with portions of 1 teaspoon of strained lemon juice, until all is in.

10. *Shrimp Sauce* (for broiled, boiled, or fried fish).— Make 1 cup of Drawn Butter Sauce (No. 9), add slowly to 2 egg yolks, stirring constantly. Add $\frac{2}{3}$ cup cooked shrimps chopped into moderate-sized pieces; 1 teaspoon of strained lemon juice, 1 tablespoon of minced parsley, plus a little salt and cayenne pepper.

11. *Fennel Sauce* (for fatty fish especially, including Eels, Mackerel, Bluefish, Swordfish, etc.).—Chop fine 3 or 4 sprigs of fennel, then parboil and let cool in cold water, then drain. In a saucepan heat 2 tablespoons olive oil, and when heated blend with $\frac{1}{2}$ cup melted butter; bring to a boil. Then add the fennel, stir and season with salt, pepper, nutmeg.

12. *Horseradish Sauce* (for broiled or boiled fish especially).—Bring to a boil 1 cup of fish stock and 4 tablespoons of grated horseradish. Let simmer for 20 minutes. Add then 1 cup of Drawn Butter Sauce (No. 9) and a

tablespoon of thick cream and ¾ cup of soft bread crumbs.
Bring to a boil again, season with salt and pepper and take
off fire. Add slowly to 2 egg yolks, stirring constantly. If
for *boiled* fish, blend 1 tablespoon of prepared mustard.

13. *Egg Sauce* (for boiled pieces of fish especially).—
Blend 1½ cups of Drawn Butter Sauce (No. 9) into two
egg yolks, while stirring, also 3 hard-cooked eggs chopped
into moderate-sized pieces. Add 1 tablespoon of minced
parsley, 1 teaspoon of strained lemon juice, salt and a
few grains of cayenne.

14. *Caper Sauce* (for boiled fish especially).—Blend
into 1 cup of Drawn Butter Sauce (No. 9) ⅓ cup of washed
and drained capers.

15. *Anna Lobster Sauce.*—Blend 3 tablespoons of flour
with 3 tablespoons of butter, pour in gradually 1½ cups of
cream, and 1 tablespoon meat extract. Then add 1 tablespoon of lobster coral, ½ cup cooked diced lobster, and salt
and pepper.

16. *Hollandaise Sauce* (for boiled fish especially).—In
a bowl place ½ cup butter, and cover it with cold water,
and work with a spoon. Divide in 3 parts. One part
mix with 2 egg yolks in a double boiler saucepan and 1
tablespoon of strained lemon juice. Heat in the double
boiler until melted, then add one other third of the butter,
and let thicken; then add the final third. Beat continuously.
Slowly add ⅓ cup boiling water, while stirring. Cook for
1 minute, then add salt and a little cayenne. (If sauce
tends to curdle, add 2 tablespoons of heavy cream and 2 of
boiling water, pouring slowly and heating.)

17. *Mustard Sauce* (for broiled or boiled fish especially).—Blend in 1 tablespoon of prepared mustard with
1 cup of Drawn Butter Sauce (No. 9). But keep the sauce
hot, without boiling, in a double boiler if it is not to be
served at once.

18. *Pimento Sauce* (for fried or boiled fish especially).—
Blend 3 tablespoons of flour into 3 tablespoons of melted
butter, then stir in gradually 1 cup of scalded milk or
cream. Bring to a boil, then add salt, pepper, few grains

of cayenne, few grains of nutmeg. Finally, before taking off fire, add ½ cup of pimento puree, which is made by forcing through a fine sieve one can of pimentos, drained.

19. *Orange Sauce* (for fatty fish especially, baked, broiled or boiled).—Simmer together gently 5 strips of fresh orange peel, 1 onion thinly sliced and 1 cup of fish stock. Let simmer for 20 minutes. Then strain and reduce to one half by boiling. Then add the juice of a small orange, also salt and pepper. Boil again for several minutes and then add 2 tablespoons of port wine. Then before it comes to a boil again add 1 tablespoon of sweet butter blended with 1 tablespoon flour. Boil 3 minutes and take off fire.

20. *Sauce Meunière.*—This is to be prepared when required, by melting 3 tablespoons of butter to the point of brownness; then when the fish is ready, sprinkle a few drops of fresh lemon juice on it, also some finely minced parsley, and then pour the melted brown butter over it.

21. *Sauce Remoulade* (cold, for shrimp and other cold seafood especially).—Mix the raw yolk of an egg with 1 riced hard-cooked egg yolk; beat in 1 tablespoon of olive oil. Mix in then 2 tablespoons of chopped shallots, 3 minced gherkins, 2 teaspoons of capers, 1 teaspoon minced parsley, 1 teaspoon chopped garlic, ½ teaspoon salt. Then add 1 cup of olive oil gradually, drop by drop, beating with each addition. Finally beat in 1½ tablespoons of lemon juice.

22. *Almond Sauce* (cold, for cold fish).—Crush together in a mortar ½ ounce of almonds which have been finely chopped, and 1 ounce of pistachio nuts. Add one-half tablespoon of cold white sauce and then force through a fine sieve, after which add 3 beaten egg yolks, ½ teaspoon of salt, and ¼ teaspoon pepper. Beat all together and blend in 2 cups of olive oil and the juice of one lemon. Then add 1½ tablespoons of mixed chopped chives, parsley and 1 clove of garlic and some tarragon. Cook over hot water for 3 minutes and press through a sieve.

23. *Onion Sauce* (for boiled or broiled fish).—Boil 3 large onions in milk, then press through sieve. Blend in 2 tablespoons of butter with 2 tablespoons of flour, and add

to the onion, and blend in 1 cup of sour cream, salt and pepper. Thin down with some fish sauce or milk if necessary.

24. *Gooseberry Sauce* (for mackerel especially).—Blend 3 tablespoons of flour into 3 tablespoons of butter, then add a pint of milk and let simmer for 20 minutes. Meantime stew 1 lb of green gooseberries in a little water, and when tender press through a sieve, together with 1 teaspoon of chopped onion. Stir this into the milk sauce, season with salt, pepper and 1 teaspoon of sugar.

25. *Creamed Parsley* (*or Dill*) *Sauce* (for any boiled or broiled fish).—Blend 2 tablespoons of butter into 2 tablespoons of flour, then add 1 cup of cream. Also bring 1 cup of veal stock to a boil, and pour in. Add then 2 tablespoons of chopped parsley (or dill), and then simmer in a double boiler for 15 minutes, being careful not to boil.

26. *Cardinal Sauce.*—Add 1 tablespoon lobster coral, finely chopped, to 1 cup medium white sauce; season with salt, pepper, nutmeg. Simmer for 15 minutes, then press through fine strainer. Reheat, add 2 tablespoons cream, 2 teaspoons lemon juice.

27. *Mushroom Sauce.*—Peel $\frac{1}{2}$ cup of button mushrooms, removing stems, and fry them lightly in 1 tablespoon of butter, tossing the saucepan occasionally. Drain off butter, add $1\frac{1}{2}$ cups brown sauce, salt and pepper; reheat.

28. *Piquant Sauce.*—Chop fine 1 small onion, add 2 tablespoons tarragon vinegar and boil until well reduced. Then add 1 cup brown sauce. 1 tablespoon halved capers, 1 tablespoon coarsely chopped gherkin, salt and pepper; bring to a boil, let simmer for 5 minutes.

29. *Sauce Bercy.*—Cook over hot fire, until well reduced, $\frac{1}{4}$ cup of Chablis (white wine) and $\frac{1}{4}$ cup fish stock, together with 1 tablespoon of chopped shallot. Add 1 cup velouté sauce (white sauce made with fish stock) and 4 tablespoons butter and 1 teaspoon minced parsley.

30. *Shallot Sauce.*—Cook together 2 tablespoons tarragon vinegar and 1 tablespoon finely chopped shallots, until vinegar is reduced to 1 tablespoon. Then add 1 tablespoon

tomato paste or concentrated tomato soup, and 1 cup strained fish stock (or clam broth). Blend 2 tablespoons cold fish stock with 1 teaspoon corn-starch, and add to the sauce. Cook until clear. Season with salt, few grains cayenne, and 1 teaspoon of minced parsley.

31. *Hollandaise Sauce Supreme* (for any fish except the fatty ones).—Make Hollandaise Sauce (No. 16) above, but do not add boiling water. Remove from fire after last of the butter is blended in; add twelve cooked shrimp, one half can of French mushrooms, two truffles cut in slices, and 2 tablespoons of boiling fish stock. Heat through over hot water; serve hot over the fish.

32. *Black Butter Sauce* (for any fish except fatty ones). —Melt 5 tablespoons of butter in a frying pan until it browns. Add 8 parsley leaves, heat again for one minute, then put in 1 teaspoon of vinegar. Pour into a sauce bowl and serve hot over the fish.

33. *Espagnole Wine Sauce* (for any fish).—Melt $\frac{1}{3}$ cup butter and brown. Blend in $\frac{1}{3}$ cup sifted flour, stirring. Let simmer very slowly for 20 minutes, stirring frequently. Then let cool, and add gradually brown stock, actively stirring. Cook over slow heat, stirring constantly until thick. Simmer in double-boiler 15 minutes, stirring occasionally. Add $\frac{1}{2}$ teaspoon salt and 2 tablespoons Chablis (white wine).

The brown stock is made by melting 2 tablespoons butter in a saucepan. Have ready 1 lb veal neck (cut into small pieces, bones and all), $\frac{1}{2}$ lb chopped ham, 1 lb chopped beef. Fry *one-half* of the meats first until brown, add 1 onion, chopped, 1 carrot, chopped, 1 celery stalk, chopped, also 1 garlic clove, minced; 2 sprigs parsley, 1 sprig thyme, 1 bay leaf, 2 cloves, 6 peppercorns. Fry for 3 minutes. Add the *other* half of the meats, and cover with 3 pints cold water or broth. Bring to a boil slowly and simmer for 2 hours. Strain, skim off the fat, reduce to one-half (3 cups) by boiling, and skim several times.

34. *Creole Sauce* (for any fish).—Heat 2 tablespoons

of olive oil, and fry for 10 minutes in it one diced pimento, one diced onion, and ½ cup of uncooked diced ham. Then add 2 cloves of garlic, minced, 1 cup thick tomato pulp, ½ tablespoon sugar, ½ teaspoon salt, ¼ teaspoon pepper, ¼ teaspoon paprika, ⅛ teaspoon cayenne. Cook for 30 minutes.

35. *Cucumber-Tomato Sauce* (for any fish).—Peel 4 tomatoes and 1 cucumber, removing seeds, and dice them. Add 1 chopped onion, ½ teaspoon salt. Bring to a boil in a saucepan with ¼ cup water, simmer for 30 minutes. Add two tablespoons of vinegar, and a few drops of tabasco sauce.

36. *Vinaigrette Sauce* (for any fish).—Mix well 1 tablespoon each of chopped onion, chopped pickle, chopped parsley, with one teaspoon prepared mustard, 2 tablespoons olive oil, 1 to 2 teaspoons vinegar. Then add 1 hard-cooked egg, finely chopped.

37. *Curry Sauce* (for any fish).—Melt 3 tablespoons of butter in a saucepan and fry 1 small onion, sliced, until brown. Then add 1 tablespoon good curry powder and 2 tablespoons flour. Stir and cook gently for 2 or 3 minutes, then add 2 cups of good stock and let come to a boil. Then put in 1 sliced tomato, and salt to taste. Simmer for 20 minutes, then strain and serve.

38. *Tomato Sauce* (for any fish).—Melt 2 tablespoons of butter in a saucepan, then add 2 tablespoons ham, finely diced, and 2 shallots, chopped. Let cook, but not brown. Then add 1 bay leaf, 1 sprig of thyme, 10 peppercorns, 1 tablespoon vinegar and 1 lb of tomatoes, sliced. Sprinkle 1 tablespoon flour over mixture, add ½ cup water; boil 20 minutes, until well reduced. Pass it through a fine sieve, season and serve.

39. *Oyster Sauce* (or Mussel or Clam Sauce).—Cook 10 oysters (or clams or mussels) in their own liquor with several sprigs of parsley and thyme for 15 minutes. In a separate saucepan cook 3 tablespoons butter, 3 tablespoons flour, without browning, then add the drained oyster liquor (with some water added, if necessary to make one pint),

and also add ½ teaspoon salt, ¼ teaspoon black pepper. Let boil for 12 minutes, until a thick consistency. Then put in 10 *fresh* oysters, chopped. Heat through and serve.

40. *Sauce Chambord* (for any fish, especially baked).— Brown one large onion, minced, in 1 tablespoon of butter, without burning. Add 3 large tomatoes, chopped fine, with their juice, also 1 sprig of thyme, 2 sprigs of parsley, 2 mashed cloves, 4 allspice (ground), 1 bay leaf, 1 thinly sliced truffle (if available), 6 thinly sliced mushrooms. Let them brown for 10 minutes. Then add 1 pint oyster liquor, 1 teaspoon salt, ½ teaspoon black pepper. Add 12 oysters, chopped fine (and 3 or 4 shrimp or pieces of lobster, if available). Let simmer 20 minutes, season again if necessary, and serve.

(For other sauces not listed here, see index, under Sauces).

XVI

The Story of Long Island Seafood and Fishing

ENTIRELY surrounded by many types of waters, and with the great warm Gulf Stream so relatively near that a hefty seaman could row out to it from the South Shore on a good day, Long Island might easily be visualized as a "natural fishing pier" jutting out 118 miles into the ocean, at an advantageous place, both as to fish and as to market.

This "natural fishing pier" attracts both the amateur and the professional fishermen, and it has been said— seriously, too—that it is a toss-up whether the amateurs or the professionals take the most fish out of Long Island waters! From this one may guess the enormous extent of the fishing for fun that goes on there.

But let us give a little more than a look to the men who, winter and summer, fair weather or foul, make their living getting fish on Long Island. It is a picturesque business, but it is also a hardy and sometimes a dangerous business. The risks which the famous fishermen off the Grand Banks of Nova Scotia take, and the tales of their courage and hardihood, are sometimes duplicated on Long Island, for the Atlantic Ocean is a hard taskmaster anywhere.

Let us start with the first fisherman's harbor near New York—Sheepshead Bay, a region known to millions because it is on the subway line from New York City, near Coney Island, Manhattan Beach and Rockaway. In this bay one may see the fishing boats; the amateurs' boats mingling with the professionals'. From Sheepshead Bay go out into mid-ocean the "draggers" of the beam-trawler type, who take Whiting, Fluke, Dabs and Sardines. They bring in their decks loaded with the fish, if they are lucky, and some of these boats sell fish right off their decks, or from a stand on the street near their docks. Most of them of course sell for the market. Practically all Sheepshead fish boats are "draggers."

The next fish wharf eastward is at Baldwin. Here a motley group of fishing methods prevail. The "gill netters," "hauler-netters" mingle with the draggers; and there are also "hand-liners" catching cod. The draggers from here catch Fluke, Porgies and Squid (a fish which only the Italians seem to know how to prepare. The Squid is the ink-fish, which little boys often read about, which squirts a dark ink-like fluid into the water when attacked). The hauler-netters operate from "ocean traps," which are located off of Jones Beach and Point Lookout. "Pot fishermen" in this neighborhood capture lobsters and sea bass. The hand-liners operate from boats 3 to 10 miles off-shore, from Sheepshead Bay to Fire Island. Haddock were also once taken in this region, but have moved to other regions.

At Freeport another group of fishermen operate draggers of the beam-trawler type. Hard and soft shell clams begin at this point to be plentiful, and amateur fishermen make Freeport one of their main centers. At Seaford, eels are the prominent catch.

At Bayshore, Islip and West Sayville, we strike into "big business" in seafood. The type of fishing here is mainly of two varieties: the "trap fishermen" and the "balloon netters." The trap fishermen operate both ocean traps and bay traps; the ocean traps being located near Fire Island Inlet. These traps gather a very broad variety of fish— mackerel predominating, unless it isn't a good mackerel year. Weakfish, Bluefish, Butterfish, Porgies, Squid, several varieties of Tuna are taken in considerable quantity. One variety of Tuna called Horse Mackerel runs from 300 to 800 pounds in weight; School Tuna is only from 10 to 50 pounds. Both are good commercial fish—and of course also good sport fishermen's catches. Bonito and Albacore are also taken, but aren't considered good eating. Albacore is palmed off as Tuna sometimes by fish sharpers. At certain times in the year Bunkers or Menhaden over-run the traps, but nobody eats them because of excess bones and oil content. In this vicinity eels are also important.

In Great South Bay, from February to April, flounder is also taken by fykes in considerable quantity. Flounder is (as I have elsewhere indicated) of a numerous, varied family, and Long Island has three sizes. In the Moriches and Shinnecock Bays, and at Oyster Bay and Cold Spring Harbor, the smaller-size flounders prevail. At other nearer-to-ocean points the flounder sizes increase.

The "balloon netters" differ from the trawler draggers only in the fact that they go after fish from *above* the ocean bottom, whereas the draggers go after fish right *on* the ocean bottom.

Along Fire Island Beach, from Cherry Grove to West Hampton, there operate the seiners, using Moriches and Eastport as their harbors. At the far Eastern end of Long Island other main fish centers are operated, at Amagansett, Montauk, Greenport, Orient. Trap fishing is done here, and very large quantities of Striped Bass taken. Of course here also is a big center for the amateur fishermen, the terminus of the railroad's special fishermen's trains. Swordfish, Weakfish and other sportmen's fish are plentiful. Marlin, Bluefish, Bonito are very gamey fish also, and men of all kinds, from tired bookkeeper to "big shots" like Al Smith, come here to match their wits against the wary wrigglers. It is a sight to see the special train of fishermen unload at Fort Pond Beach and begin their day of fun. To look at the docks where these fishermen get on the boats you would think a crowded Hudson river excursion was getting started. During June, July and August, wealthy sportsmen come to troll for broadbill swordfish at Montauk, for nowhere are they more abundant. No mere harpoon work (such as the commercial fishermen use) will do for these smart anglers; they want him on a big hook and a stout line, and then they'll stack their wits against those of the big fish, to see if they can land the 200 to 500 pounders. For the still bigger Tuna the amateur fishermen go 10 or 14 miles out to sea. Between June and September the 20 to 150 pounders are more common; the record is 705 lbs. They are tough fish, known to bite a lead squid in half, and run out 2000 feet of 24-thread line. Naturally, most amateur fishermen are not going after big fish, but just a good catch of gamey fish—Sea Bass, Blackfish, Porgy, Weakfish, Bluefish. It's a great sight, an occasion, as you stand on a bobbing fishing boat off of Montauk, to see, almost as far as the eye can reach, bluefish, 2 to 12 lbs in weight, dotted thickly all over the sea surface. Equally great a sight is a vast horde of Weakfish, riding up northward early in May on the Gulf Stream, taking a left turn into the bays around Montauk. "The weaks are in!" is the exciting word passed along. The weakfish run is almost as regular as the earth spinning on its axis. At the time of this special annual weakfish run—one of the fish marvels of the sea—the railroads run special trains to the Greenport dock. A weakfish may have a pusillanimous name, but on the other end of the line, zipping along with his orange-colored fins, he is fully worthy of his better name, sea trout (he gets his weakfish name from his peculiar mouth).

The fishermen standing in hip boots in the surf on the shore go in for striped bass fishing, since the striped bass like to come in-shore after clams and crabs. This is no child's play, either, for striped bass weigh up to 40 lbs in September, October, November. Other fishermen like the classic comfort of an old rowboat in Peconic Bay, or the North Shore Bays, and gradually fill a tub with Porgies, Flounders, Weakfish, Kingfish, "Snappers" (young bluefish). There may be great excitement one day when a big school of Tinker Mackerel appears—enabling one fisherman to catch enough to salt down a barrel or two of them! From flounder in early spring to cod in late fall, the Long Island fisherman has plenty to do.

The seafood of Long Island may be listed as follows:

Alewives	Scup (Porgy)	Whitebait
Albacore	Sea Bass	Clams (hard)
Bluefish	Sea Robins	Clams (soft)
Snapper Bluefish	Shad	Clams (surf)
Bonito	Shark	Clams (razor)
Butterfish	Skate	Conchs (whelks)
Cod	Sole	Crabs (hard)
Cunner (Bergall)	Spanish Mackerel	Crabs (soft)
Dogfish	Striped Bass	Crabs (oyster)
Eels	Swordfish	Lobsters
Flounders	Tautog (Black-	Mussels
Fluke	fish)	Periwinkles
Haddock	Tuna	Oysters
Herring	Weakfish (Sea	Squid
Kingfish	Trout)	Scallops (sea)
Mackerel	Whiting	Scallops (bay)

On the North Shore (Port Jefferson, Northport) the commercial fishermen take mostly Flounders, but also some Dogfish—of two types: the Horn Dogfish, not very edible, and the Smooth Dogfish, which is becoming more and more popular because of its excellent white meat. The Italians like it very much. Skate is also caught here; once not so highly regarded as food, but today better appreciated, for the edible flippers have no bones. (At one time ingenious fish sellers punched round pieces out of them and sold them for sea scallops!). Blowfish (sometimes called Chicken Fish, and at one Long Island restaurant peppered with paprika and called Long Island Red Snapper!) is also taken on the North Shore, and is an odd but quite delicious fish.

LONG ISLAND OYSTER FARMING

Probably Long Island oysters have made Long Island more famous than anything else, for the Gardiners Bay, the Robbins Island, the Peconic Bay and the Blue Point oysters are known and eaten almost all over America.

Oysters once were so common around New York and Long Island, even along the Hudson river, that they were the ordinary man's staple food. The gourmet, therefore, didn't deign to eat them at all! The poor man lived on oysters because they were so easy to pick up, often for the gathering at no expense, anywhere on almost any waterfront. Such an easy-to-obtain food is always rather despised; and, as a matter of fact, it wasn't the good oyster we know today, since today's oysters are carefully and scientifically farmed, under rigid sanitary inspection laws. The pollution of nearby New York waters was a hazard which more meticulous folk didn't care to risk; this hazard becoming so great to public health that laws were passed even before the Revolution, to prevent their sale from May 1 to September 1. This law, amended to May 15 to September 1, still is in effect. Oysters from nearby waters have long ago entirely disappeared. At one time Rockaway oysters were the best, and "Princess Bays" and "Saddle Rock" oysters were also known; but these oyster beds had to retreat before advancing New York.

Oysters then, prior to scientific farming, actually became scarce, and then is when the gourmet began to appreciate them; also when the scientific oyster culture produced more tasty ones. After the Civil War it became evident that a system of private grants was necessary to conserve Long Island oyster beds.

Nowadays Long Island has three large centers of shellfish production. Perhaps the most important is centered at Greenport and draws oysters from the surrounding waters. Next in importance is the West Sayville shipping center, using the product from Great South Bay. Oyster Bay is the third large producing point. Minor shipping places are scattered around the Island, such as New Suffolk, Northport, Bay Shore, Baldwin and Freeport; while almost all the towns bordering on the seashore make some shellfish shipments.

Closely related to the oyster industry are the clamming, scallop and mussel enterprises, these being mostly carried on by the so-called baymen and tongers. Great numbers of the men concerned with these crops are employed during the busy fall and winter season by the private companies, so that, all in all, the shellfish production has fairly steady employment the year round.

In general, the oyster business is "sea farming," and about the only essential difference between sea farming and land farming is that the crops of the sea farmer are out of sight under water. Sea farming involves, first of all, the obtaining of seed by the planting of shells and spawners on chosen natural setting areas. This work is accomplished chiefly in Connecticut waters, although Long Island produces itself appreciable quantities of seed, or, as it is termed in the industry, "set." The under-water farms must be cleaned and made ready to plant, and, during the five or six years required to grow the oyster to marketable size, there must be frequent transplantations to thin out the stock, and to give protection from the voracious enemies such as drills and starfish. There are also many other processes of cultivation. Private oyster grounds must be protected against oyster pirates and thieves; this involves large sums of money annually. Oysters are especially prepared for market by planting on special fattening beds. All these operations require considerable boat tonnage and a great amount of labor to man the vessels and prepare the product for market. These under-water farms are sometimes owned outright, some are leased from the state, while others are leased from the towns owning the adjacent bay bottoms. Since sea farming resembles land farming so closely, it seems practical that the control of the under-water bottoms should be vested in absolute ownership just as they are on land. In some of the other states with natural shellfish resources more extensive than New York's, such as Maryland and Virginia, the leasing of oyster beds has not been encouraged, and, as a result, these states have sadly depleted and ruined their shellfish business.

At the present time, the great market in Baltimore is forced to call upon Long Island oyster producers for a large part of their supply, when it should be obtained from Chesapeake Bay, at Baltimore's own back door.

Some operate oyster farms on Long Island with areas hardly exceeding three or four acres, and, while such small enterprises may not yield a total livable income, nevertheless, carried on in conjunction with fishing or clamming, or some such enterprise, they seem to produce satisfactory income.

A very important aspect of the Long Island oyster industry is that, by its able sea farming efforts, it produces a crop *superior on the whole to that of any other oyster-producing state in the U. S.* This may be noted in the fact that oysters in New York are shipped mainly in the shell, which means that the industry is supplying the most exacting of shellfish demands. Taken by and largely throughout the country, ninety percent of the oysters shipped from the producing points are sold as opened or shucked oysters. In New York State more than one-half the oysters are shipped *in the shell.* One reason for this is the methods of cultivation enabling the grower to produce well-shaped nicely meated, plump oysters of superlative flavor, and it is not unusual to see Long Island oysters quoted in the markets at twice the price of oysters from some of the Southern states. This is not to say that the oysters from the Southern states are an inferior brand, because practically all oysters grown on the Eastern seaboard are the same species, but the Long Island variety is grown, handled and marketed with a very much higher degree of *care.*

A few statistics will not be amiss: There are a total of 34,185 acres of Long Island waters held for shellfish cultivation; 87 boats used, $526,000 in equipment, and 545 employees. About 700,000 bushels of seed oysters are planted yearly, and about 1,200,000 bushels of marketable oysters sold yearly, and 85,227 bushels of cultivated clams. The dollar value of these oysters and clams sold is about $3,000,-000 annually.

The above is on *private* grounds. On *public* grounds on Long Island, 1,171 shellfish permit holders take out annually about 150,000 bushels of hard shell clams, 40,000 bushels of soft shell clams, 51,000 bushels of oysters, 17,000 bushels of scallops, and 12,000 bushels of mussels.

The Long Island oysters travel far. New York is the largest customer; next, the oyster-loving city of Philadelphia. Shell oysters from Long Island are shipped to Europe, to Canada, to South America, and all around the U. S. Opened fresh oysters, and quick frozen oysters are expanding the American market rapidly. We are close to becoming truly national lovers of the oyster, and of course for excellent gourmet and nutritional reasons.

Shad.—The shad which come to Long Island and New York waters in April make an interesting story. They move up the Bay and up the Hudson to spawn as soon as ocean temperature hits 56° F., which it usually does early in April. They go as far as Albany, 150 miles away, taking 3 weeks for the journey, and along the way lose their saltiness, because of the river's fresh water. They also grow thinner as they move up the river, because they sense the polluted waters and stop feeding. Returning after spawning, they are not good fishing or eating. As they come up into New York bay early in April, the roe shad (female) carries the roe that is such a delicious gourmet item, and that is why, from Coney Island upward, half way to Albany, the shad fishing in April is active, and why New York and Long Island around that time feeds heavily on shad roe (some new and interesting recipes for which are in this book).

Long Island Seafaring Activity

The "salt sea tang" of Long Island is accentuated by other things than its unique geographical position in the ocean. It is a great, unique hive of sea and seafaring activity, as these points clearly indicate:

(1) One-fourth of all the sea trade of the U. S., with over 200 foreign ports, is done from Long Island shores; more sea-trade than Manhattan Island itself! Brooklyn has

docks for 700 ships at a time; with new plans for making a great ship basin out of Jamaica Bay.

(2) Uncle Sam's greatest navy yard, "mother of navy yards" (Brooklyn Navy Yard) is there, employing 9,000, building and repairing our warships.

(3) The world's greatest radio towers are located on it, able to communicate instantaneously with 34 different overseas countries (at the rate of 200 words a minute—twice as fast as a man talks). Long Island was the birthplace of American wireless; in Babylon in 1901 the first wireless conversation occurred with a ship at sea; a very historic occasion, indeed.

(4) At the Sperry Gyroscope Company's quarters have been trained over 8,000 ships' officers and sailors from 30 nations, in the use of navigation instruments, and of seaplanes which, with the use of the gyro-pilot, steer to a course automatically without human hands.

(5) The new North Beach Airport is the world's greatest international airport, terminus of the new trans-Atlantic and other airlines.

(6) The largest volume and variety of foods and spices brought to any port is brought to Long Island docks; its vast shiploads of coffee, fruits, sugar, dates, cloves, pepper, sage, coconuts, smoked fish, cheese, cocoa, spices, etc., make it a genuine "isle of spices."

(7) The most highly colored romance of sea treasure belongs to Long Island; the famous pirate, Captain Kidd, hid his treasure chests on Gardiners Island.

(8) Whaling once had its capital on Long Island; Northport, Huntington, Port Jefferson, Cold Spring Harbor, Sag Harbor, Southampton were once whaling ports. There exist many mementos of these days, and old whaling captains are still alive to tell tall tales.

(9) The Gulf Stream and Caribbean hurricanes bring all kinds of strange tropic birds to Long Island, making the Island a veritable bird sanctuary. Although only 120 varieties of birds nest on Long Island, a hundred other varieties are "visitors"—many with gay, exotic plumage. The Roose-

belt Bird Sanctuary at Oyster Bay marks Theodore Roosevelt's special interest in Long Island birds, aroused when a boy by these strange bird visitors to Long Island. A fish hawk marked at Orient Point was later found dead *in Brazil*. A European widgeon shot on Long Island had been banded in Iceland. Labrador ducks once made Long Island their winter home—but no more; Long Island is too populated!

(10) Sea romance was written on Long Island. James Fennimore Cooper wrote *Sea Lions* at Orient Point Inn. Walt Whitman, great American poet, was born on Long Island, south of Huntington.

(11) Yachting and motorboating is developed on Long Island as nowhere else; 25,000 motorboats alone ply Long Island waters, and most of the international races are run in its bays. Freeport alone has 1,000 sailboats.

(12) At Southold is a Marine Museum, and at Sag Harbor is a Whalers' Museum (also a whalers' church) in which are tools and relics of the whaling trade—harpoons, cutting spades, blubber hooks, leg hooks, ship models, sailors' whalebone carvings, etc.

WHAT THE INDIANS GOT FOR LONG ISLAND

Like Manhattan, Long Island was bought from the Indians by the Dutch, for a mere "song." But Long Island brought a higher price than Manhattan since it was more valuable to the Indians because of its seafood and fertile ground. Different Long Island Indian tribes had different names for Long Island. "Pachonahellick" was the name given it by the tribe which sold it. "Sewanahaka" was a name used by other tribes. The following is a copy of the deed transferring Long Island from the Indians to the white man (in 1661):

Before me, Johanes La Montagne, appointed by the Hon. Director-General and Council of New-Netherland as Vice-Director and Commissary of Fort Orange and the village of Beverwyck, three savages and a squaw appeared, to wit: Machsapeen, alias Macsach Niemanau, Sansewanou, Pamanseen and the squaw Nipapoa, who are together owner of the island called Pachonahellick, and declared in presence of Aepjen and Nitamorit, both Sachems of the Mahicanders, that they have sold, ceded and conveyed, as they herewith sell, cede and convey as real and actual property to and in behalf of Andries Herbertsen and Rutger Jacobsen, inhabitants of the village of Beverwyck, the aforesaid island Pachonahellick, situate in this river opposite Bethlehem and called Long or Mahicander's Island by the Dutch, together with all the rights and privileges, which they possess, in consideration for a certain sum paid to them in goods, which they, the sellers, acknowledge to have received to their satisfaction. This done in the village of Beverwyck in presence of Gerrit Bancker and Johannes Proovost, called as witnesses, this Feb. 8, 1661.

It was signed: This x x x is the mark of Macsach Niemanou, this --- is the mark of Sansewanou, this is the mark n n n of Pamenseen, this is the mark // of Nipapoa, this I Aepjen, this Oo of Nitamorit. Gerrit Bancker, Johannes Provoost.

A Patent for the } Agrees with the original
above was issued } To my knowledge
on the 10th of March 1661 } *La Montagne,* Commissary

Note: For the above island the following was paid:

6 rugs	12 lbs of powder
10 coats of duffel	30 lbs lead
a 30 pounds kettle	3 dozen knives
60 strings of wampum	12 cans brandy
10 hatchets	1 half barrel of beer
8 adzes	10 pounds of tobacco
2 guns	

Did the Indians make a fish or clam chowder in the "30 lbs kettle"? Quite undoubtedly! The squaw Nipapoa probably fed the tribes a fish chowder feast from it to celebrate the sale! And, equally certainly, there was no milk in that chowder!

Index

313

A CATALOGUE OF SELECTED DOVER BOOKS
IN ALL FIELDS OF INTEREST

A CATALOGUE OF SELECTED DOVER BOOKS
IN ALL FIELDS OF INTEREST

LEATHER TOOLING AND CARVING, Chris H. Groneman. One of few books concentrating on tooling and carving, with complete instructions and grid designs for 39 projects ranging from bookmarks to bags. 148 illustrations. 111pp. 7⅞ x 10.
23061-9 Pa. $2.50

THE CODEX NUTTALL, A PICTURE MANUSCRIPT FROM ANCIENT MEXICO, as first edited by Zelia Nuttall. Only inexpensive edition, in full color, of a pre-Columbian Mexican (Mixtec) book. 88 color plates show kings, gods, heroes, temples, sacrifices. New explanatory, historical introduction by Arthur G. Miller. 96pp. 11⅜ x 8½.
23168-2 Pa. $7.50

AMERICAN PRIMITIVE PAINTING, Jean Lipman. Classic collection of an enduring American tradition. 109 plates, 8 in full color—portraits, landscapes, Biblical and historical scenes, etc., showing family groups, farm life, and so on. 80pp. of lucid text. 8⅜ x 11¼.
22815-0 Pa. $4.00

WILL BRADLEY: HIS GRAPHIC ART, edited by Clarence P. Hornung. Striking collection of work by foremost practitioner of Art Nouveau in America: posters, cover designs, sample pages, advertisements, other illustrations. 97 plates, including 8 in full color and 19 in two colors. 97pp. 9⅜ x 12¼.
20701-3 Pa. $4.00
22120-2 Clothbd. $10.00

THE UNDERGROUND SKETCHBOOK OF JAN FAUST, Jan Faust. 101 bitter, horrifying, black-humorous, penetrating sketches on sex, war, greed, various liberations, etc. Sometimes sexual, but not pornographic. Not for prudish. 101pp. 6½ x 9¼.
22740-5 Pa. $1.50

THE GIBSON GIRL AND HER AMERICA, Charles Dana Gibson. 155 finest drawings of effervescent world of 1900-1910: the Gibson Girl and her loves, amusements, adventures, Mr. Pipp, etc. Selected by E. Gillon; introduction by Henry Pitz. 144pp. 8¼ x 11⅜.
21986-0 Pa. $3.50

STAINED GLASS CRAFT, J.A.F. Divine, G. Blachford. One of the very few books that tell the beginner exactly what he needs to know: planning cuts, making shapes, avoiding design weaknesses, fitting glass, etc. 93 illustrations. 115pp.
22812-6 Pa. $1.50

CONSTRUCTION OF AMERICAN FURNITURE TREASURES, Lester Margon. 344 detail drawings, complete text on constructing exact reproductions of 38 early American masterpieces: Hepplewhite sideboard, Duncan Phyfe drop-leaf table, mantel clock, gate-leg dining table, Pa. German cupboard, more. 38 plates. 54 photographs. 168pp. 8⅜ x 11¼. 23056-2 Pa. $4.00

JEWELRY MAKING AND DESIGN, Augustus F. Rose, Antonio Cirino. Professional secrets revealed in thorough, practical guide: tools, materials, processes; rings, brooches, chains, cast pieces, enamelling, setting stones, etc. Do not confuse with skimpy introductions: beginner can use, professional can learn from it. Over 200 illustrations. 306pp. 21750-7 Pa. $3.00

METALWORK AND ENAMELLING, Herbert Maryon. Generally conceded best all-around book. Countless trade secrets: materials, tools, soldering, filigree, setting, inlay, niello, repoussé, casting, polishing, etc. For beginner or expert. Author was foremost British expert. 330 illustrations. 335pp. 22702-2 Pa. $3.50

WEAVING WITH FOOT-POWER LOOMS, Edward F. Worst. Setting up a loom, beginning to weave, constructing equipment, using dyes, more, plus over 285 drafts of traditional patterns including Colonial and Swedish weaves. More than 200 other figures. For beginning and advanced. 275pp. 8¾ x 6⅜. 23064-3 Pa. $4.00

WEAVING A NAVAJO BLANKET, Gladys A. Reichard. Foremost anthropologist studied under Navajo women, reveals every step in process from wool, dyeing, spinning, setting up loom, designing, weaving. Much history, symbolism. With this book you could make one yourself. 97 illustrations. 222pp. 22992-0 Pa. $3.00

NATURAL DYES AND HOME DYEING, Rita J. Adrosko. Use natural ingredients: bark, flowers, leaves, lichens, insects etc. Over 135 specific recipes from historical sources for cotton, wool, other fabrics. Genuine premodern handicrafts. 12 illustrations. 160pp. 22688-3 Pa. $2.00

THE HAND DECORATION OF FABRICS, Francis J. Kafka. Outstanding, profusely illustrated guide to stenciling, batik, block printing, tie dyeing, freehand painting, silk screen printing, and novelty decoration. 356 illustrations. 198pp. 6 x 9. 21401-X Pa. $3.00

THOMAS NAST: CARTOONS AND ILLUSTRATIONS, with text by Thomas Nast St. Hill. Father of American political cartooning. Cartoons that destroyed Tweed Ring; inflation, free love, church and state; original Republican elephant and Democratic donkey; Santa Claus; more. 117 illustrations. 146pp. 9 x 12. 22983-1 Pa. $4.00 23067-8 Clothbd. $8.50

FREDERIC REMINGTON: 173 DRAWINGS AND ILLUSTRATIONS. Most famous of the Western artists, most responsible for our myths about the American West in its untamed days. Complete reprinting of *Drawings of Frederic Remington* (1897), plus other selections. 4 additional drawings in color on covers. 140pp. 9 x 12. 20714-5 Pa. $3.95

DRIED FLOWERS, Sarah Whitlock and Martha Rankin. Concise, clear, practical guide to dehydration, glycerinizing, pressing plant material, and more. Covers use of silica gel. 12 drawings. Originally titled "New Techniques with Dried Flowers." 32pp. 21802-3 Pa. $1.00

ABC OF POULTRY RAISING, J.H. Florea. Poultry expert, editor tells how to raise chickens on home or small business basis. Breeds, feeding, housing, laying, etc. Very concrete, practical. 50 illustrations. 256pp. 23201-8 Pa. $3.00

HOW INDIANS USE WILD PLANTS FOR FOOD, MEDICINE & CRAFTS, Frances Densmore. Smithsonian, Bureau of American Ethnology report presents wealth of material on nearly 200 plants used by Chippewas of Minnesota and Wisconsin. 33 plates plus 122pp. of text. $6^1/8$ x $9^1/4$. 23019-8 Pa. $2.50

THE HERBAL OR GENERAL HISTORY OF PLANTS, John Gerard. The 1633 edition revised and enlarged by Thomas Johnson. Containing almost 2850 plant descriptions and 2705 superb illustrations, Gerard's Herbal is a monumental work, the book all modern English herbals are derived from, and the one herbal every serious enthusiast should have in its entirety. Original editions are worth perhaps $750. 1678pp. $8^1/2$ x $12^1/4$. 23147-X Clothbd. $50.00

A MODERN HERBAL, Margaret Grieve. Much the fullest, most exact, most useful compilation of herbal material. Gigantic alphabetical encyclopedia, from aconite to zedoary, gives botanical information, medical properties, folklore, economic uses, and much else. Indispensable to serious reader. 161 illustrations. 888pp. $6^1/2$ x $9^1/4$. USO 22798-7, 22799-5 Pa., Two vol. set $10.00

HOW TO KNOW THE FERNS, Frances T. Parsons. Delightful classic. Identification, fern lore, for Eastern and Central U.S.A. Has introduced thousands to interesting life form. 99 illustrations. 215pp. 20740-4 Pa. $2.50

THE MUSHROOM HANDBOOK, Louis C.C. Krieger. Still the best popular handbook. Full descriptions of 259 species, extremely thorough text, habitats, luminescence, poisons, folklore, etc. 32 color plates; 126 other illustrations. 560pp. 21861-9 Pa. $4.50

HOW TO KNOW THE WILD FRUITS, Maude G. Peterson. Classic guide covers nearly 200 trees, shrubs, smaller plants of the U.S. arranged by color of fruit and then by family. Full text provides names, descriptions, edibility, uses. 80 illustrations. 400pp. 22943-2 Pa. $3.00

COMMON WEEDS OF THE UNITED STATES, U.S. Department of Agriculture. Covers 220 important weeds with illustration, maps, botanical information, plant lore for each. Over 225 illustrations. 463pp. $6^1/8$ x $9^1/4$. 20504-5 Pa. $4.50

HOW TO KNOW THE WILD FLOWERS, Mrs. William S. Dana. Still best popular book for East and Central USA. Over 500 plants easily identified, with plant lore; arranged according to color and flowering time. 174 plates. 459pp. 20332-8 Pa. $3.50

HOUDINI ON MAGIC, Harold Houdini. Edited by Walter Gibson, Morris N. Young. How he escaped; exposés of fake spiritualists; instructions for eye-catching tricks; other fascinating material by and about greatest magician. 155 illustrations. 280pp. 20384-0 Pa. $2.50

HANDBOOK OF THE NUTRITIONAL CONTENTS OF FOOD, U.S. Dept. of Agriculture. Largest, most detailed source of food nutrition information ever prepared. Two mammoth tables: one measuring nutrients in 100 grams of edible portion; the other, in edible portion of 1 pound as purchased. Originally titled Composition of Foods. 190pp. 9 x 12. 21342-0 Pa. $4.00

COMPLETE GUIDE TO HOME CANNING, PRESERVING AND FREEZING, U.S. Dept. of Agriculture. Seven basic manuals with full instructions for jams and jellies; pickles and relishes; canning fruits, vegetables, meat; freezing anything. Really good recipes, exact instructions for optimal results. Save a fortune in food. 156 illustrations. 214pp. 6 1/8 x 9 1/4. 22911-4 Pa. $2.50

THE BREAD TRAY, Louis P. De Gouy. Nearly every bread the cook could buy or make: bread sticks of Italy, fruit breads of Greece, glazed rolls of Vienna, everything from corn pone to croissants. Over 500 recipes altogether. including buns, rolls, muffins, scones, and more. 463pp. 23000-7 Pa. $3.50

CREATIVE HAMBURGER COOKERY, Louis P. De Gouy. 182 unusual recipes for casseroles, meat loaves and hamburgers that turn inexpensive ground meat into memorable main dishes: Arizona chili burgers, burger tamale pie, burger stew, burger corn loaf, burger wine loaf, and more. 120pp. 23001-5 Pa. $1.75

LONG ISLAND SEAFOOD COOKBOOK, J. George Frederick and Jean Joyce. Probably the best American seafood cookbook. Hundreds of recipes. 40 gourmet sauces, 123 recipes using oysters alone! All varieties of fish and seafood amply represented. 324pp. 22677-8 Pa. $3.00

THE EPICUREAN: A COMPLETE TREATISE OF ANALYTICAL AND PRACTICAL STUDIES IN THE CULINARY ART, Charles Ranhofer. Great modern classic. 3,500 recipes from master chef of Delmonico's, turn-of-the-century America's best restaurant. Also explained, many techniques known only to professional chefs. 775 illustrations. 1183pp. 6 5/8 x 10. 22680-8 Clothbd. $17.50

THE AMERICAN WINE COOK BOOK, Ted Hatch. Over 700 recipes: old favorites livened up with wine plus many more: Czech fish soup, quince soup, sauce Perigueux, shrimp shortcake, filets Stroganoff, cordon bleu goulash, jambonneau, wine fruit cake, more. 314pp. 22796-0 Pa. $2.50

DELICIOUS VEGETARIAN COOKING, Ivan Baker. Close to 500 delicious and varied recipes: soups, main course dishes (pea, bean, lentil, çheese, vegetable, pasta, and egg dishes), savories, stews, whole-wheat breads and cakes, more. 168pp. USO 22834-7 Pa. $1.75

CREATIVE LITHOGRAPHY AND HOW TO DO IT, Grant Arnold. Lithography as art form: working directly on stone, transfer of drawings, lithotint, mezzotint, color printing; also metal plates. Detailed, thorough. 27 illustrations. 214pp.
21208-4 Pa. $3.00

DESIGN MOTIFS OF ANCIENT MEXICO, Jorge Enciso. Vigorous, powerful ceramic stamp impressions — Maya, Aztec, Toltec, Olmec. Serpents, gods, priests, dancers, etc. 153pp. 6⅛ x 9¼.
20084-1 Pa. $2.50

AMERICAN INDIAN DESIGN AND DECORATION, Leroy Appleton. Full text, plus more than 700 precise drawings of Inca, Maya, Aztec, Pueblo, Plains, NW Coast basketry, sculpture, painting, pottery, sand paintings, metal, etc. 4 plates in color. 279pp. 8⅜ x 11¼.
22704-9 Pa. $4.50

CHINESE LATTICE DESIGNS, Daniel S. Dye. Incredibly beautiful geometric designs: circles, voluted, simple dissections, etc. Inexhaustible source of ideas, motifs. 1239 illustrations. 469pp. 6⅛ x 9¼.
23096-1 Pa. $5.00

JAPANESE DESIGN MOTIFS, Matsuya Co. Mon, or heraldic designs. Over 4000 typical, beautiful designs: birds, animals, flowers, swords, fans, geometric; all beautifully stylized. 213pp. 11⅜ x 8¼.
22874-6 Pa. $4.95

PERSPECTIVE, Jan Vredeman de Vries. 73 perspective plates from 1604 edition; buildings, townscapes, stairways, fantastic scenes. Remarkable for beauty, surrealistic atmosphere; real eye-catchers. Introduction by Adolf Placzek. 74pp. 11⅜ x 8¼.
20186-4 Pa. $2.75

EARLY AMERICAN DESIGN MOTIFS, Suzanne E. Chapman. 497 motifs, designs, from painting on wood, ceramics, appliqué, glassware, samplers, metal work, etc. Florals, landscapes, birds and animals, geometrics, letters, etc. Inexhaustible. Enlarged edition. 138pp. 8⅜ x 11¼.
22985-8 Pa. $3.50
23084-8 Clothbd. $7.95

VICTORIAN STENCILS FOR DESIGN AND DECORATION, edited by E.V. Gillon, Jr. 113 wonderful ornate Victorian pieces from German sources; florals, geometrics; borders, corner pieces; bird motifs, etc. 64pp. 9⅜ x 12¼.
21995-X Pa. $2.50

ART NOUVEAU: AN ANTHOLOGY OF DESIGN AND ILLUSTRATION FROM THE STUDIO, edited by E.V. Gillon, Jr. Graphic arts: book jackets, posters, engravings, illustrations, decorations; Crane, Beardsley, Bradley and many others. Inexhaustible. 92pp. 8⅛ x 11.
22388-4 Pa. $2.50

ORIGINAL ART DECO DESIGNS, William Rowe. First-rate, highly imaginative modern Art Deco frames, borders, compositions, alphabets, florals, insectals, Wurlitzer-types, etc. Much finest modern Art Deco. 80 plates, 8 in color. 8⅜ x 11¼.
22567-4 Pa. $3.00

HANDBOOK OF DESIGNS AND DEVICES, Clarence P. Hornung. Over 1800 basic geometric designs based on circle, triangle, square, scroll, cross, etc. Largest such collection in existence. 261pp.
20125-2 Pa. $2.50

EARLY NEW ENGLAND GRAVESTONE RUBBINGS, Edmund V. Gillon, Jr. 43 photographs, 226 rubbings show heavily symbolic, macabre, sometimes humorous primitive American art. Up to early 19th century. 207pp. 8⅜ x 11¼.
21380-3 Pa. $4.00

L.J.M. DAGUERRE: THE HISTORY OF THE DIORAMA AND THE DAGUERREOTYPE, Helmut and Alison Gernsheim. Definitive account. Early history, life and work of Daguerre; discovery of daguerreotype process; diffusion abroad; other early photography. 124 illustrations. 226pp. 6⅙ x 9¼.
22290-X Pa. $4.00

PHOTOGRAPHY AND THE AMERICAN SCENE, Robert Taft. The basic book on American photography as art, recording form, 1839-1889. Development, influence on society, great photographers, types (portraits, war, frontier, etc.), whatever else needed. Inexhaustible. Illustrated with 322 early photos, daguerreotypes, tintypes, stereo slides, etc. 546pp. 6⅛ x 9¼.
21201-7 Pa. $5.00

PHOTOGRAPHIC SKETCHBOOK OF THE CIVIL WAR, Alexander Gardner. Reproduction of 1866 volume with 100 on-the-field photographs: Manassas, Lincoln on battlefield, slave pens, etc. Introduction by E.F. Bleiler. 224pp. 10¾ x 9.
22731-6 Pa. $4.50

THE MOVIES: A PICTURE QUIZ BOOK, Stanley Appelbaum & Hayward Cirker. Match stars with their movies, name actors and actresses, test your movie skill with 241 stills from 236 great movies, 1902-1959. Indexes of performers and films. 128pp. 8⅜ x 9¼.
20222-4 Pa. $2.50

THE TALKIES, Richard Griffith. Anthology of features, articles from Photoplay, 1928-1940, reproduced complete. Stars, famous movies, technical features, fabulous ads, etc.; Garbo, Chaplin, King Kong, Lubitsch, etc. 4 color plates, scores of illustrations. 327pp. 8⅜ x 11¼.
22762-6 Pa. $5.95

THE MOVIE MUSICAL FROM VITAPHONE TO "42ND STREET," edited by Miles Kreuger. Relive the rise of the movie musical as reported in the pages of Photoplay magazine (1926-1933): every movie review, cast list, ad, and record review; every significant feature article, production still, biography, forecast, and gossip story. Profusely illustrated. 367pp. 8⅜ x 11¼.
23154-2 Pa. $6.95

JOHANN SEBASTIAN BACH, Philipp Spitta. Great classic of biography, musical commentary, with hundreds of pieces analyzed. Also good for Bach's contemporaries. 450 musical examples. Total of 1799pp.
EUK 22278-0, 22279-9 Clothbd., Two vol. set $25.00

BEETHOVEN AND HIS NINE SYMPHONIES, Sir George Grove. Thorough history, analysis, commentary on symphonies and some related pieces. For either beginner or advanced student. 436 musical passages. 407pp.
20334-4 Pa. $4.00

MOZART AND HIS PIANO CONCERTOS, Cuthbert Girdlestone. The only full-length study. Detailed analyses of all 21 concertos, sources; 417 musical examples. 509pp.
21271-8 Pa. $4.50

THE BEST DR. THORNDYKE DETECTIVE STORIES, R. Austin Freeman. The Case of Oscar Brodski, The Moabite Cipher, and 5 other favorites featuring the great scientific detective, plus his long-believed-lost first adventure — 31 New Inn — reprinted here for the first time. Edited by E.F. Bleiler. USO 20388-3 Pa. $3.00

BEST "THINKING MACHINE" DETECTIVE STORIES, Jacques Futrelle. The Problem of Cell 13 and 11 other stories about Prof. Augustus S.F.X. Van Dusen, including two "lost" stories. First reprinting of several. Edited by E.F. Bleiler. 241pp.
20537-1 Pa. $3.00

UNCLE SILAS, J. Sheridan LeFanu. Victorian Gothic mystery novel, considered by many best of period, even better than Collins or Dickens. Wonderful psychological terror. Introduction by Frederick Shroyer. 436pp. 21715-9 Pa. $4.00

BEST DR. POGGIOLI DETECTIVE STORIES, T.S. Stribling. 15 best stories from EQMM and The Saint offer new adventures in Mexico, Florida, Tennessee hills as Poggioli unravels mysteries and combats Count Jalacki. 217pp. 23227-1 Pa. $3.00

EIGHT DIME NOVELS, selected with an introduction by E.F. Bleiler. Adventures of Old King Brady, Frank James, Nick Carter, Deadwood Dick, Buffalo Bill, The Steam Man, Frank Merriwell, and Horatio Alger — 1877 to 1905. Important, entertaining popular literature in facsimile reprint, with original covers. 190pp. 9 x 12. 22975-0 Pa. $3.50

ALICE'S ADVENTURES UNDER GROUND, Lewis Carroll. Facsimile of ms. Carroll gave Alice Liddell in 1864. Different in many ways from final Alice. Handlettered, illustrated by Carroll. Introduction by Martin Gardner. 128pp. 21482-6 Pa. $1.50

ALICE IN WONDERLAND COLORING BOOK, Lewis Carroll. Pictures by John Tenniel. Large-size versions of the famous illustrations of Alice, Cheshire Cat, Mad Hatter and all the others, waiting for your crayons. Abridged text. 36 illustrations. 64pp. 8¼ x 11. 22853-3 Pa. $1.50

AVENTURES D'ALICE AU PAYS DES MERVEILLES, Lewis Carroll. Bué's translation of "Alice" into French, supervised by Carroll himself. Novel way to learn language. (No English text.) 42 Tenniel illustrations. 196pp. 22836-3 Pa. $2.00

MYTHS AND FOLK TALES OF IRELAND, Jeremiah Curtin. 11 stories that are Irish versions of European fairy tales and 9 stories from the Fenian cycle — 20 tales of legend and magic that comprise an essential work in the history of folklore. 256pp. 22430-9 Pa. $3.00

EAST O' THE SUN AND WEST O' THE MOON, George W. Dasent. Only full edition of favorite, wonderful Norwegian fairytales — Why the Sea is Salt, Boots and the Troll, etc. — with 77 illustrations by Kittelsen & Werenskiöld. 418pp.
22521-6 Pa. $3.50

PERRAULT'S FAIRY TALES, Charles Perrault and Gustave Doré. Original versions of Cinderella, Sleeping Beauty, Little Red Riding Hood, etc. in best translation, with 34 wonderful illustrations by Gustave Doré. 117pp. 8⅛ x 11. 22311-6 Pa. $2.50

THE FITZWILLIAM VIRGINAL BOOK, edited by J. Fuller Maitland, W.B. Squire. Famous early 17th century collection of keyboard music, 300 works by Morley, Byrd, Bull, Gibbons, etc. Modern notation. Total of 938pp. 8⅜ x 11.
ECE 21068-5, 21069-3 Pa., Two vol. set $12.00

COMPLETE STRING QUARTETS, Wolfgang A. Mozart. Breitkopf and Härtel edition. All 23 string quartets plus alternate slow movement to K156. Study score. 277pp. 9⅜ x 12¼. 22372-8 Pa. $6.00

COMPLETE SONG CYCLES, Franz Schubert. Complete piano, vocal music of Die Schöne Müllerin, Die Winterreise, Schwanengesang. Also Drinker English singing translations. Breitkopf and Härtel edition. 217pp. 9⅜ x 12¼.
22649-2 Pa. $4.00

THE COMPLETE PRELUDES AND ETUDES FOR PIANOFORTE SOLO, Alexander Scriabin. All the preludes and etudes including many perfectly spun miniatures. Edited by K.N. Igumnov and Y.I. Mil'shteyn. 250pp. 9 x 12. 22919-X Pa. $5.00

TRISTAN UND ISOLDE, Richard Wagner. Full orchestral score with complete instrumentation. Do not confuse with piano reduction. Commentary by Felix Mottl, great Wagnerian conductor and scholar. Study score. 655pp. 8⅛ x 11.
22915-7 Pa. $10.00

FAVORITE SONGS OF THE NINETIES, ed. Robert Fremont. Full reproduction, including covers, of 88 favorites: Ta-Ra-Ra-Boom-De-Aye, The Band Played On, Bird in a Gilded Cage, Under the Bamboo Tree, After the Ball, etc. 401pp. 9 x 12.
EBE 21536-9 Pa. $6.95

SOUSA'S GREAT MARCHES IN PIANO TRANSCRIPTION: ORIGINAL SHEET MUSIC OF 23 WORKS, John Philip Sousa. Selected by Lester S. Levy. Playing edition includes: The Stars and Stripes Forever, The Thunderer, The Gladiator, King Cotton, Washington Post, much more. 24 illustrations. 111pp. 9 x 12.
USO 23132-1 Pa. $3.50

CLASSIC PIANO RAGS, selected with an introduction by Rudi Blesh. Best ragtime music (1897-1922) by Scott Joplin, James Scott, Joseph F. Lamb, Tom Turpin, 9 others. Printed from best original sheet music, plus covers. 364pp. 9 x 12.
EBE 20469-3 Pa. $6.95

ANALYSIS OF CHINESE CHARACTERS, C.D. Wilder, J.H. Ingram. 1000 most important characters analyzed according to primitives, phonetics, historical development. Traditional method offers mnemonic aid to beginner, intermediate student of Chinese, Japanese. 365pp. 23045-7 Pa. $4.00

MODERN CHINESE: A BASIC COURSE, Faculty of Peking University. Self study, classroom course in modern Mandarin. Records contain phonetics, vocabulary, sentences, lessons. 249 page book contains all recorded text, translations, grammar, vocabulary, exercises. Best course on market. 3 12" 33⅓ monaural records, book, album. 98832-5 Set $12.50

150 MASTERPIECES OF DRAWING, edited by Anthony Toney. 150 plates, early 15th century to end of 18th century; Rembrandt, Michelangelo, Dürer, Fragonard, Watteau, Wouwerman, many others. 150pp. 8⅜ x 11¼.　　21032-4 Pa. $3.50

THE GOLDEN AGE OF THE POSTER, Hayward and Blanche Cirker. 70 extraordinary posters in full colors, from Maîtres de l'Affiche, Mucha, Lautrec, Bradley, Cheret, Beardsley, many others. 9⅜ x 12¼.　　22753-7 Pa. $4.95
21718-3 Clothbd. $7.95

SIMPLICISSIMUS, selection, translations and text by Stanley Appelbaum. 180 satirical drawings, 16 in full color, from the famous German weekly magazine in the years 1896 to 1926. 24 artists included: Grosz, Kley, Pascin, Kubin, Kollwitz, plus Heine, Thöny, Bruno Paul, others. 172pp. 8½ x 12¼.　　23098-8 Pa. $5.00
23099-6 Clothbd. $10.00

THE EARLY WORK OF AUBREY BEARDSLEY, Aubrey Beardsley. 157 plates, 2 in color: Manon Lescaut, Madame Bovary, Morte d'Arthur, Salome, other. Introduction by H. Marillier. 175pp. 8½ x 11.　　21816-3 Pa. $3.50

THE LATER WORK OF AUBREY BEARDSLEY, Aubrey Beardsley. Exotic masterpieces of full maturity: Venus and Tannhäuser, Lysistrata, Rape of the Lock, Volpone, Savoy material, etc. 174 plates, 2 in color. 176pp. 8½ x 11.　21817-1 Pa. $3.75

DRAWINGS OF WILLIAM BLAKE, William Blake. 92 plates from Book of Job, Divine Comedy, Paradise Lost, visionary heads, mythological figures, Laocoön, etc. Selection, introduction, commentary by Sir Geoffrey Keynes. 178pp. 8½ x 11.
22303-5 Pa. $3.50

LONDON: A PILGRIMAGE, Gustave Doré, Blanchard Jerrold. Squalor, riches, misery, beauty of mid-Victorian metropolis; 55 wonderful plates, 125 other illustrations, full social, cultural text by Jerrold. 191pp. of text. 8⅛ x 11.
22306-X Pa. $5.00

THE COMPLETE WOODCUTS OF ALBRECHT DÜRER, edited by Dr. W. Kurth. 346 in all: Old Testament, St. Jerome, Passion, Life of Virgin, Apocalypse, many others. Introduction by Campbell Dodgson. 285pp. 8½ x 12¼.　　21097-9 Pa. $6.00

THE DISASTERS OF WAR, Francisco Goya. 83 etchings record horrors of Napoleonic wars in Spain and war in general. Reprint of 1st edition, plus 3 additional plates. Introduction by Philip Hofer. 97pp. 9⅜ x 8¼.　　21872-4 Pa. $2.50

ENGRAVINGS OF HOGARTH, William Hogarth. 101 of Hogarth's greatest works: Rake's Progress, Harlot's Progress, Illustrations for Hudibras, Midnight Modern Conversation, Before and After, Beer Street and Gin Lane, many more. Full commentary. 256pp. 11 x 14.　　22479-1 Pa. $6.00
23023-6 Clothbd. $13.50

PRIMITIVE ART, Franz Boas. Great anthropologist on ceramics, textiles, wood, stone, metal, etc.; patterns, technology, symbols, styles. All areas, but fullest on Northwest Coast Indians. 350 illustrations. 378pp.　　20025-6 Pa. $3.50

HOW TO SOLVE CHESS PROBLEMS, Kenneth S. Howard. Practical suggestions on problem solving for very beginners. 58 two-move problems, 46 3-movers, 8 4-movers for practice, plus hints. 171pp.   20748-X Pa. $2.00

A GUIDE TO FAIRY CHESS, Anthony Dickins. 3-D chess, 4-D chess, chess on a cylindrical board, reflecting pieces that bounce off edges, cooperative chess, retrograde chess, maximummers, much more. Most based on work of great Dawson. Full handbook, 100 problems. 66pp. 7⅞ x 10¾.   22687-5 Pa. $2.00

WIN AT BACKGAMMON, Millard Hopper. Best opening moves, running game, blocking game, back game, tables of odds, etc. Hopper makes the game clear enough for anyone to play, and win. 43 diagrams. 111pp.   22894-0 Pa. $1.50

BIDDING A BRIDGE HAND, Terence Reese. Master player "thinks out loud" the binding of 75 hands that defy point count systems. Organized by bidding problem—no-fit situations, overbidding, underbidding, cueing your defense, etc. 254pp.   EBE 22830-4 Pa. $2.50

THE PRECISION BIDDING SYSTEM IN BRIDGE, C.C. Wei, edited by Alan Truscott. Inventor of precision bidding presents average hands and hands from actual play, including games from 1969 Bermuda Bowl where system emerged. 114 exercises. 116pp.   21171-1 Pa. $1.75

LEARN MAGIC, Henry Hay. 20 simple, easy-to-follow lessons on magic for the new magician: illusions, card tricks, silks, sleights of hand, coin manipulations, escapes, and more —all with a minimum amount of equipment. Final chapter explains the great stage illusions. 92 illustrations. 285pp.   21238-6 Pa. $2.95

THE NEW MAGICIAN'S MANUAL, Walter B. Gibson. Step-by-step instructions and clear illustrations guide the novice in mastering 36 tricks; much equipment supplied on 16 pages of cut-out materials. 36 additional tricks. 64 illustrations. 159pp. 6⅝ x 10.   23113-5 Pa. $3.00

PROFESSIONAL MAGIC FOR AMATEURS, Walter B. Gibson. 50 easy, effective tricks used by professionals —cards, string, tumblers, handkerchiefs, mental magic, etc. 63 illustrations. 223pp.   23012-0 Pa. $2.50

CARD MANIPULATIONS, Jean Hugard. Very rich collection of manipulations; has taught thousands of fine magicians tricks that are really workable, eye-catching. Easily followed, serious work. Over 200 illustrations. 163pp. 20539-8 Pa. $2.00

ABBOTT'S ENCYCLOPEDIA OF ROPE TRICKS FOR MAGICIANS, Stewart James. Complete reference book for amateur and professional magicians containing more than 150 tricks involving knots, penetrations, cut and restored rope, etc. 510 illustrations. Reprint of 3rd edition. 400pp.   23206-9 Pa. $3.50

THE SECRETS OF HOUDINI, J.C. Cannell. Classic study of Houdini's incredible magic, exposing closely-kept professional secrets and revealing, in general terms, the whole art of stage magic. 67 illustrations. 279pp.   22913-0 Pa. $2.50

MANUAL OF THE TREES OF NORTH AMERICA, Charles S. Sargent. The basic survey of every native tree and tree-like shrub, 717 species in all. Extremely full descriptions, information on habitat, growth, locales, economics, etc. Necessary to every serious tree lover. Over 100 finding keys. 783 illustrations. Total of 986pp.
20277-1, 20278-X Pa., Two vol. set $8.00

BIRDS OF THE NEW YORK AREA, John Bull. Indispensable guide to more than 400 species within a hundred-mile radius of Manhattan. Information on range, status, breeding, migration, distribution trends, etc. Foreword by Roger Tory Peterson. 17 drawings; maps. 540pp.
23222-0 Pa. $6.00

THE SEA-BEACH AT EBB-TIDE, Augusta Foote Arnold. Identify hundreds of marine plants and animals: algae, seaweeds, squids, crabs, corals, etc. Descriptions cover food, life cycle, size, shape, habitat. Over 600 drawings. 490pp.
21949-6 Pa. $4.00

THE MOTH BOOK, William J. Holland. Identify more than 2,000 moths of North America. General information, precise species descriptions. 623 illustrations plus 48 color plates show almost all species, full size. 1968 edition. Still the basic book. Total of 551pp. 6½ x 9¼.
21948-8 Pa. $6.00

AN INTRODUCTION TO THE REPTILES AND AMPHIBIANS OF THE UNITED STATES, Percy A. Morris. All lizards, crocodiles, turtles, snakes, toads, frogs; life history, identification, habits, suitability as pets, etc. Non-technical, but sound and broad. 130 photos. 253pp.
22982-3 Pa. $3.00

OLD NEW YORK IN EARLY PHOTOGRAPHS, edited by Mary Black. Your only chance to see New York City as it was 1853-1906, through 196 wonderful photographs from N.Y. Historical Society. Great Blizzard, Lincoln's funeral procession, great buildings. 228pp. 9 x 12.
22907-6 Pa. $6.00

THE AMERICAN REVOLUTION, A PICTURE SOURCEBOOK, John Grafton. Wonderful Bicentennial picture source, with 411 illustrations (contemporary and 19th century) showing battles, personalities, maps, events, flags, posters, soldier's life, ships, etc. all captioned and explained. A wonderful browsing book, supplement to other historical reading. 160pp. 9 x 12.
23226-3 Pa. $4.00

PERSONAL NARRATIVE OF A PILGRIMAGE TO AL-MADINAH AND MECCAH, Richard Burton. Great travel classic by remarkably colorful personality. Burton, disguised as a Moroccan, visited sacred shrines of Islam, narrowly escaping death. Wonderful observations of Islamic life, customs, personalities. 47 illustrations. Total of 959pp.
21217-3, 21218-1 Pa., Two vol. set $7.00

INCIDENTS OF TRAVEL IN CENTRAL AMERICA, CHIAPAS, AND YUCATAN, John L. Stephens. Almost single-handed discovery of Maya culture; exploration of ruined cities, monuments, temples; customs of Indians. 115 drawings. 892pp.
22404-X, 22405-8 Pa., Two vol. set $8.00

THE MAGIC MOVING PICTURE BOOK, Bliss, Sands & Co. The pictures in this book move! Volcanoes erupt, a house burns, a serpentine dancer wiggles her way through a number. By using a specially ruled acetate screen provided, you can obtain these and 15 other startling effects. Originally "The Motograph Moving Picture Book." 32pp. 8¼ x 11.   23224-7 Pa. $1.75

STRING FIGURES AND HOW TO MAKE THEM, Caroline F. Jayne. Fullest, clearest instructions on string figures from around world: Eskimo, Navajo, Lapp, Europe, more. Cats cradle, moving spear, lightning, stars. Introduction by A.C. Haddon. 950 illustrations. 407pp.   20152-X Pa. $3.00

PAPER FOLDING FOR BEGINNERS, William D. Murray and Francis J. Rigney. Clearest book on market for making origami sail boats, roosters, frogs that move legs, cups, bonbon boxes. 40 projects. More than 275 illustrations. Photographs. 94pp.
20713-7 Pa. $1.25

INDIAN SIGN LANGUAGE, William Tomkins. Over 525 signs developed by Sioux, Blackfoot, Cheyenne, Arapahoe and other tribes. Written instructions and diagrams: how to make words, construct sentences. Also 290 pictographs of Sioux and Ojibway tribes. 111pp. 6⅛ x 9¼.   22029-X Pa. $1.50

BOOMERANGS: HOW TO MAKE AND THROW THEM, Bernard S. Mason. Easy to make and throw, dozens of designs: cross-stick, pinwheel, boomabird, tumblestick, Australian curved stick boomerang. Complete throwing instructions. All safe. 99pp.   23028-7 Pa. $1.50

25 KITES THAT FLY, Leslie Hunt. Full, easy to follow instructions for kites made from inexpensive materials. Many novelties. Reeling, raising, designing your own. 70 illustrations. 110pp.   22550-X Pa. $1.25

TRICKS AND GAMES ON THE POOL TABLE, Fred Herrmann. 79 tricks and games, some solitaires, some for 2 or more players, some competitive; mystifying shots and throws, unusual carom, tricks involving cork, coins, a hat, more. 77 figures. 95pp.   21814-7 Pa. $1.25

WOODCRAFT AND CAMPING, Bernard S. Mason. How to make a quick emergency shelter, select woods that will burn immediately, make do with limited supplies, etc. Also making many things out of wood, rawhide, bark, at camp. Formerly titled Woodcraft. 295 illustrations. 580pp.   21951-8 Pa. $4.00

AN INTRODUCTION TO CHESS MOVES AND TACTICS SIMPLY EXPLAINED, Leonard Barden. Informal intermediate introduction: reasons for moves, tactics, openings, traps, positional play, endgame. Isolates patterns. 102pp. USO 21210-6 Pa. $1.35

LASKER'S MANUAL OF CHESS, Dr. Emanuel Lasker. Great world champion offers very thorough coverage of all aspects of chess. Combinations, position play, openings, endgame, aesthetics of chess, philosophy of struggle, much more. Filled with analyzed games. 390pp.   20640-8 Pa. $3.50

MOTHER GOOSE'S MELODIES. Facsimile of fabulously rare Munroe and Francis "copyright 1833" Boston edition. Familiar and unusual rhymes, wonderful old woodcut illustrations. Edited by E.F. Bleiler. 128pp. 4½ x 6⅜. 22577-1 Pa. $1.00

MOTHER GOOSE IN HIEROGLYPHICS. Favorite nursery rhymes presented in rebus form for children. Fascinating 1849 edition reproduced in toto, with key. Introduction by E.F. Bleiler. About 400 woodcuts. 64pp. 6⅞ x 5¼. 20745-5 Pa. $1.00

PETER PIPER'S PRACTICAL PRINCIPLES OF PLAIN & PERFECT PRONUNCIATION. Alliterative jingles and tongue-twisters. Reproduction in full of 1830 first American edition. 25 spirited woodcuts. 32pp. 4½ x 6⅜. 22560-7 Pa. $1.00

MARMADUKE MULTIPLY'S MERRY METHOD OF MAKING MINOR MATHEMATICIANS. Fellow to Peter Piper, it teaches multiplication table by catchy rhymes and woodcuts. 1841 Munroe & Francis edition. Edited by E.F. Bleiler. 103pp. 4⅝ x 6.
22773-1 Pa. $1.25
20171-6 Clothbd. $3.00

THE NIGHT BEFORE CHRISTMAS, Clement Moore. Full text, and woodcuts from original 1848 book. Also critical, historical material. 19 illustrations. 40pp. 4⅝ x 6. 22797-9 Pa. $1.00

THE KING OF THE GOLDEN RIVER, John Ruskin. Victorian children's classic of three brothers, their attempts to reach the Golden River, what becomes of them. Facsimile of original 1889 edition. 22 illustrations. 56pp. 4⅝ x 6⅜.
20066-3 Pa. $1.25

DREAMS OF THE RAREBIT FIEND, Winsor McCay. Pioneer cartoon strip, unexcelled for beauty, imagination, in 60 full sequences. Incredible technical virtuosity, wonderful visual wit. Historical introduction. 62pp. 8⅜ x 11¼. 21347-1 Pa. $2.00

THE KATZENJAMMER KIDS, Rudolf Dirks. In full color, 14 strips from 1906-7; full of imagination, characteristic humor. Classic of great historical importance. Introduction by August Derleth. 32pp. 9¼ x 12¼. 23005-8 Pa. $2.00

LITTLE ORPHAN ANNIE AND LITTLE ORPHAN ANNIE IN COSMIC CITY, Harold Gray. Two great sequences from the early strips: our curly-haired heroine defends the Warbucks' financial empire and, then, takes on meanie Phineas P. Pinchpenny. Leapin' lizards! 178pp. 6⅛ x 8⅜. 23107-0 Pa. $2.00

WHEN A FELLER NEEDS A FRIEND, Clare Briggs. 122 cartoons by one of the greatest newspaper cartoonists of the early 20th century — about growing up, making a living, family life, daily frustrations and occasional triumphs. 121pp. 8½ x 9½.
23148-8 Pa. $2.50

THE BEST OF GLUYAS WILLIAMS. 100 drawings by one of America's finest cartoonists: The Day a Cake of Ivory Soap Sank at Proctor & Gamble's, At the Life Insurance Agents' Banquet, and many other gems from the 20's and 30's. 118pp. 8⅜ x 11¼. 22737-5 Pa. $2.50

BUILD YOUR OWN LOW-COST HOME, L.O. Anderson, H.F. Zornig. U.S. Dept. of Agriculture sets of plans, full, detailed, for 11 houses: A-Frame, circular, conventional. Also construction manual. Save hundreds of dollars. 204pp. 11 x 16.
21525-3 Pa. $5.95

HOW TO BUILD A WOOD-FRAME HOUSE, L.O. Anderson. Comprehensive, easy to follow U.S. Government manual: placement, foundations, framing, sheathing, roof, insulation, plaster, finishing — almost everything else. 179 illustrations. 223pp. 7⅞ x 10¾.
22954-8 Pa. $3.50

CONCRETE, MASONRY AND BRICKWORK, U.S. Department of the Army. Practical handbook for the home owner and small builder, manual contains basic principles, techniques, and important background information on construction with concrete, concrete blocks, and brick. 177 figures, 37 tables. 200pp. 6½ x 9¼.
23203-4 Pa. $4.00

THE STANDARD BOOK OF QUILT MAKING AND COLLECTING, Marguerite Ickis. Full information, full-sized patterns for making 46 traditional quilts, also 150 other patterns. Quilted cloths, lamé, satin quilts, etc. 483 illustrations. 273pp. 6⅞ x 9⅝.
20582-7 Pa. $3.50

101 PATCHWORK PATTERNS, Ruby S. McKim. 101 beautiful, immediately useable patterns, full-size, modern and traditional. Also general information, estimating, quilt lore. 124pp. 7⅞ x 10¾.
20773-0 Pa. $2.50

KNIT YOUR OWN NORWEGIAN SWEATERS, Dale Yarn Company. Complete instructions for 50 authentic sweaters, hats, mittens, gloves, caps, etc. Thoroughly modern designs that command high prices in stores. 24 patterns, 24 color photographs. Nearly 100 charts and other illustrations. 58pp. 8⅜ x 11¼.
23031-7 Pa. $2.50

IRON-ON TRANSFER PATTERNS FOR CREWEL AND EMBROIDERY FROM EARLY AMERICAN SOURCES, edited by Rita Weiss. 75 designs, borders, alphabets, from traditional American sources printed on translucent paper in transfer ink. Reuseable. Instructions. Test patterns. 24pp. 8¼ x 11.
23162-3 Pa. $1.50

AMERICAN INDIAN NEEDLEPOINT DESIGNS FOR PILLOWS, BELTS, HANDBAGS AND OTHER PROJECTS, Roslyn Epstein. 37 authentic American Indian designs adapted for modern needlepoint projects. Grid backing makes designs easily transferable to canvas. 48pp. 8¼ x 11.
22973-4 Pa. $1.50

CHARTED FOLK DESIGNS FOR CROSS-STITCH EMBROIDERY, Maria Foris & Andreas Foris. 278 charted folk designs, most in 2 colors, from Danube region: florals, fantastic beasts, geometrics, traditional symbols, more. Border and central patterns. 77pp. 8¼ x 11.
USO 23191-7 Pa. $2.00

Prices subject to change without notice.
Available at your book dealer or write for free catalogue to Dept. GI, Dover Publications, Inc., 180 Varick St., N.Y., N.Y. 10014. Dover publishes more than 150 books each year on science, elementary and advanced mathematics, biology, music, art, literary history, social sciences and other areas.